ADVANCE PRAISE FOR
GET A FINANCIAL LIFE:

Wake up, Generation X! Beth Kobliner is telling you it's time to smell the latte: There's more to managing your money than putting out a cup for tips on the coffee bar, and if you don't do something now, the biscotti of your golden years will be from Milk Bone. In *Get A Financial Life*, Kobliner serves a rich, smooth brew of common sense on everything from paying off your student loan to saving for (gasp) your own kid's college education. The advice is thoughtful, precise and up-to-date. But the simple step-by-step explanations make getting a financial life easier than steaming the perfect froth on a cappuccino.

> Saul Hansell,
> Business Reporter,
> *The New York Times*

With all those new choices, personal financial decision-making is getting more and more complicated, even for the computer generation. Beth Kobliner's book provides a much-needed and sensible guide.

> Paul A. Volcker,
> Former Chairman,
> Federal Reserve Board

One of the best guides to help young people get a handle on money matters.

> Burton G. Malkiel,
> Chemical Bank Chairman's Professor
>   of Economics, Princeton University;
> author, *A Random Walk Down Wall Street*

If you're young—and you follow the rules in this book—you won't worry whether there's Social Security down the road.

Ray Brady,
Economics Correspondent,
CBS Evening News

Shaw said youth is wasted on the young. I suspect the Kobliner financial wisdoms will work out well at all our ages.

Paul A. Samuelson,
Institute Professor Emeritus, MIT;
Nobel Laureate in Economics

Laying a solid financial foundation is one of the most important and rewarding tasks facing young people today. In *Get a Financial Life*, Beth Kobliner has created a great guide that will make the job much easier and a lot more fun.

Dean Shepherd,
Anchor, CNBC

At forty-seven, I no longer qualify as young, but I have six children who will soon need "a financial life." This is the kind of basic, readable book they should have.

Stuart Varney,
CNN Business News

HERE'S WHAT THE EXPERTS ARE SAYING
ABOUT INDIVIDUAL CHAPTERS OF
GET A FINANCIAL LIFE:

Chapter 3 (Debt):

The "Debt and the Material World" chapter provides straightforward solutions to the problems of personal debt that plague many young people today.

>   Durant Abernethy,
>   President,
>   National Foundation for Consumer Credit

Chapter 4 (Banking):

It's tough to get ahead, and Beth Kobliner has some solid advice in her banking chapter that will help you make every dollar count. Who has time to learn things the *hard* way?

>   Fritz Elmendorf,
>   Vice President,
>   Consumer Bankers Association

Chapter 5 (Investing):

Kobliner's easy, can-do writing style and command of the investment material make this book essential reading for all those who find investments hopelessly complex.

>   Lewis J. Altfest, Ph.D., CFA,
>   President,
>   L. J. Altfest & Co.

Chapter 6 (Retirement):

Kobliner's discussion of do-it-yourself retirement plans is top-notch—clear, concise and comprehensive.

> Karen Ferguson,
> Director, Pension Rights Center;
> coauthor, *Pensions in Crisis*

Chapter 7 (Housing):

There are very few sources of *practical*, step-by-step advice for young households getting started in the housing market. Beth Kobliner's book fills this gap in an accessible, accurate, and valuable way.

> John Tuccillo,
> Vice President and Chief Economist,
> National Association of Realtors

Chapter 8 (Insurance):

Many authors explain basic principles of personal insurance, but Beth Kobliner also provides practical and usable advice for young adults, and she does it all in a clear, readable style.

> Eric A. Wiening, CPCU, ARM, AU,
> Assistant Vice President,
> American Institute for Chartered
> Property Casualty Underwriters

Chapter 9 (Taxes):

Beth Kobliner's book provides a road map for avoiding tax potholes on your travels throughout your financial life.

> Jeff J. Saccacio,
> Partner,
> Coopers & Lybrand L.L.P.

PERSONAL FINANCE IN YOUR TWENTIES AND THIRTIES

BETH KOBLINER

GET A
FINANCIAL
LIFE

A FIRESIDE BOOK

Published by Simon & Schuster

New York   London   Toronto

Sydney   Tokyo   Singapore

FIRESIDE
Rockefeller Center
1230 Avenue of the Americas
New York, NY 10020

FIRESIDE and colophon are registered trademarks
of Simon & Schuster, Inc.

Designed by Katy Riegel

Manufactured in the United States of America

10

Library of Congress Cataloging-in-Publication Data

Kobliner, Beth.
    Get a financial life : personal finance in your twenties and thirties /
Beth Kobliner.
        p.   cm.
    1. Finance, Personal.   2. Young adults—Finance, Personal.   I. Title.
HG179.K59   1996
332.024—dc20   96-6309
                                                                  CIP

ISBN 0-684-81213-4

Figure 5-1, page 106, © *Stocks, Bonds, Bills, and Inflation 1995 Yearbook™*,
Ibbotson Associates, Chicago (annually updates work by Roger G. Ibbotson and
Rex A. Sinquefield). Used with permission. All rights reserved.

To my parents,
who taught me how to handle money,
and to Sylvia Porter,
who gave me the opportunity to write about it

SPECIAL ACKNOWLEDGMENTS

This book is really a collaborative effort of literally hundreds of individuals. Beginning on page 255, I've listed the more than 500 sources to whom I turned for expertise. This special section, however, acknowledges those people who have made contributions above and beyond the call of duty.

First, the financial experts. Thanks go to senior manager at Price Waterhouse Kent Allison; investment advisor Lew Altfest; vice president and chief economist of Fannie Mae David Berson; investment advisor Jack Bonné; quantitative modeling consultant Ed Chang; fee-only insurance consultant Glenn Daily; vice president of communications of the Consumer Bankers Association Fritz Elmendorf; fee-only financial planner Steven Enright; public affairs officer of the IRS Wilson Fadely; director of the Pension Rights Center Karen Ferguson; pension expert extraordinaire Martin Fleisher; tax partner at Deloitte & Touche Jerry Gattegno; vice president of HSH Associates Keith T. Gumbinger; director of the Women's Pension Project at the Pension Rights Center Cindy Hounsell; life insurance actuary with the Consumer Federation of America James Hunt; tax advisor and senior tax partner at Goldstein Golub Kessler & Co. Stuart Kessler; tax expert and professor of law at Vanderbilt University L. Harold Levinson; banking expert at Bank Rate Monitor Gail Liberman; vice president of the Vanguard Group Brian Mattes; president of Wholesale Insurance Network (WIN) Keith Maurer; credit card guru and president of RAM Research Corp. Robert McKinley; banking expert and chairman of Moebs Services Michael Moebs; principal at Furash & Company Edward L. Neumann; financial planner at Ayco Company L.P. Glenn Pape; insurance expert Irving Pfeffer; vice president of underwriting at Norwest Mortgage Sharon Ridenour; tax attorney Diane Rivers; tax attorney Martin M. Shenkman; research analyst with the Center for Study of Responsive Law Janice Shields; financial planner at David L. Babson & Co. Bill Speciale; insurance consultant Morey Stettner; retirement expert Paul Westbrook; and assistant vice president of American Institute for CPCU and Insurance Institute of America Eric A. Wiening.

Next, I would like to thank my coworkers at *Money* who have helped in various ways. They include Caroline Donnelly, Richard Eisenberg, Judy Feldman, Carla Fried, Eric Gelman, Jordan Goodman, Bonnie Hilton Green, Holly Ketron, Lani Luciano, Kelly Smith, and Patti Straus. I would especially like to thank Gary Belsky and Walter Updegrade for their incredibly valuable feedback. My gratitude also goes to Tyler Mathisen, executive editor of *Money*, who taught me what good writing is, and Frank Lalli, the managing editor of *Money*, who has been a mentor to me at many stages of my career and particularly throughout this book project.

Many friends and colleagues also offered valuable input at various stages. They include Rick Allen, Andrew Bradfield, Richard Burgheim, Larry Burke, Fran Claro, Joe Claro, Paul Cohen, Jon Cowan, Adam Feldman, James Gates, Lynn Goldner, Glenn Hodes, Jonathan Karp, Sam Kerstein, Skye Ketron, John Kildahl, Janet Klosklo, Michelle Kosch, Steve Kotsen, Kathy Landau, Michael Kantor, Harold Kobliner, Kenneth Kobliner, Perry Kobliner, Shirley Kobliner, Carmen Morais, Vanessa O'Connell, Max Phillips, Parker Reilly, Ruby Reilly, Robin Reinowitz, Mark Safire, William Safire, Rebecca Scott, Rebecca Belle Shaw, Anne Morgan Spalter, Michael Spalter, and Dave Zinczenko. I especially want to thank Danielle Claro, whose insight, humor, and remarkable editing skills were a godsend.

I would like to thank Gordon Kato, who believed in this book from the beginning, and Lisa Bankoff and Abigail Rose at ICM.

I owe gratitude to Bob Asahina, Sue Fleming-Holland, Mark Gompertz, Christine Lloreda, and Rachel Rader at Simon & Schuster, and am especially thankful to my incredible twentysomething editor at Simon & Schuster, Sarah Pinckney, who is smart, talented, and an absolute pleasure to deal with.

And most of all, I would like to thank my husband, David, who has never failed to offer complete, unwavering love and devotion. He is my inspiration.

CONTENTS

INTRODUCTION

Many people in my generation—specifically, those now in their twenties and thirties—do not expect to live as well as their parents.

It's no wonder.

The bulk of our crowd came of age financially just in time to take part in the gore but not the glory of the go-go eighties—missing out on the stock market and real estate booms and cutting our teeth on major market downturns and an economic recession. The youngest are now graduating from college and facing a particularly tough job market. And even those of us who have jobs aren't living on Easy Street. In inflation-adjusted dollars, Americans 25 to 34 years old today have incomes that are about 20% less on average than those of our 1970s counterparts. It's not surprising that many of us are convinced we'll never be able to afford the homes we grew up in or the lifestyles we became accustomed to as kids.

Despite the gloomy statistics, there is some good news: There's a lot you can do to improve your odds. In fact, getting your financial life in order is not hard to do if you start taking control now. All it takes is a modest amount of knowledge—much less than you might think—and a little effort. This book will show you how to manage the money you *do* have and make it grow.

Unlike most personal finance books, this one focuses exclusively on what you need to know when you're just starting to pay serious attention to money matters—whether you earn $15,000 or $150,000, whether you're single or married, whether you're financially inclined or financially challenged.

You will learn how to eke out the most you can from your paycheck and discover smart ways to reduce your debt. You'll find out how to shop for everything from auto loans to mortgages. You'll get straightforward advice on how to select mutual funds. You'll pick up tax strategies that could save you hundreds of dollars a year.You'll discover how to reduce outrageous bank fees. And you will get unbiased advice on what kind of insurance you need and what kind you should avoid.

This book will provide answers to specific questions, including: How do you get a low-rate credit card? Should you contribute to your company's 401(k) plan? How do you determine whether you should buy or rent a home? When does it make sense to start investing? How can you find out what's in your credit report? Should you buy or lease a car? How can you get a mortgage with a small down payment?

If the thought of reading an entire book on personal finance leaves you cold, don't despair. Chapter 1 offers a summary of some of the most important steps you'll need to take, and "Financial Cramming" review sections at the end of each chapter highlight key concepts. If you take the plunge and read on, you'll see that achieving your financial goals can be a lot easier than you think—that is, if you take advantage of the one major benefit you have on your side: time.

1

CRIB NOTES

A "Cheat Sheet" for Time-Pressed Readers

I F YOU PREFER CNN Headline News to the newspaper and opt for the *Cliffs Notes* over actual books, this chapter is made for you. It cuts to the chase and offers you the most important steps toward a good financial start. So if you don't have the patience to read the entire book right now, adopting one or two of these strategies will put you ahead of the game.

Of course, as someone's mother once said, cheaters only cheat themselves. And while this chapter is a good launching point, ignoring the remaining eight chapters is a little like relying on a friend's ten-minute summary of *Moby Dick*—you'll get the basic plot line but never understand it in any real depth. Still, the following crib notes should give you a quick-and-dirty rundown on the basics. I've tried to list them in rough order of importance, but your priorities may depend on your own situation.

1. Insure yourself against financial ruin.

It's not surprising that people don't like to talk about insurance. It's expensive, confusing, and mostly about sickness and death. But if you're interested in getting adequate medical care in case of a serious accident or illness, and would prefer not to bankrupt yourself and your family in the process, there really is no higher financial priority than health insurance.

If you work for a company that offers employees health insurance, you're lucky; participating in your employer's group plan will probably cost you much less than buying a policy on your own, and the coverage you get is likely to be more comprehensive than any individual policy you could afford. You may even have more than one type of health insurance plan to choose from through your employer. When deciding among offerings, make sure you consider not only price but also the type of coverage you will receive. If, for example, you're thinking about joining a type of plan called a **health maintenance organization** (HMO), inquire about exactly what is covered, ask about the procedure for seeing specialists, and find out what happens if you want to visit a doctor outside the HMO. Although HMOs are generally less expensive, if you come down with a serious illness and want to see a specialist outside your HMO network, you may have to foot the entire bill yourself. Before you sign up for any health insurance plan, talk to coworkers about their experiences with the various options.

If the company you work for does not offer insurance, you'll have to pay for it yourself. If you recently graduated from college, see if you can extend coverage from your parents' plan for a few years. If you're job hunting, at the very least get temporary coverage. If you're employed but your company doesn't offer you insurance, see if there are any organizations you can join (a trade association, for example) that will allow you to purchase health insurance at a group rate. This can be much less expensive than purchasing individual coverage. Since plans vary dramatically from state to state, your best bet if you're on your own is simply to call the major insurers and HMOs in your area and see what they have to offer. Also call Quotesmith (800-556-9393), USAA (800-531-8000), and your local Blue Cross/Blue Shield company for quotes. And if you're having trouble getting coverage because of a medical condition, your state insurance department may be able to provide you with the names of companies that will cover you. (See page 182 for the phone number of your state's office.)

Another type of protection you may want to consider is life insurance, but only if you have children or if someone else is financially dependent on you. If you don't have dependents, you don't need life insurance. If you do, the type you should buy is called **term insurance,** which is relatively inexpensive. There are several services that will scan their multicompany databases free of charge and mail you a list of some of the least expensive policies. Try the Wholesale Insurance Network (WIN) (800-808-5810), Quotesmith (800-556-9393), SelectQuote (800-343-1985), and Termquote (800-444-8376). One warning: If you deal with a life insurance agent, be prepared to hear a big pitch for a type of policy known as **cash value life insurance.** Ignore it. While it's more profitable for the agent, it's probably not a good deal for you.

Depending on your current financial situation, you may also want to consider protecting your earning power with disability insurance. A disability policy will pay you an income (typically 60% to 70% of your current salary) if you're injured or very sick, and are unable to work for an extended period of time. Depending on the state in which you're employed, you may already be covered by a mandatory disability insurance program and/or by insurance provided voluntarily by your employer as part of your standard employee benefits package. Even if you are, it's a good idea to find out how much coverage you currently have, whether it's possible to buy more, and what it would cost you. As with health insurance, the least expensive way to buy disability insurance is generally through an employee benefits plan. If it's not available to you through your employer's plan, look into purchasing some on your own, though you'll probably find that it's pretty expensive. Some companies that specialize in disability insurance are Unum Life Insurance (800-227-8138), Paul Revere (800-843-3426), and Provident Life and Accident (615-755-1011). Also try USAA (800-531-8000), the Wholesale Insurance Network (800-808-5810), and Termquote (800-444-8376).

For additional tips on purchasing all types of insurance, see Chapter 8.

2. Pay off your debt the smart way.

Whether you're drowning in debt or just have a few manageable loans, more often than not the smartest financial move you can make is to take any savings you have (above and beyond money you need for essentials such as rent, food, and health insurance) and pay off your high-rate loans. The reason is simple: You can "earn" more by paying off a loan than you can by saving and investing. Paying off a credit card that has a 17% interest rate is equivalent to earning 17% on an investment—an extremely attractive rate of return. (Actually, it's even better than that; it's the equivalent of earning 17% *after taxes*.) If you want a full explanation of this concept, turn to page 48. Otherwise, take my word for it.

If you can't pay off your high-rate debt immediately, take steps to reduce the interest rate you pay. One of the simplest ways is to apply for a low-interest-rate credit card. For a list of low-rate credit card issuers, send a request and $4 (check or money order) to Bankcard Holders of America, 524 Branch Drive, Salem, VA 24153, or call 703-389-5445. Another good source is RAM Research's *CardTrak*, P. O. Box 1700, Frederick, MD 21702; the charge is $5.

If you have several different types of debt—say, a credit card balance on a card with a 17% interest rate, a car loan with a 12% rate, and a student loan at 9%—pay off the loan with the highest interest rate first. One strategy you may want to consider is stretching out your student loan payments over 15 years instead of 10 years by signing up for the Federal Direct Consolidation Loan program. (To see if you're eligible, call the Department of Education at 800-4FED-AID.) This will reduce your monthly student loan payment and leave you with extra cash. Use this money to pay off your credit card balance faster. Once you've gotten rid of your credit card debt, start paying off your auto loan faster. After you wipe out that loan, too, increase your student loan payments to at least their initial levels.

The only time it doesn't make sense to kill your debt is when the interest rate you're being charged is *lower* than the rate you can receive on an investment. If, for example, you have a special student loan with a 3% rate, you'd be better off maintaining your usual payment schedule on the loan and putting your cash into an investment that pays you an after-tax rate greater than 3%.

For detailed information on credit cards, auto loans, student loans, home equity loans, and credit reports, see Chapter 3.

3. Start contributing to a tax-favored retirement savings plan.

Okay, okay—the last thing on your mind is retirement. But if you're lucky enough to work for a company that offers a retirement savings plan like a 401(k), you should take advantage of it.

There are several reasons to participate in a 401(k). For starters, many employers will match a portion of the amount you put into such a plan. That means the company will contribute a set amount—say, 50 cents—for every dollar you contribute, up to a specified dollar amount. That's an immediate 50% return on your money! (In fact, if your company offers such a fabulous matching deal, you should probably contribute to the plan even before paying off your credit card debt.) In addition, the federal government allows you to delay paying taxes on the money you contribute to a retirement savings plan. That translates into an immediate tax break of hundreds of dollars each year. If, for example, you contribute $1,000 to a retirement savings plan, you're entitled to deduct the full amount at tax time, reducing your taxable income by $1,000. If you're in the 28% tax bracket, that's a savings of $280. (You are probably in this tax bracket in 1996 if you are single and your taxable income is between $24,000 and $58,150, or if you are married and you and your spouse's combined taxable income is between $40,100 and $96,900.)

Be forewarned that you're likely to come across people who'll tell you you're too young to lock up your money in a retirement savings plan. Ignore them. While it's true that you won't be able to withdraw your money until you reach age 59½ without paying a 10% penalty, many plans allow employees to borrow against their retirement savings at favorable rates. What's more, your money will grow tax-free in a retirement plan for years. The benefits of tax-free growth could easily outweigh the penalty you'd have to pay for making an early withdrawal. And if you switch jobs, you may be able to move your 401(k) money into your new employer's plan.

The easiest way to start contributing is to contact your employee benefits office and ask to have a set percentage of each paycheck automatically transferred to your company plan. Try to contribute the maximum allowed by law. If you can't afford to stash away this much, at least contribute the maximum amount for which you're eligible to receive matching funds.

If you aren't lucky enough to work for an employer who offers a 401(k) or a similar company retirement plan (and possibly even if you are), you should start investing in an **individual retirement account (IRA)**. The most you can contribute to an IRA is $2,000 annually; if at all possible, contribute this amount every year. The tax advantages of an IRA are very similar to those of a 401(k). But IRAs don't have all the advantages of 401(k)s, so putting money in an IRA is somewhat less pressing than enrolling in your company-sponsored plan. For starters, with an IRA you don't have the benefit of an employee matching program. Also, you can't borrow money from an IRA before you reach age 59½ the way you can with most 401(k)s; if you need to get at your money, you'll have to pay the 10% penalty. As of this writing, however, Congress is considering modifying the IRA rules so that savers can borrow from their accounts for medical emergencies and down payments on first homes. If this happens, investing in an IRA will be a no-brainer for anyone who isn't eligible for a 401(k). But even if these rules don't change, the advantage of tax-free growth for many years is extremely beneficial; if you have to make an early withdrawal from your IRA, you'll often still come out ahead, even after factoring in the penalty.

If your employer *does* offer a 401(k) or a similar tax-favored retirement savings plan, you should contribute to that plan before thinking about an IRA. Once you've hit the maximum on your company retirement plan, you can decide whether or not to contribute to an IRA as well. If you do, you'll get the benefit of tax-deferred growth. However, the fact that you're eligible to contribute to a company-sponsored plan may make your IRA contributions non-deductible, depending on your income level.

For more information on tax-favored retirement savings plans and answers to commonly asked questions, see Chapter 6.

4. Reduce your monthly banking fees.

If you're like most people, you don't pay much attention to your bank, despite the fact that it's the center of your financial universe. But by becoming aware of bank charges, you may be able to save hundreds of dollars a year.

Two of the most burdensome bank fees are checking charges and automated teller machine (ATM) fees. To reduce these charges and possibly eliminate them entirely, shop around for a bank that waives them for customers who maintain a specified minimum balance. Some banks require you to maintain the minimum in a checking account only; others will waive monthly checking charges as long as the combined balances in your checking and savings accounts meet the minimum requirement. Either way, look for a bank with a low minimum. While some banks require you to keep as much as $3,000 in the bank to get free checking and ATM use, others require you to keep just $100. Even if you have enough money to meet the higher minimum balance requirements, it still makes sense to find a bank with low balance requirements. That way you won't have to tie up large sums of cash in a bank account that pays a pitifully low interest rate.

Before you switch banks, ask whether yours will waive its minimum balance requirement if you sign up for **direct deposit** (which would mean that your entire paycheck would be deposited automatically into your checking or savings account each pay period); some banks will. You should also find out if you're eligible to join any credit unions, which are special not-for-profit banks that tend to have lower minimum balance requirements and lower fees all around. For help in finding a credit union, call the Credit Union National Association at 800-358-5710.

For more tips on banking smart, see Chapter 4.

5. Build an emergency cushion with an automatic savings plan.

If you find it impossible to save any money, you're not alone. But once you've gotten rid of your high-rate debt and taken care of Crib Notes 2, 3, and 4, it's time to start. A relatively painless way to do it is to enroll in an **automatic savings plan.** These plans allow you to have money withdrawn automatically from each paycheck and funneled into a bank account or mutual fund. (See Crib Note 6 for a brief discussion of mutual funds.)

If you're trying to accumulate a balance in a savings account large enough to qualify for free checking, see if your bank offers an automatic savings program. If it does, contact your company's payroll office and ask if you can have a portion of each paycheck—say, $50—deposited into your savings account and the rest put in your checking account. If your employer doesn't offer this option, your bank can probably offer you an alternative way to save automatically. If, for example, you deposit your entire paycheck into your checking account on the first and fifteenth of every month, you might ask your bank to withdraw a fixed amount from your checking account on the sixth and the twentieth and transfer it to your savings account. Use the money in your checking account to pay your living expenses, and consider the money in your savings account off-limits.

Once you've met the minimum balance requirement for free checking at your bank, you're ready to invest in a special type of mutual fund called a **money market fund**. Money market funds are considered nearly as safe as bank savings accounts and tend to pay higher interest rates. Although they are also sold by brokerage firms and certain banks, you're probably better off with one that's offered by a low-cost mutual fund company. (For my suggestions on specific low-cost mutual fund companies that offer money market funds, see Crib Note 6.) Find out if the fund company and your employer will allow you to have the amount you want to invest automatically deducted from your paycheck and deposited into the fund. If not, the next best option is to have the fund company automatically siphon the cash out of your bank checking account once or twice a month.

No matter what type of automatic savings plan you choose, your goal should be to save at least three months' worth of living expenses in a money market fund before you even think about the more aggressive investments discussed in Crib Note 6. To figure out what three months' worth of living expenses amounts to, use the worksheet in Chapter 2.

For virtually everything you need to know about money market funds, see Chapter 5.

6. Begin investing in stock and bond mutual funds.

Once you have your three-month savings cushion in place in a money market fund, it's time to get a bit more aggressive with your investments. The advantage of **stocks** and **bonds** over money market funds is that they've historically tended to earn higher rates of return for investors over long periods of time, and many experts predict that they will continue to do so in the future. You may need these higher returns to stay ahead of **inflation**. (For a discussion of inflation and why you need to worry about it, see Chapter 5.)

The downside of stocks and bonds is that they're riskier than money market funds. Translation: You can lose money by investing in them. Only you can decide how much risk you're willing to take for the chance to earn higher returns over time, but one reasonable approach might be to put about half of your holdings into stocks, one-third into bonds, and the rest in money market funds.

If you do decide to put some of your money in stocks and bonds, I recommend that you do so by investing in stock mutual funds and bond mutual funds. A **mutual fund** is a type of investment that pools together the money of thousands of people. It's headed by a fund manager, who invests the entire sum in a variety of stocks, bonds, and/or money market instruments. (Sorry, but to find out exactly what these are, you'll need to read Chapter 5.) I recommend that you consider only **no-load mutual funds**. A load is a fee that some mutual fund companies charge each time you put money in or take money out of a fund. Avoid investing in load funds—they don't perform any better on average than no-load funds, so there's no point in paying the extra fees.

Although stock funds are considered somewhat riskier than bond funds, they have also performed somewhat better over the years. If you decide to invest in a stock fund, I recommend that you limit yourself to a type known as a **stock index fund**. Three companies that offer stock index funds with relatively low management fees are Vanguard (800-662-7447), Charles Schwab (800-2NO-LOAD), and T. Rowe Price (800-638-5660). Vanguard has the lowest fees and the largest selection of index funds, but you'll need at least $3,000 to open an account there. Schwab requires a minimum initial investment of $1,000, while T. Rowe Price allows investors to get started by putting in just $50 a month.

Bonds are generally less risky than stocks but riskier than money market funds. Holding bonds as well as stocks will help to diversify your investments, thus reducing your overall risk. Two companies that offer no-load bond funds with low expenses are Vanguard (800-662-7447) and USAA (800-531-8181). While there are several different types of bond funds, a reasonable approach would be to choose an **intermediate term bond fund** that invests in government securities or highly rated corporations.

To learn more about bond funds, stock funds, and investing in general—you guessed it—you'll have to read Chapter 5.

7. Think about buying a house or apartment.

At a certain point in life you may start to feel that you should buy a home. But deciding that it makes sense to purchase a place of your own involves more than simply comparing your monthly rent with the monthly mortgage payments you'd make as an owner. A range of financial factors—including the tax break you'll get from buying, the fees you'll pay when you buy, and how long you plan to live in the new home—should enter into your decision. For a discussion of some of these factors and information on where you can get software to help analyze your situation, turn to Chapter 7.

Many people who are ready to buy a home have difficulty coming up with a down payment. If you're in this position, don't despair. Several options are available to you. Start by calling your state housing office to see if it offers any low down payment mortgage programs for which you're eligible. The advantage of these state programs is that they typically charge lower interest rates than you can get on a bank mortgage. (For the phone number of your state housing office, see pages 158–59.)

Your next step is to get information on Federal National Mortgage Association (Fannie Mae) and Federal Home Loan Mortgage Corporation (Freddie Mac) loans. Fannie Mae and Freddie Mac are "quasi-governmental" agencies that were organized to help banks and mortgage companies expand their mortgage offerings to all types of borrowers. Fannie and Freddie offer several low down payment loan programs. When you shop around, ask lenders if they participate in Fannie's "Community Home Buyer's Program" and "FannieNeighbors," and in Freddie's "Affordable Gold." They'll know what you mean. For several free booklets from Fannie Mae on purchasing a home, call 800-688-HOME.

If you don't qualify for one of these programs, a third alternative is the Federal Housing Administration (FHA) loan program. FHA loans require only a very small down payment—between 2% and 4% of the price of the home, depending on the amount you borrow—and they're usually easier to qualify for, but the deal you get may not be quite as good. Contact a lender or your local Housing and Urban Development (HUD) office for more information on FHA loans.

If you don't qualify for any of these programs, don't give up. There are many lenders out there that offer creative options. Some allow down payments of as little as 3%, and some require no down payment at all as long as a friend or relative is willing to pledge assets as collateral.

For more housing-related tips for buyers and renters, see Chapter 7.

8. Get smart about taxes.

Nobody likes paying taxes. One way to reduce the portion of your paycheck that goes to Uncle Sam is to take as many tax deductions as you are eligible for. Deductions are specific expenses that the government allows you to subtract from your income before calculating the amount of tax you're required to pay.

The government allows you to take advantage of deductions in either of two distinct ways. The easiest approach is to take the **standard deduction,** which is simply a fixed dollar amount ($4,000 for singles and $6,700 for couples in 1996) that you subtract from your income. Although all taxpayers are permitted to take the standard deduction, depending on your circumstances you may wind up paying less if you **itemize** your deductions instead. Itemizing means listing separately the specific items that are deductible under the current tax laws and then subtracting their total cost from your income.

If you choose to itemize your deductions, you'll have to fill out a tax form called a 1040 (also known as the long form) rather than the simpler 1040A or 1040EZ. You'll then have to list your deductions on an attachment to Form 1040 called Schedule A. Among the types of expenses you may be allowed to deduct are state and local taxes you've paid, donations you've made to a charity, and certain moving, job-hunting, business travel, and education expenses.

The only way to find out if you can save money on your taxes by itemizing instead of taking the standard deduction is to fill out a copy of Schedule A and see if the amount you're allowed to deduct is greater than the standard deduction. Even if you find that you won't save money by itemizing this year, this exercise will help you get better acquainted with some common types of deductions and may help you plan things in a way that could reduce your tax bite next year.

To get tax forms and a general instruction book from the IRS, call 800-TAX-FORM and ask for Tax Publication 17, called *Your Federal Income Tax*. Also consider using your computer to help you prepare your taxes. For about $35 you can purchase software that provides you with the forms and instructions you'll need, performs all the necessary calculations, and prints out completed forms you can send to the IRS. Two programs worth considering are TurboTax (or MacInTax for Macs) and TaxCut.

For specific ways to cut your tax bill, see Chapter 9.

2

TAKING STOCK OF YOUR FINANCIAL LIFE

Figuring Out Where You Are
and Where You Want to Go

I F YOU'RE LIKE a lot of people, you're not sure where your money goes. After you pay for the basics such as rent, food, and utilities, most of what's left disappears. The concept of setting aside any money for the future seems like a cruel joke.

But, hey, you're still young. There's plenty of time to get your financial life in order, you keep telling yourself. You'll get control once you start earning more, right?

Well, unfortunately, there's no guarantee it will get any easier. Unlike fine wine or a bad haircut, financial management skills do not necessarily improve with age. Although your paycheck will increase as you get older (God willing), your financial obligations will also grow.

The good news is that if you start paying attention to your finances today, you can develop some habits that will help you for the rest of your financial life. For example, by regularly saving a small amount now, you will be rewarded with a very big payoff later on. If you're 25 years old and put as little as $5 a day into a savings program offered by your employer, you could well be a millionaire by age 65. (Of course, a million dollars 40 years from now is likely to be worth a lot less than it's worth today, but you get the idea.) The point is, you need to start right away. This chapter will help you get organized so you can begin.

PUTTING A PRICE TAG ON YOUR GOALS

Most of us have one or two specific financial dreams that we would love to realize within the next few years. You may want to buy a car by the time you're 25. You may long to own a house by age 30. You may hope to have a feeling of financial security by age 35. Or you may simply want to move out of your parents' place as soon as possible.

The first step toward turning your financial fantasy into an achievable goal is calculating the dollar value of your dream. If you're not sure what that figure is, use the following guidelines:

- **A home.** The median-priced home for first-time home buyers in 1994 was $125,000. To qualify for a home loan, you usually need to make a down payment of between 3 percent and 20 percent of the total price; you also need to pay about 5% to the bank for "closing costs." So for a $125,000 home, you would need to have saved somewhere between $10,000 and $31,250. Of course, these figures could be higher or lower depending on where you live. There are some "no down payment" mortgages available as well. (For details, see Chapter 7.)

- **A new car.** Expect to make a down payment of 10% to 20% on a new automobile. To buy a $20,000 car, you will need to have from $2,000 to $4,000 in cash.

- **A financial emergency cushion.** Generally, an acceptable financial cushion is equal to at least three months' worth of living expenses. This amount will probably guard against a total and immediate disruption of your life if, for example, you lose your job. Although saving for a home, a car, or any other tangible item seems like a lot more fun, accumulating enough for a financial emergency cushion is something you should consider a necessity.

LEARNING HOW
TO REACH YOUR GOALS

Once you've determined what your goals are, you're ready to work toward achieving them. Use the following table (Figure 2-1) to help. It gives you a rough idea of how much you'll need to put aside each month to end up with a specific dollar amount in a set number of years. The table assumes that inflation will be 4% and the money you put away will earn a rate of return of 8% before taxes. (Of course no one can know what will happen to inflation and interest rates in the future, but these are considered moderate estimates.) It also assumes that your combined federal, state, and local tax rate is 33 percent for the next 10 years.* The table factors in tax rates because you will have to pay taxes each year on the earnings you receive on certain investments. (For details on figuring out your tax rate, see Chapter 9.)

If you tend to be a good saver, you may not be fazed by the amount you'll need to save each month. If you're like most people, though, you'll probably have to save more than you think you can spare. Don't get discouraged. The next part of this chapter will help you figure out how to get this money from your current income. Even though you may ultimately decide you have to adjust your planned goal—or the amount of time it will take for you to reach it—at least you'll be on your way toward making it happen.

---

* Here's how I got the 33%: If in 1996 you are single and earn between $24,000 and $121,300 per year or are married and together earn between $40,100 and $147,700, your federal tax rate is either 28% or 31%. Depending on where you live, your state and local taxes might be about 5%; 28% plus 5% is 33%. One thing to keep in mind: If you itemize your tax deductions, you get to deduct the state taxes you pay. This will have the effect of reducing your rate somewhat.

Figure 2-1

HOW MUCH DO YOU NEED TO SAVE EACH MONTH TO MEET YOUR GOAL?

Look across the top row and find the dollar amount that corresponds to your goal. Now look down the far-left column and locate the number of years in which you hope to achieve your goal. The point at which your goal and the number of years intersect is the amount you need to save each month.*

YOUR GOAL

Years to Reach Your Goal	$1,000	$2,000	$3,000	$5,000	$7,000	$10,000	$20,000	$30,000	$50,000	$70,000	$100,000
1	$84	$168	$253	$421	$589	$842	$1,684	$2,525	$4,209	$5,893	$8,418
2	43	85	128	213	298	426	852	1,278	2,130	2,982	4,260
3	29	57	86	144	201	287	575	862	1,437	2,012	2,874
4	22	44	65	109	153	218	436	654	1,090	1,527	2,181
5	18	35	53	88	124	176	353	529	882	1,235	1,765
6	15	30	45	74	104	149	297	446	744	1,041	1,487
7	13	26	39	64	90	129	258	387	644	902	1,289
8	11	23	34	57	80	114	228	342	570	798	1,140
9	10	20	31	51	72	102	205	307	512	717	1,024
10	9	19	28	47	65	93	186	279	465	652	931

*The goals listed across the top row of this table are in constant dollars. That means that if your goal is to buy a car in five years that's equivalent to a $20,000 car today, you need to set aside $353 every month to end up with a sum that has the same purchasing power that $20,000 currently has. In other words, you don't have to worry about inflation eroding the value of the $20,000; the table factors it in for you. The amount you need to put into your account every month is simply the figure listed in the table (in this example, $353).

Sources: Price Waterhouse, The Ayco Company

FIGURING OUT WHERE YOUR MONEY GOES

Saving isn't easy for most people, and putting aside a fixed amount each month seems like an impossible task. But the fact is, you probably *can* save—even if you feel like you're barely making ends meet now. The key is getting a handle on your current spending habits and then reevaluating your priorities. This section will help you do the necessary financial soul searching it often takes to achieve specific goals.

The first step is to keep a detailed spending diary for two weeks so that you can get a better sense of your regular cash expenditures. Get a little notebook and write down everything you spend money on. This sounds like a tedious exercise, but you'll find it's a very useful way to track your cash flow. Once you've done that, you're ready to fill out the worksheet (Figure 2-2). The point of the worksheet is to help you first see where your money goes and then set priorities.

Keep in mind when you fill out the worksheet that it's not necessary to be exact. Use your pay stubs and your bank statements to come up with reasonable estimates in the income section. For the outflow section, look at your pay stubs, your spending diary, your checkbook, and your credit card statements. Don't forget that this worksheet helps you examine your *monthly* expenses. For large expenses (such as tuition, travel, and furniture) come up with a monthly estimate. For expenses that vary from month to month (such as car repairs or clothing) take an average from four or five months' worth of entries in your checkbook. (If you make most major purchases with a credit card, use your credit card statements, too.) If possible, choose a month from each season so you can calculate a more accurate average.

Once you have completed the worksheet, subtract your total outflow from your total income. If you come up with a negative number, that means you're spending more than you're taking in, and you're going to have to cut back. To do this you will need to think about your priorities and make some tough choices. Would you be able to save $150 a month by cooking at home rather than eating out every other night? Do you spend as much on clothes as you do on rent? Are you spending too much money on gifts, especially around holiday time? Are you subscribing to more magazines than you can actually read? Is your car costing more than it's worth? These are some of the questions to consider.

With these questions in mind, go back over the entire outflow section. Consider where you can cut back—and by how much. Once you've done that, star those items that you feel are absolute necessities. (For most of us that includes mortgage or rent, groceries, utilities, student loan payments, and health insurance premiums— although even here, many of us can cut back if we need to.) Subtract your outflow on necessities from your total income. The answer (which is positive, hopefully) is the amount of discretionary income you have left. Some of that money should be set aside to meet your goals, and the rest is for items that are not necessities. At this point it should be clear whether or not you need to adjust the size of your goal or the number of years in which you can realistically hope to attain it.

FINANCIAL RULES
OF THUMB

To help you evaluate whether your current spending and saving habits are right on track, wildly off base, or somewhere in between, I've listed a few financial rules. Like an ideal weight or relationship, these rules of thumb will give you financial ideals to strive for. Realistically, they aren't always possible to attain, but it's good to set high goals. Use the worksheet to help with your calculations.

- **The Debt Rule: Your total debt (not including your mortgage) should be less than 20% of your annual take-home pay.** To see if you meet this standard, list all the money you owe, including unpaid balances on your student loans, your credit cards, your car loan, and any other lines of credit, and add these amounts together. If the total exceeds 20% of your

Figure 2-2

WORSHEET:
A MONTH IN YOUR FINANCIAL LIFE

INCOME (what you take in each month):

Salary (before tax) _____

Pay from extra jobs (before tax) _____

Investment income, such as interest, earnings,
   and dividends (before tax) _____

Scholarships _____

Other _____

   TOTAL INCOME PER MONTH (BEFORE TAX) _____

OUTFLOW (what you pay out each month):

Federal, state and local income tax and FICA
   (get this figure from your pay stubs) _____

Tax on investment income* _____

Mortgage or rent _____

Savings (amount regularly saved each month,
   such as before-tax 401(k) contributions) _____

Groceries _____

Gas and Electricity _____

Telephone _____

Eating out (including morning coffee, snacks,
   and lunches out) _____

Clothes _____

Student loan payments _____

Car loan payments _____

Car expenses (gas, repairs, maintenance) _____

Public transportation (bus, train, taxi costs) _____

Health insurance premiums _____

Homeowners/renters insurance premiums _____

Auto insurance premiums	_____
Disability insurance premiums	_____
Life insurance premiums	_____
Home expenses (furnishings, maintenance)	_____
Laundry, dry cleaning	_____
Tuition	_____
Child care	_____
Medical and dental expenses not covered by insurance	_____
Bank fees	_____
Hobbies	_____
Night life	_____
Movies, theater, cable TV	_____
Computer software, CDs, cassettes	_____
Gifts	_____
Vacations	_____
Magazines, newspapers, books	_____
Personal care (haircuts, toiletries, cosmetics)	_____
Health club fees	_____
Membership fees, charitable contributions	_____
Pets, pet care	_____
Miscellaneous	_____
TOTAL OUTFLOW PER MONTH	_____

TOTAL MONTHLY INCOME _____

minus TOTAL MONTHLY OUTFLOW _____

equals your MONTHLY CASH FLOW _____

*To estimate the tax on your investment income, multiply the amount of interest you receive for the month by your tax bracket. If you don't know your tax bracket, multiply the interest by 0.33 to get a rough idea.

THE ART OF NEGOTIATION: WHEN A SAVER MARRIES A SPENDER

Anne and Marc moved in together in June and started to plan a March wedding. Anne's parents said they'd be willing to contribute $10,000 for the event, so the couple figured out that they'd need to pitch in $5,000 of their own to have the wedding of their dreams. The problem was coming up with the cash. Anne, who is frugal and likes being debt-free, felt that with some careful planning they could accumulate the money. After all, they each earned about $35,000. Marc, however, thought that raising that kind of cash was out of the question. He already *owed* more than $3,000 to various credit card companies and didn't see how he could possibly save the money. Why couldn't they just wait and see how much cash they received as wedding presents and then charge the rest? After two weeks of discussion (actually, arguments), they decided to list their income and expenses and see if they could work out the problem. By writing things down, Marc quickly realized that if he cut out expensive lunches (he spent four times as much as Anne did) and put off buying clothes for work until the spring (he spent twice as much as she did on suits), he could come up with a good chunk of change. He also was forced to acknowledge that having Anne as a roommate actually made saving much easier; it cut his rent, utilities, and basic phone charges in half. The end result: Anne and Marc each set aside $150 every two weeks in a joint bank account earmarked for wedding expenses only.

annual take-home pay, see Chapter 3 for tips on reducing your debt. Of course, anyone with student loans probably fails the debt-rule test. (The $10,000 in student loans I had when I graduated from college represented more than 60% of my take-home pay!) Fortunately, mortgage lenders tend to be more forgiving of borrowers with student loans than of those with lots of credit card debt. For this reason you may want to exclude your student loans from this calculation. Just make sure the total of all your other loans, especially credit card balances, falls well below this 20% mark.

- **The Housing Rule: Spend no more than 30% of your monthly take-home pay on rent or mortgage payments.** This rule may or may not apply depending on where you live. If you live in a small town or a city like St. Louis or Cleveland, this may sound reasonable. But if you live in New York City, San Francisco, or Miami, for example, you probably won't meet this guideline unless you share a place with roommates or you don't mind living in a closet.

- **The Savings Rule: Save at least 10% of your take-home pay each month.** It's critical to think of your savings as a fixed monthly expense that's part of your budget, just like your car payments and your rent. While there's no magical reason to save exactly 10%, it's a good target to shoot for. Include in that 10% the money you set aside to meet your short-term goals as well as the funds you put in a company retirement plan. If you can save more, you should. In fact, some hard-core financial planners recommend that you should save 10% in retirement savings plans alone, plus another 5% outside of your retirement plan. See Chapters 4, 5, and 6 for details on where and how to save.

HEY, BIG SPENDER

Because of the way our tax system works, the cost of buying something is higher than you think. Here's why: Say you find a great jacket for $70, and you buy it. If you were in the 30% tax bracket, you actually had to earn $100 in order to pay for the jacket. That's because $100 taxed at 30% is $70. Keep this in mind on your next shopping spree.

GETTING YOUR FINANCIAL LIFE IN ORDER

It's easier to gain control of your finances if you're organized. Here are some tips:

- **Set up a financial filing system.** To get your paperwork organized, you need a place to put items such as credit card statements and bank statements. The easiest way to do this is with file folders and an inexpensive cardboard filing cabinet. Ideally, you should file paperwork as soon as you receive it. Since almost no one who has a life really does that, set up an "in box" in which you stash away stuff that needs to be filed, and then do all your filing once a month. Here's a rundown of the folders you'll need (many of which are described in greater detail in Chapter 9):

    —*Auto Loans.* Save loan agreements that list the terms of your loan.

    —*Auto (Other).* Keep your purchase agreement, certificate of title, and any warranty you may have. Also hold on to warranties and receipts from repair work.

—*Bank Statements.* Also include canceled checks in this file. Pull out checks for items that may be deductible on your taxes or related to home improvements and stick them in the proper folders.

—*Brokerage Accounts.* If you happen to have any, keep statements that show purchases and sales of investments. You'll also need to hold on to stock or bond certificates.

—*Credit Cards.* Set up a different folder for each card you have. Throw your credit card receipts into these folders. When you get statements, make sure they match your receipts. Once you've done that, pluck out receipts for those purchases that may be tax deductible and put them in the appropriate folder for tax-deductible items.

—*Home Improvements.* Keeping track of these expenses will pay off if you ever decide to sell your home.

—*Home (Purchase).* Hang on to your closing statement and all the documents related to the purchase.

—*Insurance.* You'll need separate folders for auto, home, rental, life, health, and disability insurance. Keep your policies, descriptive literature, copies of any claims that you make, and statements of reimbursement.

—*Individual Retirement Accounts (IRAs).* See Chapters 6 and 9 for details.

—*Mortgage Interest Payments.* If you own a home, hold on to statements related to these payments.

—*Mutual Funds.* File your year-end transaction statements here.

—*Pension Plan/Retirement Plan Statements.* Keep all "summary plan descriptions" you receive from your employer, and save quarterly statements from your retirement savings plan. Also hang on to documents relating to other employee benefits, such as profit-sharing plans.

—*Personal Documents.* Store important documents such as your passport, Social Security card, and marriage certificate here.

—*Property Tax/Real Estate Tax.* These payments are deductible, so hold on to statements related to them.

—*Salary.* Keep your weekly pay stubs, your year-end pay stub, and any written information you receive regarding your bonus.

—*Student Loans.* Save your original loan agreement and your monthly statements.

—*Tax-Deductible Items.* If you don't have many deductible expenses, use this as a catch-all folder. Otherwise, you may want to set up separate folders for each specific type of deduction you can take.

—*Tax Returns.* Each January you receive "W-2s" from your employer and "1099s" from a variety of sources including employers, banks, and mutual fund companies. Save them in this file. Also hold on to copies of your tax returns, tax-related forms, and any supporting documentation. Create a new folder for each year.

—*Warranties, Rebates, Receipts.* Hold on to these for all major purchases. The receipts will help you if you ever need to verify to an insurance company that a particular item was stolen or ruined in a fire.

• **Know what to save and what to throw away.** Some people are pack rats who habitually save every scrap of paper. (I am the worst offender.) The fact is, you don't need to keep all receipts and bills. In general, you'll want to hold on to receipts related to tax-deductible expenses or those that are necessary to take advantage of a warranty. You'll also want to keep receipts of major purchases for insurance purposes. Below is a detailed list of what you need to save and what you can toss.

Throw out now:

—*Old phone bills* (unless you intend to deduct a portion of your phone bill on your taxes)

—*Supermarket receipts*

—*Old utility bills*

Throw out after one year:

—*Canceled checks* (except those you need for tax or insurance purposes)

—*Store receipts and credit card statements* (except those you need for tax or insurance purposes, or for proof of purchase necessary for a warranty)

Throw out after three years:

—*Bank statements* (which you may need to produce if you're audited)

Save forever:

—*Birth certificate*

—*College transcripts*

—*Credit card agreement* (for as long as you have the card)

—*Diplomas*

—*Divorce decree and property agreement*

—*Home improvement receipts* if you own your home (see Chapter 9)

—*Home inventory* (see Chapter 8)

—*Insurance policies*

—*Loan agreements*

—*Marriage certificate*

—*Passport* (current one)

—*Pension-plan and retirement-plan documents*

—*Receipts for major purchases* that you'll need as proof in case of a fire or burglary

—*Social Security card*

—*Stock purchase agreements*

—*Tax returns, additional tax forms and supporting documentation.* (Actually, you can probably throw out the supporting documentation, like receipts, three years after you file your return. See Chapter 9 for details.)

—*Warranties* (for as long as they last)

—*Work performance reviews, memos on job performance*

—*Year-end pay stubs and bonus statements*

—*Year-end transaction statements from mutual fund companies*

• **Consider using a computer to help.** One way to track your spending, as well as get a clearer sense of your total financial picture, is to use personal finance software. If you and your partner fight about money, a computer budgeting program can be especially helpful because it offers an organized, objective way of seeing how your money is actually being spent. One of the main features of these programs is a checkbook management spreadsheet that automatically balances your checkbook. The programs make it easy for you to calculate what portion of your income falls into various categories, such as "housing," "clothes" and "telephone." At the end of a few months you can see how much you spent in each category, and you might learn something useful. For example, you might discover that you eat out twice as much in the winter as you do in the summer, you use three times as much electricity in the summer as you do in the winter, or you spend three times as much on clothes as you do on anything else.

Good personal finance programs can also help you with basic financial planning. Many include worksheets that enable you to quickly figure out what your monthly payments would be on a given loan or how much you'd need to save each year at a given interest rate to achieve a specific goal. Most allow you to print checks from your computer. You may also want to consider paying your bills electronically; most personal finance programs have arrangements with bill-paying services that allow you to pay via modem for about $10 a month. (For details on other ways to pay your bills electronically, see Chapter 4.)

At the time of this writing, the most popular personal finance software is Quicken (it sells for about $50). Another highly rated program is Managing Your Money (about $40). But the world of personal finance software is changing rapidly; for the latest on which programs work best, visit the library and consult a recent issue of *PC Magazine* that rates personal finance software.

If your financial life is fairly simple, or if you're not comfortable using a computer, you probably shouldn't bother with this type of software; it could bog you down rather than help you out.

FINANCIAL CRAMMING

- To calculate how much you need to save each month to reach specific financial goals, look at Figure 2-1 on page 33. Although it's based on several assumptions about inflation, your tax bracket, and the rate you'll be able to earn on investments, it will still give you a rough idea of how much money you'll need to set aside.

- Keep a spending diary for two weeks. By forcing yourself to write down everything you spend money on, you will get a better sense of why your cash seems to disappear each month.

- Consider these guidelines when evaluating your financial fitness: Spend no more than 30% of your monthly take-home pay on housing and dedicate at least 10% of your take-home pay to savings. Also, don't allow your total debt (not including your mortgage or rent) to exceed 20% of your annual take-home pay.

- Gain control of your finances by setting up a filing system and developing regular bill-paying habits. And take a look at the latest personal finance software, which can help you keep track of your spending.

3

DEBT AND THE
MATERIAL WORLD

Finding the Best Loans and
Getting Yourself Out of Hock

S UPPOSE YOU'RE 30 years old and owe
$3,500 on your credit card. The interest rate
on your card is 18%. If you regularly make the minimum payment
required by the credit card issuer, when will you be debt-free?
(Drum roll, please.) The answer is . . . when you are 70 years old. By
then you would have paid $9,431 in interest, plus the original
amount you borrowed. Amazing.

The point of this chilling example is clear: Carrying a lot of credit
card debt—or, for that matter, lots of any type of debt—can be
hazardous to your financial health for a very long time. Unfortunately, debt is a problem many of us are intimate with.

Whether you're trying to dig your way out of debt or simply
looking for a low-cost loan, this chapter provides tips on managing
your credit card debt, shopping for student loan repayment plans,
locating attractive auto loans, and weighing the benefits of home
equity loans. It will also provide you with an inside look at how your
credit habits affect your credit report, the report card of your financial life.

TWO POINTERS FOR ANYONE
WITH DEBT

Before I plunge into the nitty-gritty details of credit cards, student loans, and auto loans, there are two basic principles you should know:

- **If you have savings, pay off your high-rate debt.** In most cases, the very best investment you can make is to pay off your credit cards and auto loans. This is because the interest rates on such debt are higher than the rates you can expect to receive from most investments. Paying off a loan with a 16% interest rate, for instance, is in effect paying yourself a 16% rate of return, *tax-free*. That's a rate even Wall Street big shots would be thrilled to get.

     For a better understanding of why it is beneficial to pay off your debt, consider the following example. Say you have a choice between paying off a $1,000 loan and keeping $1,000 in a bank savings account. The loan has an annual interest rate of 16%, and the bank savings account pays a rate of 4% after taxes. If you keep the $1,000 in the bank for a year, you will earn $40 in interest on it while paying $160 in interest on the loan, ending up with a $120 loss. But if you forget about the savings account and instead pay off the loan immediately, you will earn no interest and will also pay no interest. Clearly it's better to break even than to pay $120 in interest.

- **Transfer debt from high-interest-rate loans to lower-rate loans.** The process of transferring debt from high-rate loans to lower-rate loans is known as **refinancing**. Obviously, it's better to pay 8% to borrow money than it is to pay 18%. If you currently have credit card debt that you can't pay off entirely, apply for a low-rate credit card that allows you to transfer your current debt to it. If you have student loans or auto loans, you may also be able to lower the rates you're paying by refinancing. (For details, see the sections on credit cards, student loans, and auto loans that follow.)

CREDIT
CARDS

Whether you're a sensible user or big-time abuser of credit cards, there are steps you can take to reduce your costs. This section will show what they are.

How to Find the Right Card for You

Despite what the ads say, whether your card has a Visa seal or MasterCard logo is not that important. These are just membership organizations. It's the bank or company that *issues* the card—such as Citibank or AT&T Universal—that matters. Issuers control the rates, fees, and other factors that are critical to you.

Look for a credit card that best suits your own personal spending habits. If you usually carry a balance from month to month, get the lowest interest rate you can. But if you always pay off your balance in full, the rate doesn't matter. Your priority is to find a card that doesn't charge an annual fee and does provide a **grace period,** which is a period of time lenders give you before they start charging interest. If you pay off your entire balance each month, you may also want to consider special "give-back" cards that offer frequent-flyer mileage or credits toward a car for every dollar you charge. If you have a troubled credit history or have a tough time controlling your credit card spending, you may want to consider a secured card or a debit card. (More on these options follows.)

Although there are hundreds of different credit cards available, most of us need no more than three. Limiting your access to credit is a smart move whether you're a binge shopper or a model of self-control. That's because lenders with the most attractive rates tend to reject prospective borrowers based on their *potential* to run up a lot of debt.

How to Get a Low-Rate Credit Card

If you don't have enough cash to pay off your credit card balance immediately, you'll want to get a low-rate card and transfer your debt to it. The way it generally works is that the low-rate issuer provides you with checks that you can use to pay off the balances on high-rate cards. The details of how this system works vary from card to card, so you need to read the fine print before you sign up. Some low-rate issuers, for example, offer you a 25-day grace period before interest accumulates on the money you borrow; others tack on transfer fees and start charging you interest the moment the checks are cashed.

Unfortunately, it's not easy to qualify for the lowest of the low-rate cards: Only about four in ten applicants are approved. Here are details on some of the requirements. The list was prepared by Bankcard Holders of America, a group that educates consumers about credit cards.

- **Salary.** In most cases, you need to earn at least $10,000 a year.

- **Stability.** Most issuers want to see that you've been at your job for at least a year. It also helps if you've lived in the same residence for a year.

- **Debt.** Your monthly debt divided by your income, or **debt-to-income ratio,** typically shouldn't be more than 35% to 45%. To figure this out, add up the amount you pay each month on rent or mortgage, auto loans, and student loans, and the minimum monthly payments on credit cards. To get the percentage, divide this total by your monthly income before taxes.

- **Usage.** To measure credit card usage, issuers calculate the ratio of your outstanding debt to your potential debt (that's the sum of the credit limits on all your cards). For example, if you have a $1,000 credit limit and outstanding debt of $900, your **usage ratio** is 90% ($900 divided by $1,000). This ratio should not exceed 80% if you have two cards and should not exceed 65% if you have three or more cards.

Bill-paying habits. If you have recently been 30 days late [pa]ying a credit card bill or if you were late more than 60 days in the last four years, you will have a harder time getting a low [...]

[For a] list of low-[...] and no-fee issuers, send a request and $4 [(check or money order) to] Bankcard Holders of America, 524 Branch [...]WA 241[...] or call 703-389-5445. Another good source is [...] Card [...], P. O. Box 1700, Frederick, MD 21702; [...] to include your name and address with [...] you have a[c]cess to a computer, check out RAM's [...]earch.com—which is fast and free.) [...]-rate credit card issuers in personal fi-nance magazines such as *Money*. If you belong to a credit union, na-tional association, or labor union, you might be able to get a card with a relatively low rate. Also investigate local banks, which sometimes offer lower rates than large national institutions.

Pointers for Those Who Carry a Balance

More than two thirds of credit card users carry a balance from month to month. While your goal is to pay off your credit card debt entirely, until you can, take note of the following suggestions:

- **Pay your bill the day you get it.** Most credit cards have a grace period, which begins the day your purchases are made or posted (officially recorded), and lasts until the due date specified on the bill. As long as you pay your bill in full by the due date, you won't be charged interest. Unfortunately, with most cards the grace period exists only for those credit card users who pay their full balance each month. If you don't regularly pay off your bill in full, you will be charged interest immediately on any new purchases you make. In other words, if you carry a balance from month to month—even a very small balance—you lose the grace period. To reduce your interest charges, pay your bill as soon as you get it.

- **Find out how interest is calculated.** Most lenders calculate interest using a system called the **average daily balance method including new purchases.** Here's how it works: The issuer divides up the year into 30-day periods known as billing cycles. On the last day of each billing cycle, the issuer mails your bill. Say you owe $500. If you pay the entire amount by the due date, you won't pay any interest. But if you leave even just $1 unpaid, expect a nasty surprise on your next bill. Interest charges won't be calculated on just $1 balance; instead, they will be based on the *average daily balance* of the billing cycle. In this case, your balance would be $500 for 25 days of the billing cycle, and $1 for the last five days, resulting in an average daily balance of $417.

  Another method, the **two-cycle average daily balance method including new purchases,** can be even more costly for you. Basically it allows the issuer to calculate interest based on the two most recent billing cycles. If you sometimes carry a balance and sometimes pay in full, avoid cards that use the two-cycle method. Several major credit card issuers use it. To find out if yours does, check the back of your billing statement, where the method is usually printed in tiny type. For an illustration of just how expensive these methods can be, see the box on page 54.

- **Pay more than the monthly minimum and resist skip-a-payment offers.** Many banks have lowered the monthly minimum payment from 4% of your outstanding balance to 2%. But if you pay only 2% rather than 4% on a $1,000 balance, it will take you about 12 more years and $1,415 more to finally pay it off (assuming a minimum payment of $10). Ideally, you'll pay your balance in full each month. If you can't, pay as much as possible. Also, resist the temptation to go for the skip-a-payment deals offered by many issuers. What they often don't make clear is that you will still be charged interest on your outstanding balance for that month.

- **If you can't get a low-rate credit card, apply for one with a teaser rate.** A teaser rate is a low rate that applies for a year or less. After that period, the rate usually increases dramatically. If you think you can pay off your entire credit card debt before the teaser inflates, transfer your high-rate debt to a card with a low teaser rate. If, for example, you transfer a $2,000 balance from a 16% card to one with a 7% teaser rate, you would save about $90 in interest payments if you paid off the balance in six months. But read the rules of your new low-rate card carefully before you use it to make purchases; some cards stipulate the low rate applies only to transferred balances, not to new purchases, and some tack on hefty transfer fees.

If You Can't Get a Regular Credit Card, Try a Secured Card

If you've never had any credit or you've defaulted on a loan within the last few years, it may be difficult to find a lender who will give you a standard credit card. One option to consider is a **secured credit card.** With a secured card the issuer requires you to provide collateral by depositing money into a special savings account. The issuer usually allows you to charge an amount equal to the sum you keep in the savings account, although in some cases you're permitted to charge less than the amount on deposit, and in other cases slightly more. You can't withdraw the money from the savings account while you have the card.

If you've misused credit in the past but your problem is now under control, you can probably qualify for a secured card. Once you've demonstrated that you can handle a secured card, issuers will be more willing to take a chance on giving you a regular credit card.

Secured cards often charge higher interest rates than traditional credit cards, and most have annual fees. And although some issuers pay interest on the required savings account, others do not. That's why you should shop around. To get a report listing details about several dozen secured cards, send $10 to RAM Research Special Report, Secured Credit Cards, P. O. Box 1700, Frederick, MD 21702. For a shorter Secured Credit Card List, send $4 to Bankcard Holders of America, 524 Branch Drive, Salem, VA 24153.

A NASTY CARD SURPRISE

Kathy and Michael went on a honeymoon to Hawaii and charged all their expenses on a credit card. A week after they got home, the $5,000 credit card bill arrived. They had enough money to pay the whole bill, but Michael decided to pay it over the course of two months so he wouldn't fall below the minimum balance he needed to get free checking at his bank. He wrote a check for $4,900 and mailed it out by the due date. When the next credit card bill came, Michael was shocked to discover that although he owed only $100 from the previous balance, he also owed $63 in interest. Because he didn't pay off his balance entirely, he was charged interest for the average daily balance of the billing cycle—in this case, about $4,180. The lesson: Don't carry a balance if you can help it. (By the way, if Kathy and Michael had a card that used the two-cycle method, they could have owed as much as $138 in interest!)

Get a Debit Card as a Way of Disciplining Yourself

If you have trouble controlling your spending, consider cutting up your credit cards and using a **debit card** instead. Like a credit card, a debit card is a plastic card that you can use to make purchases. Unlike a credit card, which allows you to borrow money, a debit card simply enables you to use money you already have. When you pay by debit card, the money is withdrawn from your bank checking account. With certain types of debit cards, the funds get siphoned out of your account the day you use the card, and with others it could take several days. A growing number of banks offer debit cards with Visa and MasterCard logos, allowing you to use the cards wherever you would use an ordinary credit card, even abroad. You can use these debit cards at ATMs, too. If your bank offers a debit card, ask if there are any annual or monthly fees. Also, if you use a debit card, document your debit card purchases the same way you would record purchases made by check.

Some Final Tips on Credit Cards

Whether you carry a balance or not, here are a few more pointers that will save you some money.

- **Ask your current card company for a better deal.** Because the credit card business is very competitive these days, you may be able to talk a credit card representative into lowering your rate or eliminating your annual fee. Call the 800 number and explain in a friendly but assured manner that you're thinking of canceling your card if your request isn't met. Say that your other cards have lower interest rates and no fees (but be prepared for the phone rep to ask you to name names). If you hold your ground, there's a good chance the rep will check your record and then offer you some break on the rate or fee, especially if you pay your bills on time.

- **Don't use your credit card for cash advances.** Most credit cards can be used to obtain cash from an ATM. When you get a cash advance from an ATM, you are borrowing money from the credit card company in a more expensive way since many issuers charge higher interest rates on cash advances than they do on purchases. And most cash advances don't have a grace period; interest begins accruing the moment you get the advance. On top of the interest you may have to pay a one-time fee of as much as $20 or 5% of the amount you withdraw. You should also stay away from the "convenience checks" some issuers include with your statements (unless you're using them to transfer balances from higher-rate cards). These usually work the same way as cash advances, and you'll be charged accordingly.

Figure 3-1

HOW MANY MONTHLY PAYMENTS
YOU'LL NEED TO KILL YOUR DEBT

This table can help you get a rough sense of how long it will take you to get rid of your credit card debt entirely, regardless of how much you have. Here's how it works: Look down the far-left column and ask yourself what percent of your debt you can comfortably commit to pay off each month. If, for example, you have $1,000 in debt, you may decide that you can pay off 3% of $1,000, or $30, every month until the balance is completely wiped out. Now look across the top row and find the annual interest rate charged by your credit card. Say it's 18%. The point at which 3% intersects with 18% is the number of months it will take you to pay off your debt. In this case the answer is 47 months. But if you're able to refinance that debt with a credit card that charges only a 10% annual rate, the number of monthly payments you'd make would be 39.

		ANNUAL INTEREST RATE					
		8%	10%	12%	14%	16%	18%
Payment as a % of Initial Debt	2%	61	65	70	75	83	93
	3%	38	39	41	42	44	47
	4%	27	28	29	30	31	32
	5%	21	22	22	23	23	24
	10%	10	10	11	11	11	11
	15%	7	7	7	7	7	7
	20%	5	5	5	5	5	5
	25%	4	4	4	4	4	4

Source: AT&T Universal Card Services

- **Before you sign up, evaluate give-back cards carefully.** With a give-back card, whenever you charge, you earn points toward some product or service. Most give-back deals make sense only if you pay off your entire balance each month. That's because the interest rates they charge are often higher than the rates you can get if you shop around. These higher rates can offset any benefit you get from the card. Also, most give-back deals, especially airline cards that allow you to earn frequent-flyer miles for every dollar you charge, pay off only if you charge a lot. You have to charge thousands of dollars (recently the figure was typically $25,000) to get one free round-trip ticket from an airline card. If you don't carry a balance and you don't spend very much, look for a give-back card that does not charge an annual fee—for example, the Sunoco MasterCard, which offers rebates on gas.

STUDENT LOANS

If you're having trouble paying back your loans—or you're simply looking for a way to reduce your interest payments—this section can help.

How to Reduce The Cost of Your Student Loans

Here are two strategies to consider:

- **Refinance to a lower rate.** If you currently have federal student loans, you may be able to consolidate and transfer them to a new lower rate loan under a program introduced by Uncle Sam in 1994. The Federal Direct Consolidation Loan program, as it is lovingly called, allows people to combine their major federal student loans into one massive loan. The interest rate on this new consolidated loan is variable, meaning it will increase or decrease depending on what's happening in the economy, but it won't ever rise above 8.25% (at least that's what the current rules say). If the rate you're paying on your student loans is higher than 8.25%, find out if you can take advantage of this program. For more information call 800-4FED-AID.

- **Prepay your student loans.** If you're not loaded down by credit card debt or other high-rate debt, consider paying back your student loans faster than you're required to under your current payment schedule. One simple way to do this is to double the monthly payment you make. This will save you a substantial amount of interest in the long run. Say you have a $10,000 loan with an interest rate of 7.43%. If you assume interest rates remain the same and you pay back your loan over ten years, your monthly payment will be $118. If you double that amount and pay $236 a month, you will pay off your loan in four years and two months and save more than $2,500 in interest. Remember, prepayment makes sense only if the interest rates on your loans are *higher* than the rates you can earn on an investment.

Federal Repayment Options

The standard way of paying back student loans is by making equal monthly payments for 10 years. If you currently hold student loans from one of the major federal loan programs and you're having trouble making your monthly payments, you may be eligible for one of several repayment options from the Federal Direct Consolidation Loan program. The details are highlighted below. For eligibility requirements and more information, call the Department of Education at 800-4FED-AID.

- **Graduated repayment.** This option allows you to make lower payments in the early years of your loan. Your payments will then increase every two years. The repayment period can extend from 12 to 30 years, depending on the size of your loan. The drawback is that you will pay more interest with this method than with the standard repayment option.

- **Income-contingent repayment.** To ease the burden if you're in a low-paying job, this plan enables you to have your monthly payments determined by your salary and your debt load. The percentage of your monthly income you pay can range from 4% (for loans of $1,000 or less) to 15% (for loans of $56,000 or more). Your payments will rise and fall based on fluctuations in your income. If you're married and file a joint tax return, your joint income is used to calculate the required monthly payments.

- **Extended repayment.** This option allows you to stretch out your loan repayment over a period of 12 to 30 years, depending on the loan amount. While this will reduce your monthly payment, it will increase the total amount you pay.

Other Repayment Options

Some banks and servicers may have programs that are competitive with Uncle Sam's offerings. For example, the Student Loan Marketing Association (Sallie Mae), a company that services about one third of all student loans, offers a loan consolidation program that allows borrowers who make their first 48 scheduled payments on time to reduce their interest rate by one or two percentage points for the remaining **term,** or length of time during which the loan lasts. And if you agree to have your loan payments automatically deducted from your checking or savings account each month, Sallie will reduce your interest rate by an additional quarter of a percentage point. Sallie also has its own version of graduated, extended, and income-contingent plans, as well as other special repayment programs. If Sallie Mae is not servicing your loan, your bank or agency may be willing to sell your loan to Sallie if you ask. Call 800-643-0040 for details.

Special Breaks if You Can't Make Your Payments

Federal rules spell out exactly why and for how long you can put off repaying your student loans. A government-approved delay is called a **deferment**. Deferment rules change every few years, so figuring out whether you qualify for a deferment can get pretty confusing. In general, deferments are granted for many different reasons. For instance, if you're unemployed, a part-time student, a full-time student, a full-time unpaid volunteer, or a recipient of an approved graduate fellowship, you may qualify for a deferment. Also, if you teach full time in a public or nonprofit elementary or secondary school in what is considered a teacher-shortage area, you may be able to defer for up to three years. (Each state has its own definition of a teacher-shortage area.)

During deferment periods the government sometimes pays the interest for you. That's the case with all "subsidized Stafford loans" and most "Perkins loans." With all other student loans, you will eventually have to pay the interest that accrues during the deferment period. To learn more about deferments, contact the institution that's handling your loans. If you don't qualify for a deferment, all hope is not lost. Loan servicers can offer you time off from making

A SMART MOVE IF YOU HAVE CREDIT CARD AND STUDENT LOAN DEBT

The interest rates on your student loans are probably lower than the interest rates on your credit cards. If this is the case, you should pay off your credit card debt faster than you pay off your student loans. By extending the number of years over which you pay back your student loans, you can reduce monthly student loan payments and free up some cash to pay off your credit cards. Once you've wiped out your credit card debt, increase your student loan payments to at least their original levels.

payments through a process known as **forbearance.** Forbearance can be granted for a variety of reasons, many of which are based on the discretion of the institution that's holding your loan. You will be responsible for the interest that accrues on any type of loan during a period of forbearance. Again, speak to someone at the institution that is servicing your loan for details.

CAR LOANS

Once you get a car loan with a high interest rate, you're probably stuck with it; it's nearly impossible to find a lender who will refinance a car loan with a lower-rate loan. (If you own a home, you may have the option of transferring your auto debt to a home equity loan. See the next section for details.) For this reason it's smart to shop carefully for a loan when you buy a car. For instance, a 7% rate versus a 9% rate on a $15,000 four-year loan would save you about $675. This section will offer you some shopping advice on loans and leases.

How to Get a Good Deal on an Auto Loan

To get a good rate you're going to need to do some legwork. Here are some pointers:

- **Before you set foot in a dealership, check with a credit union and at least two banks.** Credit unions tend to charge lower rates on car loans than banks do—sometimes as much as a full percentage point lower. (For information on joining a credit union, see Chapter 4.) And in some cities the difference among bank rates can be more than four percentage points. See if your own bank is willing to bargain; you can sometimes get a half-percentage-point break if you're considered a "good customer," meaning you have anywhere from $1,000 to $5,000 (depending on the bank) in your bank account.

Also, ask your banker if you can get **preapproved** for an auto loan. Preapproval is a process by which the lender looks at your income, debts, and other financial information and determines how large a loan you can handle. There is usually no charge for this service. The benefit is that you'll be better equipped to negotiate with a car dealer once you have a ballpark figure on how big a loan you can qualify for.

- **Negotiate and settle on an exact price for the car before you discuss financing.** Sometimes dealers will give you a break on one aspect of a car purchase—say, a low-rate loan—but then jack up the price of the car to compensate. That's why it's critical to settle on the price first and then negotiate financing. In general, the sticker price is 10% to 20% higher than the price the dealer paid for the car. For all but the hottest models, you shouldn't pay the sticker price. Instead, check out annual reports in magazines such as *Money* and *Consumer Reports,* which list estimates of dealers' costs. Try to haggle with the dealer and pay just 5% or so above the price he paid.

- **Don't tell the dealer how much you can afford to spend on monthly payments.** This is often the first question a car dealer will ask. Though you should have a rough idea of the answer (see Figure 3-2), don't share that information with the dealer. The reason: Once the dealer knows, he can adjust the terms (for example, the price of the car or the interest rate you are charged) to his liking while matching your monthly payment figure.

- **Be wary of financing options that require "no money down" or a very low down payment.** The lower the down payment, the more interest you will pay over the life of the loan because a low down payment increases the size of the loan you need. If you can afford it and don't have other high-rate debt, of course, the best move is to pay the entire cost of the car upfront.

- **In general, go with the shortest term loan you can afford.**
  The average term on auto loans is about four years. If you
  don't have any other high-rate debt, get a loan with a term of
  four years or fewer. Remember, your goal is to pay off your
  highest-rate debt as fast as possible.

Figure 3-2
HOW MUCH YOU'LL PAY EACH MONTH WITH AN AUTO LOAN

This table can help you get a sense of what your monthly car payments
will be given a specific term and interest rate on a $10,000 auto loan.
Although your monthly payments are lower with a longer-term loan, the
total amount you will pay is greater. To figure out the total cost of the
car loan, multiply the monthly figure by the number of months it will
take for you to pay it off.

		INTEREST RATE						
		7%	8%	9%	10%	11%	12%	13%
Term (Months)	24	$448	$452	$457	$461	$466	$471	$475
	36	309	313	318	323	327	332	337
	48	239	244	249	254	258	263	268
	60	198	203	208	212	217	222	228

Source: Chase Automotive Finance

Some Advice on Leasing a Car

If you've been shopping for a car, you probably know that car dealers
push leasing in a big way. And if you're like most people, you've probably found the low down payment and low monthly payments extremely attractive. What you may not know is how leasing works.

When you lease, you are essentially renting a car from a leasing
company. Although it's most common to lease a car through a

dealership, a dealer is actually just the middleman who works on behalf of a leasing company. As a leasing customer you pay for the amount the vehicle depreciates during the lease period (typically two to four years) plus interest on this amount. Your monthly payments are based on the price of the car, the interest rate you're charged, the anticipated resale value of the car at the end of the leasing period, and the number of years in the leasing period.

As of this writing, auto dealers are not obligated to spell out all the details in the leasing agreement. As a result, it's easy to get taken for a ride, so it's important that you insist the dealer put the following information in writing:

- **The "interest rate."** Technically, there is no such thing as an "interest rate" where car leasing is concerned. There is, however, an implicit **lease rate,** which is the equivalent of an interest rate. The dealer should be able to calculate the lease rate for you. If your dealer balks, insist that he or she tell you the **money factor,** which is a figure used by most leasing companies to calculate their monthly charges. You can use this number to get an estimate of the effective interest rate you'll be paying: Simply multiply the money factor by 24 to come up with your answer. A money factor of 0.0042, for example, would give you an "interest rate" of about 10%.

- **The "price" of the car on which the lease is based.** In leasing lingo, the term **net capitalized cost** is basically the purchase price plus tax and minus your down payment and the value of any trade-in. Bargain down this price the same way you would if you were buying.

- **The probable value of the car at the end of the lease.** This is known as the **residual value.** To find out if the dealer is quoting you a fair residual value, consult the *Automotive Lease Guide's Residual Percentage Guide.* You can order a copy (cost: $12.50) by calling 800-418-8450. To make a leasing deal more attractive, some car manufacturers are willing to make the residual value artificially high. All other factors being equal, a high residual value is better for you because your monthly payments are based on how much the car is expected to depreciate during the time you lease it. A high residual value means that the car will not depreciate much during your lease; as a result, your payments will be lower. The only time a high residual value is a drawback is if you're planning to buy the car when the lease is over. But if you do decide to buy the car, you may be able to bargain with your leasing company and pay less than the residual value you previously agreed to in your leasing agreement. Try to do this right before the lease is up.

Before you lease you'll want to settle a number of issues. Find out, for instance, the total mileage you're allowed without being charged extra, and compare this mileage limitation with other manufacturers' offers to make sure you're getting a fair deal. Also, learn what the penalties are for getting out of the lease early. This information should be in your leasing agreement. Before you lease, check out magazines such as *Consumer Reports, Kiplinger's,* and *Money.* These publications usually have annual guides to buying and leasing cars. A computer program that will allow you to do a lease-versus-buy analysis is Expert Lease, which sells for about $50. (The deluxe version, which includes dealers' costs, residual values, and a list of rebate incentives, costs $100.) For more information, call 800-418-8450.

HOME EQUITY
LOANS

If you own a home, you have one additional loan source: You're usually allowed to borrow about 80% of your home's value *minus* the balance on your mortgage. The main advantage of a home equity loan, or HEL, is that it offers you a tax break that you don't get with student loans, credit cards, or auto loans. For this reason, in addition to using HELs to pay for home improvements, many people take out home equity loans and use the money to pay off other, higher-rate debt. The chief drawback of home equity loans is that borrowers can lose their homes if they can't make their payments. (In theory, auto lenders and credit card issuers can go after your home in most cases if you owe them money, but in practice they don't.)

Home Equity Loans and Home Equity Lines of Credit

Most banks offer both home equity loans and home equity lines of credit. With a home equity loan, you get all the money at once in a lump sum and repay it over 5 to 15 years. The interest rate on a home equity loan is typically a fixed rate, meaning it's the same throughout the life of the loan. Home equity lines of credit are different. They are similar to credit cards in that borrowers get a set credit line on which to draw over time. Each month they can make the minimum payment or pay more if they want to. Home equity lines generally have variable interest rates that can change on a monthly or annual basis.

The interest you pay on a home equity loan or line of up to $100,000 is *deductible*, meaning you can subtract it from your taxable income when you fill out your tax return. The interest on amounts above $100,000 is not deductible, with one exception: If you use the money for home improvements, you can deduct the interest on a loan of up to $1 million.

Here's what that tax break means in dollars. Say you owe $1,000 on your home equity loan and your interest rate is 10%. If you pay it off in one year, you will also pay $100 in interest. If you're in the 30% tax bracket, you will save $30 (30% of $100) at tax time if you itemize your deductions. So after you factor in your tax savings, the interest you actually paid was just $70. Another way to look at it is that the *after-tax* interest rate on a 10% home equity loan is 7%. (See Chapter 9 for details on itemizing.)

Before You Refinance Other Debt with Home Equity, Read This

Although home equity lines and loans offer attractive rates, it doesn't always make sense to transfer your high-rate debt to them.

BORROWING FROM FRIENDS AND RELATIVES

Jim wanted to pay off the $3,000 balance he owed on his credit card, which charged a rate of 18%. His parents were willing to lend him the money to do it. Here are some steps they followed to make the transaction harmonious:

- **They made sure the deal was good for both parties.** Jim agreed to pay his parents back with interest, and they settled on a rate of 8%. Not only was this a good deal for Jim, but it was also beneficial to his parents, whose money had formerly been sitting in a bank savings account earning just 4%.
- **They put everything in writing.** Jim's parents wrote up an agreement that included the interest rate charged and the dates payments were due. It might sound formal, but this helped avoid confusion.
- **They made sure there weren't any negative tax consequences.** Bizarre as it may seem, the IRS sets a minimum interest rate— the **applicable federal rate (AFR)**—that family members and friends are required to charge on certain types of loans. Even if your parents want to lend you money without charging you interest, they may owe tax on the interest they *would have* received had they charged you the AFR. If you borrow less than $10,000 to buy an item like a car or to pay off debts (as Jim did), you don't have to worry about these rules. But if you borrow the money to purchase assets like stocks and bonds or if you borrow more than $10,000 for any purchase, your parents, friends, or relatives may be expected to charge you interest. The rules are very complicated, so check one of the current tax guides for details, looking in the index under "loans." For the current AFR, call your bank or local IRS office.

Do not consider refinancing with your home's equity unless you do the following:

- **Plan to pay off your home equity line as fast as you would have paid off the loans you're refinancing.** As I mentioned, you may want to transfer your auto loan to a home equity line, but because you can decide how much you want to pay back each month with a home equity line, it can be tempting to make small monthly payments. Dragging out repayment gets expensive, so you have to be disciplined—which is why it's a smart idea to pay off your home equity line over the same number of years it would have taken to pay off your auto loan.

  Similarly, if you decide to pay off your credit card debt with a home equity line, you'll need to be diligent about paying the line off quickly. And don't start using your home equity line as a credit card substitute. Remember, if for any reason you can't make your payments—say, you lose your job or have a medical emergency—the lender will be allowed to take your home.

- **Factor in up-front fees.** Many lenders charge hundreds or even thousands of dollars in initial fees when they grant home equity loans and lines of credit; others do not. Shop carefully. And make sure that after you factor in the fees it still makes sense for you to refinance.

- **Determine whether or not you're comfortable with a variable interest rate.** The variable interest rates on some home equity lines are enticingly low, but make sure you know just how high your monthly payments could go if you stick to your self-imposed short-term payoff schedule. Ask the loan officer how much the rate can rise. Also, ask him to talk you through a worst-case scenario. Many home equity lines offer deeply discounted first-year rates that can increase several percentage points in year two.

CREDIT
REPORTS

Companies that keep your credit report, known as credit agencies or credit bureaus, are information gatherers and distributors. They supply banks and other lenders with all the details of your financial behavior. When you apply for a loan or credit card, lenders request the report and evaluate your history. Frequently, the credit bureau will be asked by the lender to summarize the information in your report into one number called a **risk score**. These risk scores are supposed to predict how likely you are to default on a loan, declare bankruptcy, or even make late payments. Unfortunately, at the time of this writing, you do not have access to your risk score, but you do have access to your credit report. Because so much rides on a credit agency's evaluation of your credit history, it is essential to check your credit report thoroughly before applying for a major loan.

Q: *What kind of information is in my credit report?*

A: Your report lists the basics, such as your age, birth date, Social Security number, current and previous addresses, current and previous jobs, and spouse's name (if you have one). The credit information describes all the credit relationships you have, such as bank credit cards, store credit cards, and student loans. Included is the date you opened each account, how much you owe, the maximum amount you can borrow, and your payment history. The report typically does not include information about your rent or utility payments but does indicate whether you've ever had any major financial problems such as defaulting on a loan or declaring bankruptcy.

Q: *How do I get a copy of my credit report?*

A: There are three major credit agencies that maintain credit reports: TRW, Equifax, and Trans Union. The information may be very different in each report.

If you haven't been denied credit but simply want to see what's in your credit report, TRW will send you a free report once a year if you request it. Call 800-392-1122 to find out what information to include in your written request. You'll have to pay for a report from the other two. The cost is $8 to get your report from Equifax (800-685-1111) or from Trans Union (216-779-7200). A few states limit or prohibit the charge for sending a copy of your credit report. To find out about your state's rules, contact the consumer protection division of your state's attorney general's office.

Q: *If I'm turned down for a loan, do I get to find out why?*
A: Yes. The Equal Credit Opportunity Act says that if your application for credit is denied, the lender must either give you an explanation for the rejection or inform you as to how you can get an explanation. If you ask for a specific reason, the lender must provide you with one. According to the Federal Trade Commission, acceptable explanations should be fairly specific—for example, you earn too little money or haven't worked long enough. Vague reasons—such as not meeting the creditor's "minimum standards"—aren't acceptable.

If the denial was due to something in your credit report, the lender must tell you the name and address of the credit agency that provided information about you. If you are denied credit, all the credit agencies are required by law to send you a free report if you request it within 30 days.

Q: *What should I do if I find a mistake in my credit report?*
A: Credit bureaus have a reputation for making mistakes. Sometimes it's simply misspelling your name or giving a wrong address, but sometimes it's a potentially damaging error—such as mistakenly showing that you've defaulted on a loan.

If you find a mistake in your report, write to the credit agency right away. It must investigate the discrepancy within a reasonable time period (generally 30 days). If the agency agrees that there's an error, request that it send a corrected version of the report to any lender that received the incorrect report within the last six months and to any employer who received the wrong information within the last two years. The credit agency is required to do this if you request it.

If there's a dispute, the burden of proof lies with the agency; unless it can verify that the information in question is correct, the agency must delete it. If you don't agree with the outcome of the investigation, write a short statement (100 words or fewer) and have the credit agency include it in your credit report. If you ask, the credit agency should send a copy of your version of the dispute free of charge to anyone who recently received the old report.

Q: *How long will my credit report show my misdeeds?*

A: Most negative information will be deleted after seven years. If you ever filed for bankruptcy, it could take ten years before your credit report will be clean. This doesn't mean you won't be able to get credit before then. Lenders usually look at your behavior in the last two years or so when evaluating your creditworthiness.

Q: *I've heard of companies that claim to repair credit ratings. Should I consider one?*

A: Definitely not. There are all kinds of sleazy firms that promise to fix credit reports. Don't waste your money on them. At best, these fly-by-night companies work the legal fine print to trip up the credit bureaus and force them to remove negative information. But most of the time these tricky maneuvers don't work, and you end up paying hundreds of dollars for nothing. Stay away from these scam artists.

Q: *I'm married. Does that mean my spouse and I have the same credit report?*

A: If you each had your own credit cards before you were married, then you each have a separate credit report. If you have a joint credit card or loan, that will be noted on both of your individual credit reports. Keep in mind that whenever you share a card or cosign a loan, you are liable for each other's debts.

It is important for you to keep at least one loan or credit card in your own name, and for your spouse to do the same so that each of you establishes a separate credit history. If you don't, you will have trouble getting credit if you get divorced or if your spouse dies.

Q: *Who can look at my credit report?*

A: The law says that credit bureaus can disclose information about you to any person or organization with a "permissible purpose" for seeing the information. That can include a lender, employer, or landlord who wants to find out about your financial habits. A copy of the report shows who made inquiries about you. Lender and landlord inquiries remain in your report for six months or longer, depending on the credit bureau; potential-employer inquiries remain for two years.

IS BANKRUPTCY AN OPTION?

Tom, A 25-year-old social worker, earns $22,000 a year and doesn't expect his salary to increase anytime soon. Unfortunately, he has more than $50,000 in student loans and $5,000 in credit card debt. Feeling desperate, he wondered if it made sense for him to declare bankruptcy.

The fact is, declaring bankruptcy, especially a certain type known as Chapter 7, can seem very appealing. You simply have to fill out a form and submit it with a fee (recently $160) at a federal bankruptcy court. At that point your creditors can't come after you; instead, they must wait for a judge's decision. If the judge permits your case to proceed, he or she will often "discharge" most of your debts, meaning absolve you of responsibility for the money you owe to creditors such as your landlord, doctors, and credit card companies. Some of your assets can be seized to pay off these creditors, but you may be able to work out a deal where you get to keep your car, home, and many of your household possessions. And it may not be

IF YOU'RE IN
SERIOUS DEBT

If you're having severe trouble making your payments, contact your lenders directly and explain your financial situation. Often you will find that a lender is willing to work with you to come up with a more flexible repayment schedule.

If your creditor has hired a debt collector to get you to pay up,

long before you can start borrowing again. A recent study found that more than one-third of those who declared bankruptcy were able to get credit within three years of filing.

Although this sounds like a great deal, it's not an option Tom—or most of us, for that matter—should consider. For starters, there's a long list of debts that can't be discharged if you file Chapter 7. Only student loans that you were supposed to begin paying back seven years ago or more, for instance, can be wiped out; newer student loans are not forgiven. What's more, bankruptcy is noted on your credit report for 10 years. True, you may be able to get some form of credit within a few years, but you probably won't be eligible for low-rate credit cards or other attractive loan deals for many years. Finally, because prospective employers will learn from your credit report that you declared bankruptcy, you may have trouble changing jobs—especially if you're trying to get a position that requires you to be financially responsible.

know your rights. Debt collectors can contact you by phone, mail, or fax, or in person. They must contact you during reasonable hours (not before 8 A.M. or after 9 P.M.) unless you agree to a different arrangement. They can't harass you or repeatedly phone you with the intent to annoy you. You can stop a debt collector from continually contacting you by sending a letter to the collection agency he represents. Under the Fair Debt Collection Practices Act, the collection agency must stop contacting you at your request except to notify you of plans to bring legal action against you.

If you need help negotiating with lenders to lower your monthly payments and possibly reduce the interest rates on your loans, you may want to contact the nonprofit Consumer Credit Counseling Service (CCCS). This service is often free for general budgeting advice and typically charges a low fee for debt repayment counseling (about $9 a month). If you can't afford to pay, CCCS says it will not turn you away. To locate an office near you, call 800-388-2227.

Unfortunately, CCCS is not perfect. There has been criticism of the organization because it's funded primarily by lenders such as credit card companies. Critics charge that CCCS has a vested interest in having debtors pay back the money they owe. They say that if someone's only recourse is to file for bankruptcy and get a fresh start, CCCS may be hesitant to point out this option because such a solution does not serve its sponsors well. If you're not satisfied with the help you receive, call the National Foundation for Consumer Credit, an umbrella group for CCCS offices nationwide; the number is 301-589-5600.

You may also want to look into other nonprofit counseling services available in your area. Some colleges and credit unions, for instance, offer such services. And you might be able to get a referral from a local bank or consumer protection office.

FINANCIAL CRAMMING

- Take any savings you have and pay off your high-rate credit card debt. Paying off a balance on a credit card that charges 18% is the equivalent of earning more than 18% interest on your money. This is by far the best investment most of us can make.

- If you have a decent credit history but can't pay off your high-rate credit card debt immediately, try to get a low-rate card and transfer your debt to it. You can find listings of low-rate cards in personal finance magazines, or you can write to one of the firms mentioned on page 51 and request a listing for about $5.

- If you currently have federal student loans, check whether you can refinance them at a lower rate under the Federal Direct Consolidation Loan program. For information call 800-4FED-AID.

- Before you visit a car dealership, check with a couple of banks (and a credit union if you belong to one) to get an idea of the current auto loan rates. Then, once you find the car you want, negotiate an exact price for a car with the dealer before you discuss the financing he has to offer.

- If you own a home, consider taking out a home equity line in order to pay off your high-rate debt. But plan to pay off your home equity line as fast as you would have paid off the loans you're refinancing.

- Before you apply for an auto loan or a low-rate credit card, get a free copy of your credit report from TRW (800-392-1122). Because each credit bureau has different information, you should also check with Equifax (800-685-1111) and Trans Union (216-779-7200). These bureaus charge $8 for a report, although the price can vary depending on where you live.

BASIC BANKING

Learn How to Get the Most
from Your Bank
for the Least Amount of
Money

CHANCES ARE YOUR parents' financial lives revolved around their bank. They kept their savings there. They got their mortgage there. They obtained their first credit card there. They probably even got their clock radio there.

But that may not be true for you, because today many of the services that were once the domain of banks are better handled elsewhere. You may have obtained an auto loan through a car dealership rather than from a bank because the dealership offered more attractive terms. Perhaps you have a General Motors credit card because it has no annual fee and allows you to earn discounts on GM cars. Or maybe you switched from a bank savings account to a money market mutual fund because it paid a better rate.

Why do you need a bank at all? The main reason is that banks offer two services that are difficult to get anywhere else: an all-purpose checking account and easy access to your cash through bank machines, also known as **automated teller machines** (**ATMs**). So the key factors to consider when choosing a bank are the costs of its checking and ATM services. If you take the time to investigate these charges before you choose a bank, you could save yourself hundreds of dollars each year. This chapter shows you how to shop for a bank. It also highlights your various savings options and offers you tips on reducing all your banking costs.

A BANK BY ANY OTHER NAME

For our purposes, it doesn't matter whether an institution calls itself a bank, a savings bank, or a savings and loan (S&L). These classifications reflect the government agency that oversees the institution and have no impact on you whatsoever. A **credit union** is a special kind of bank formed by people who have a common bond, such as a shared workplace or profession. Credit unions tend to offer lower-priced services than ordinary banks. (For details on the advantages of credit unions and how to join, see the box.)

Nearly all banks, savings banks, and S&Ls in the United States are covered by something called federal deposit insurance. It offers the guarantee that if the institution should fail, the money in your federally insured accounts (up to $100,000) will be protected. Look for signs that tell you that your money is covered by federal deposit insurance. Federally insured credit unions have signs indicating that they are protected by the National Credit Union Administration (NCUA). If you don't see a sign or sticker at your institution, ask. Keep in mind that many banks, savings banks, S&Ls, and credit unions sell *uninsured investments* these days, so it is also important to make sure that the type of account you're opening is covered by federal deposit insurance. (These uninsured investments are explained later on in this chapter.)

For simplicity, I'm going to stick with the term "bank" when discussing any of these financial institutions.

SIGN UP WITH A CREDIT UNION IF YOU CAN

Doing your banking at a credit union can often save you money. Credit unions tend to charge lower rates on loans and pay higher rates on savings accounts than ordinary banks. Even better, about two-thirds of credit unions (versus about one-quarter of ordinary banks) offer free checking with no minimum balance requirement. And credit unions typically charge less for everything from cashier's checks to bounced checks.

Before you sign up with a credit union, you'll want to see if it offers all the services you want. For instance, most credit unions do not have their own ATMs. Although they usually offer their members a card they can use at ATMs owned by other banks, the ATM fees charged by credit unions are sometimes higher than those at ordinary banks. Also, many credit unions don't return your canceled checks with your statements the way banks do.

If these drawbacks don't bother you, you should definitely see if you're eligible to join one. If you work for your city, chances are there's a credit union available to you. Your church or synagogue may have one, or your community may have a credit union whose members are people who live in the neighborhood. If you have a relative who belongs to a credit union, you might be eligible to enroll; some credit unions accept immediate family members only, while others allow extended family members to sign up. For assistance, call 800-358-5710 and ask for the phone number of your state's credit union league. The league will help you locate a credit union that you may be able to join.

FINDING A LOW-COST
CHECKING ACCOUNT

The interest rates that banks pay on savings accounts usually do not vary dramatically from bank to bank. It would be unusual to find one bank paying 3% on a savings account and another bank down the street paying 8%. The important distinction among banks has to do with the fees you pay for services and the minimum balances required to avoid such fees. And the biggest challenge you may face is finding a bank that does not require you to maintain a high minimum balance to get free checking.

Many banks do not charge monthly checking fees if you keep $500 in a checking account. But some banks in major cities have much higher minimums—from $1,000 to $3,000. If you can't maintain the minimum, you have to pay a monthly checking charge of between $3 and $10. You may also have to pay 25 cents for each check you write above a predetermined limit.

To find the best checking deal, you'll have to do some scouting around. First, make sure you fully understand your current bank's minimum balance requirements. Then ask friends and coworkers if they know of a bank that has a lower balance requirement to qualify for free checking. If they don't have any leads for you, use the Yellow Pages to pinpoint banks nearby and start calling around. In New York City, for example, at least one bank (First Nationwide) has offered totally free checking to all customers regardless of the size of their balances. In general, smaller community banks tend to offer better deals than large, big-name national banks. Keep this in mind when you hunt for an institution.

Here are some tips on reducing your checking costs:

- **Pay attention to how a bank calculates the minimum balance.** Avoid institutions that use what is called the **minimum daily balance method**. This system requires you to maintain the minimum balance every single day in order to get free checking. If your balance drops below the minimum for even one day, you will be charged a fee. Instead, look for a bank that uses the **average daily balance method**. With this method the bank adds up your daily balances and then divides that total by the number of days in the billing cycle to get an average figure. So if your bank's balance requirement is $1,000 and your account dips below that a couple of times a billing cycle, you won't be penalized as long as your *average* balance is at least $1,000.

• **See if your bank allows you to "link" accounts to meet balance requirements.** Some institutions insist that you keep a minimum amount of money in your *checking* account in order to get free checking. Others offer free checking if you maintain the minimum balance in a *combination* of accounts—including checking accounts, savings accounts, certificates of deposit (CDs), and money market accounts. Typically, the combo deal is the way to go—but pay attention to the details. In order to get free checking at some banks you must keep twice as much money in the combination of accounts as you'd have to keep in a checking account.

• **Ask your employer to deposit your paycheck directly into your bank account each month.** Some banks will waive minimum balance requirements and checking fees if you sign up for **direct deposit** through your employer. This increasingly available arrangement permits your company to deposit your entire paycheck automatically into your checking or savings account.

• **If you write only a few checks a month, consider alternatives to a regular checking account.** Many banks offer what are called "basic," "lifeline," or "no-frills" checking accounts. These accounts charge a smaller monthly fee (about $3) and limit you to eight or ten free checks per month. (Some banks waive the checking fee if you keep at least $250 in a combination of your bank accounts.) If you exceed the monthly check limit, you pay a fee for each additional check you write, so if you usually need more than eight or ten checks a month, basic banking is not for you. Also, these programs often limit your free ATM transactions to a few per month, ruling them out for many young people. But if you can comfortably comply with the restrictions, a basic banking account is a worthwhile alternative.

• **Avoid interest-bearing checking accounts that require you to maintain high minimum balances.** Checking accounts that pay interest—also called **NOW accounts**—can be very appealing. (NOW stands for—get this—negotiable orders of withdrawal.) But some banks require you to keep a minimum of $1,000 in a NOW account at all times, and a number even require an average daily balance of $2,000. If you fall below the minimum, you're slapped with a penalty. The interest rate paid on such a NOW account is often so meager that it probably doesn't make sense to tie up your money in one. Odds are you're better off sticking with a regular checking account and a savings account (which is discussed later in this chapter).

MANAGING YOUR CHECKING ACCOUNT

Once you find a low-cost checking account, you'll want to make sure you manage it wisely. If you don't, you could find yourself zapped with $20 bounced-check fees. Here are some tips that will help you avoid such outrageous charges and in general gain control of your checking account:

• **Balance your checkbook.** For some reason many people dread this chore even though it isn't difficult. Unless you're wealthy enough to keep so much cash in your checking account that you never have to worry about covering all the checks you write, you've got to balance your book. It helps to carry your check register with you so that you can record checks the minute you write them and ATM withdrawals (and deposits) as soon as you make them. If your company deposits your paycheck into your checking account, make sure to enter that deposit into your check register every payday as well. If you need help balancing your checkbook, look at the back of your bank statement; many banks provide a useful worksheet that can help you keep your checkbook in order. And if you're into computers, you may want to use a personal finance program that will do the math for you. (For details, see Chapter 2.) If you do use such a program, you'll need to enter every deposit and withdrawal you make into your computer.

• **Adopt a system that suits your financial situation.** If you tend to live from paycheck to paycheck, one way to help ensure that you have enough money in your account to cover your checks is to sign up for direct deposit and have your paycheck deposited into your checking account. With direct deposit, the money shows up in your checking account within two days of payday. The drawback to this method is that it can result in all your money sitting in a checking account that doesn't pay interest. That's why, if you opt for this system, you should sign up for an automatic savings plan at your bank. You might, for example, ask your bank to withdraw $50 a month from your checking account and transfer it into a savings account or another interest-bearing account. (For details on how these automatic savings plans work, see the box on page 91.)

If your financial situation is less hand-to-mouth, another alternative is to deposit your paycheck directly into an interest-bearing account and then transfer money into your checking account to cover checks as you write them. You'll earn more interest using this method, but if you're not extremely conscientious about transferring money into your checking account, you'll end up bouncing checks.

• **Pay your bills electronically.** One way to get your checking account in order is to pay your bills electronically. Many utility companies allow you to have your monthly payments electronically siphoned out of your checking account. There are also a handful of national bill-paying services that allow you to pay all your bills electronically via a computer and modem or by using a touch-tone telephone. You can sign up for one of these services directly or through a bank, a personal finance program (such as Quicken), or an online service (such as CompuServe). The way it generally works is that you supply the bill-paying service with a list of merchants you want to pay and the date on which the payments should be made. After setting up your system, with the touch of a button on your computer (or telephone) you can pay your bills electronically each month. Many bill-paying services allow you to prepare and date payments up to a year in advance. You can also set up your system to automatically pay recurring bills that are the same amount each month. If you sign up for a bill-paying service through your bank, you may be able to pay your bills at an ATM. The cost of many electronic bill-paying services is about $10 a month; one of the least expensive services, Payline, costs just $4 a month. (For information on Payline, call 800-572-9546.)

One general warning: Don't wait until the day a bill is due to pay it electronically. There is a lag, typically between two and five days, between the time you initiate a payment and the time a merchant actually receives it. To avoid any slip-ups, make electronic payments at least six business days before your bills are due.

- **Sign up for bounced-check protection.** Many banks offer what is called **overdraft protection.** This is basically an automatic loan that kicks in if you write a check for an amount greater than the amount you have in your checking account. The interest rate you pay on the overdrawn amount is often high (19% or so), but if you don't abuse it, the service will cost you much less than a bounced-check penalty. That said, it's important to keep in mind that you'll probably have to write a check to pay off the overdraft account; it will not automatically be paid off as you deposit money in your checking account. Also, understand that some banks allow you to access your overdraft protection via your ATM. I have a friend who ran out of money and simply withdrew the $1,000 in overdraft protection via the ATM to cover the cost of a trip to France. It took her three years and more than $1,300 to pay off the loan.

- **Don't rely on the ATM to keep track of your checking account.** One common reason people get nailed with massive bounced-check fees is that they don't realize how the check-clearing process works. If you don't keep track of the checks you write, you could find yourself in trouble. Say you have $200 in your checking account, and you mail an $80 check to the phone company. Assume it takes a week for the phone company to deposit your check. If five days go by and you suddenly remember that you need $150 to renew your health club membership, you would see at the ATM that you have $200 in your account. If you forgot about the check you wrote to the phone company, you might withdraw $150, in which case your phone company check would bounce. The point: Keep track of your checking account.

USING THE ATM WISELY

You've heard of the MTV generation? Well, most of us are part of the ATM generation, a group that relies on bank machines for survival. Just a few years ago banks didn't charge for ATM use because they wanted to encourage customers to become comfortable banking by machine. But the days of free ATMs are nearly over; now they can cost up to $2 per transaction. Here are some tips on keeping your ATM habits—and your spending—in check:

- **Limit yourself to four ATM withdrawals per month if possible.** Not only is it often expensive to withdraw $20 a day from an ATM, it's also a bad way to keep track of where your money goes. Use the worksheet you filled out in Chap-

WHY IT PAYS TO KNOW YOUR BANK MANAGER

You don't have to present your bank manager with a shiny apple each time you visit, but it's a good idea to get acquainted. You can simply say that you've signed on as a customer and just wanted to introduce yourself. If you think this sounds a little weird, invent a reason—ask about loan options or something. The point is to make sure the manager recognizes your face. If you ever have a problem, it can really help to have someone at the bank who knows you as more than just another multi-digit account number.

And if you ever encounter an outrageous fee, don't hesitate to speak up. When a friend of mine was charged $30 for two bank checks—an amount he felt was outlandishly high—he protested to the bank manager, who waived the fee. The fact is, bank managers often forgive fees for customers who complain—especially those customers who have clean banking records. And if you're penalized for something you had no control over—unknowingly depositing a bad check, for example—you should definitely talk to the bank manager; he or she may be willing to erase the charge.

ter 2 to estimate how much cash you need each week. Then pick one day a week to withdraw cash from the machine— say, every Monday. Make a pact with yourself to make that cash last for the entire week. Promise yourself that once it runs out, you won't get more. This strategy will also help you rein in your spending habits.

• **Find out what it costs to use another bank's ATM.** Some banks charge their own customers for using their ATMs. Others don't, but do charge you for using bank machines that are affiliated with other banks. The fee for using a "foreign" ATM, as it is called, could be as high as $2 per transaction.

- **Ask about the minimums for avoiding ATM fees.** Some banks require you to maintain a minimum balance in your account in order to avoid ATM fees. If you don't meet the minimum, you could be charged 25 cents per withdrawal to use your bank's ATMs, and $1 to use another bank's machine. Although that may not sound like a lot, it can add up; if you withdraw money from an ATM twice a week, half the time at your own bank and half at other banks, you could pay about $65 a year in ATM charges.

- **Know the different ATM fees your bank charges.** Some banks also charge for transactions other than withdrawals. Finding out your balance or transferring money between accounts might cost from 25 cents to $1. If you use the ATM a lot, find a bank with low transaction fees, or look for one that waives ATM charges when you maintain a low monthly minimum balance.

JOINT VERSUS SEPARATE ACCOUNTS

If you're involved with someone but not married, don't open a joint account with that person without giving it serious thought. With a joint account, either person has complete access to all the money in the account. What's more, if you break up, dividing up the money in a joint account could get ugly.

If you're not married but are involved in a serious relationship, you may decide you want to open a joint account with your partner. Many people do this for convenience and also because they think a joint account ensures that one partner will get all the money in the account in case the other dies. But this can be very tricky. Having one type of joint account with your partner, called a **joint convenience**

account, does not entitle one person to inherit all the money in the account if the other dies. With another type of joint account, called a **joint account with the right of survivorship,** the person with whom you share the account usually gets to inherit all the money in the account. An account with the right of survivorship doesn't offer your partner total protection, however; parents and other family members can protest the arrangement in court. To better protect your partner, you should also write a will.

If you're married, you and your spouse should discuss the joint account question. If you favor separate accounts but your spouse wants joint, there is a way to compromise: Consider keeping a portion of your savings in a joint account and putting a percentage—say, 5% of each paycheck—into separate accounts. That way you have the freedom to spend some of your money without having to confer with your partner. You should also discuss what will happen in case of death. In some states your parents would split your assets with your spouse if you die. Again, write a will to prevent such a situation.

MANAGING A JOINT CHECKING ACCOUNT

If you and your mate decide to have a joint checking account, you're going to need to develop a system for keeping track of the checks each of you writes. A system will help avoid bouncing checks. The best way to handle it is to put one person in charge of balancing the checkbook. Marty and Andrea use checkbooks that have carbon copies. Each time they write a check, they simply toss the carbon copy into a box located in the kitchen. They also put ATM and bank withdrawal and deposit slips into the box, as well as incoming household bills. Twice a month Andrea goes through the box, writes checks to pay all the current household bills and balances the checkbook.

DIFFERENT WAYS TO SAVE IN A BANK

Bank savings options don't offer the potential for phenomenal gains, but that's not what you're after here. You're just looking to meet the requirements for free checking and low-cost ATM usage. You'll make your fortune elsewhere.

As I said earlier, many banks will waive checking fees and give you unlimited free checking if you keep $500 in a checking account. If you don't have $500, make it your goal to build up this amount through an automatic savings program. You might want to stick with a no-frills checking account in the meantime. Once you have $500, aim to maintain that balance in your checking account. When you've accumulated more than $500, start thinking about other banking options. You may be able to find a bank that offers you free checking for keeping, say, $1,000 in a *combination* of accounts— including CDs, money market accounts, savings accounts, and checking accounts. The advantage of this arrangement is that most of these accounts pay interest. If you're not sure you can maintain the required $1,000 in combined balances, however, you're better off keeping all your money in a non-interest-bearing checking account. The reason: The interest you would earn is too low to offset the monthly checking fees you would pay if you unintentionally fell below the minimum.

If you can comfortably maintain the $1,000 combined minimum, consider keeping most of your money in accounts that pay interest and transferring money to your checking account to cover the checks you write.

Here are some details on the interest-paying accounts most banks offer:

- **Savings accounts.** This plain vanilla type of account provides you with the simplest way to keep money in the bank and earn interest on it. The big advantage of a savings account over other bank savings choices is that you don't need much money to open one. Generally there is no initial minimum deposit (but some banks do charge a monthly fee of $3 if the amount in your savings account drops below $200). Another advantage is that money in a savings account is **liquid**, meaning you can withdraw it whenever you want without paying a penalty. The bummer about savings accounts is that they tend to pay very low interest rates. Although banks occasionally raise the rates on savings accounts when interest rates in the economy rise, they are very slow to do this.

Advice: Keep only as much as you need to qualify for free checking in a savings account. If you have additional money, explore options other than a bank. (More on these options in Chapter 5.)

• **Money market accounts.** A money market account is little more than a savings account with a relatively high minimum balance requirement and a complicated name. You will likely need between $1,000 and $2,500 to open a money market account, and you may have to maintain at least $1,000 in your account at all times to avoid paying a monthly account maintenance fee. Like savings accounts, money market accounts are liquid (except for the minimum balance requirement) and usually pay a low, variable interest rate. The only extra feature you get with a money market account is that you can write a limited number of checks against it; you can't do that with a savings account.

When money market accounts were first introduced in the 1980s, they paid higher interest rates than savings accounts. Banks offered these higher rate accounts to keep customers from fleeing banks for higher paying investments offered elsewhere. But customers *did* move away from banks to invest their money elsewhere, so many banks gave up trying to compete; they stopped offering money market accounts with significantly better rates than savings accounts. Today, most money market accounts pay only slightly higher rates than savings accounts.

Advice: Consider a money market account only if (1) it pays a higher interest rate than your bank's savings account, *and* (2) the minimum balance required to avoid monthly account maintenance fees isn't much higher than the minimum required in a savings account. Unless both these criteria are met, you might as well stick with a basic savings account and put any additional cash into more attractive investments.

• **Certificates of deposit (CDs).** A certificate of deposit is a "savings product" that usually pays a fixed interest rate if you keep your money invested in it for a specified period of time (known as the CD's **term**). CDs almost always pay better rates than savings or money market accounts. With a CD you make a one-time investment and earn interest until the CD's term is complete. You do not continually add money to a CD; if you want to invest more money, you can open a new CD. You can find a CD with as short a term as three months or as long a term as ten years. A common type is a one-year CD.

At many banks you need at least $500 to open a CD. Usually, the longer the CD's term, the higher the interest rate. With a CD you give up the liquidity you have with a savings or money market account, but you are rewarded with a higher rate.

The big drawback of a CD is that if you take out the money you've deposited before the CD's term is complete, you will be hit with an early withdrawal fee. These penalties can be steep; if you withdraw money very early in the CD's term, you could lose interest plus part of your initial investment.

There's another issue to consider before choosing a CD over a savings account: When you lock yourself into a CD, you are in effect placing a bet on the direction of interest rates. Here's why. Say you deposit money in a two-year CD that promises to pay you 5%. Suppose that six months later interest rates increase dramatically, and banks are now paying 7% on two-year CDs. You have a problem. You're stuck with the 5% CD for another year and six months. Although you would like to get out of the 5% CD (and into a 7% CD), the early withdrawal penalty you'd have to pay might be so

AUTOMATIC SAVINGS PLANS

Although you're probably not going to keep your life's savings in a bank forever, a bank savings account is the first place most of us start to save. If you haven't been able to accumulate much savings on your own, have someone save *for* you. There are a couple of ways to do this. One way is to ask your company payroll office if you can have a fixed sum taken from each paycheck—say, $50 a month—and funneled directly into your bank savings account. Many employers offer such arrangements. If your employer doesn't, ask your bank to siphon off a set amount from your checking account at the same time each month and deposit that money in your savings account. (Remember to record the amount of money you withdraw in your checkbook, or else you could start bouncing lots of checks!) These "forced savings" methods offer you an effortless way to build up a nest egg. Because you don't even see the money that's being set aside, before long you also won't even miss it. (For more information on automatic savings options offered by mutual funds and retirement savings plans, see Chapters 5 and 6.)

large that it wouldn't be worth it. You won't face this risk with a savings account because the rate you receive will rise (slowly but surely) as interest rates in the economy rise. Of course, this works in reverse, too. If interest rates fall and new CDs are paying 3%, you'd be a winner with your 5% CD.

Advice: If you don't need your money for a fixed period of time, consider a CD. But before you open one, consider the return you can get with money funds, an investment you will learn about in Chapter 5. And shop around: You might be able to find CDs that pay a fixed rate that is from 1% to 3% higher than your own bank's CD rate. To find a list of banks offering the nation's highest CD rates, look in financial publications or in your local newspaper. Also, take a look at federally insured bank CDs that are sold by brokerage firms. **Brokered CDs,** as they are called, sometimes offer higher rates than CDs sold directly by banks. Two brokerage firms that have offered competitive CD rates in the past are Merrill Lynch and Smith Barney. You don't pay a commission on broker-sold CDs; brokerage firms make their money on CDs by charging the bank a fee.

If you get a CD at your own bank, you may be able to link it to your checking account for purposes of meeting your minimum balance requirement. Ask a new-accounts officer about this option.

A WARNING ABOUT BANK-SOLD INVESTMENTS

Just a few years ago banks offered only the three savings options described above (savings accounts, money market accounts, and CDs), all of which are federally insured. That's no longer the case. Today many banks sell investments, such as stock mutual funds and bond mutual funds. Although you will learn everything you ever wanted to know about mutual funds in Chapter 5, I want to mention something right away: Mutual funds, even those sold in banks, are not protected by federal deposit insurance. That means you *can* lose money with a mutual fund. Bank salespeople, who like to call themselves "financial counselors," are supposed to explain this, but they sometimes forget. As a rule, you're probably better off buying stock and bond mutual funds directly from low-cost mutual fund companies rather than from banks. That's because the vast majority of banks charge commissions on the mutual funds they sell.

FINANCIAL CRAMMING

- Shop around for a bank that offers you free checking and waives ATM fees if you maintain a low minimum monthly balance in your checking account or in a combination of accounts. This can save you hundreds of dollars a year.

- Sign up with a credit union to minimize your banking costs. To find out if you're eligible to join one, call 800-358-5710 and ask for the number of your state's Credit Union League.

- Avoid massive bounced-check charges by balancing your checkbook. If your bank offers overdraft protection, sign up for it.

- Don't put your money in a money market account just because it pays a slightly higher interest rate than a plain old savings account. To avoid monthly maintenance fees, you often have to keep more money in a money market account than you would in a savings account. As you'll see in Chapter 5, it usually doesn't pay to tie up so much money in the bank.

- If you've been charged an outrageous fee for a bank service, complain. Being forceful but polite will often help you persuade the bank's customer service rep to waive the charge.

- Resist buying mutual funds on which banks charge commissions. Instead, look into some of the low-cost mutual fund companies discussed in Chapter 5.

5

ALL YOU REALLY NEED TO KNOW ABOUT INVESTING

For New Investors, the Feeling Is Mutual (Funds)

I F YOU'RE LIKE a lot of people, you have all your money sitting in a low-paying checking or savings account. Although you know you should explore alternatives, you never seem to get around to it. Maybe you have just enough money to get by and investing doesn't seem realistic, or maybe you have no idea where to put it. But whatever your own maybes may be, the fact is that once you have enough money in your bank account to qualify for free checking, you're ready to learn about investing. Fortunately, this is a lot easier than it sounds.

Instead of betting your life's savings on some half-baked tip that promises to make you rich (but probably won't), you should be thinking about a particular, fully baked investment known as a mutual fund. In fact, you can consider mutual funds your entire investment universe, at least for now. This chapter will first explain what mutual funds are and how you can use them to meet the goals you formulated in Chapter 2. Later in the chapter you'll learn how to actually go about investing in them.

MUTUAL FUND
FUNDAMENTALS

Before I get into the details, you'll need to know what a mutual fund is. Let's break it down. Mutual means shared, or in common. A fund is a sum of money set aside for a particular purpose. A **mutual fund** is a type of investment that pools together the money of thousands of people. At the helm is a fund manager, the person (or company) in charge of investing the money. Depending on the type of fund, the fund manager will generally invest most of the fund's money in stocks, bonds, or money market instruments; these are all known as **securities.** (I'll explain what stocks, bonds, and money market instruments really are later on.)

What's So Great About Mutual Funds?

Pooling your money with the money of other people works to your advantage because it allows you to reduce the risk you take as an investor. At any given time a mutual fund is typically invested in dozens (and sometimes hundreds) of different stocks, bonds, or money market instruments. If you bought just one of these securities on your own, your success or failure would depend solely on the performance of that one security. When you invest in a mutual fund, though, you avoid putting all your eggs in one basket. So even if half the securities in the mutual fund lose value, you won't necessarily lose money; the other half may be profitable and may balance out the losses with offsetting gains. The term for this investing principle is **diversification.**

Mutual Fund Shares

When you invest in any type of mutual fund, you are technically purchasing units known as shares. As shareholders, you and thousands of others are in fact the owners of the fund. The fund's share price—meaning the price at which you can buy or sell a share in the fund—is called the **net asset value (NAV)**. Remember this term. It will not only impress your friends when you use it at parties, but it will also come in handy later in the chapter.

Two Pointers for New Mutual Fund Investors

Before going into the details of the various types of mutual funds, I'd like to take a minute to acknowledge two sad truths of investment life. Though they may seem obvious, they are often lost on many investors who should know better.

- **There's no easy way to pick a winner.** The fact that a given stock did well last year provides little or no information about how well it will do in future years. More generally, there's no proven investment strategy that will always beat the others. If people tell you otherwise, don't believe them— including the analyst from a major brokerage firm who appears on CNN, the distinguished economist who is quoted regularly in the newspaper, or your favorite uncle on your mother's side who had the foresight to buy stock in Microsoft when it was trading for half its current price.

- **In general, you don't get something for nothing.** With rare exceptions the only way to get an unusually high rate of return on your investments is to accept an unusually high level of risk. So if anyone promises you a very high return with "absolutely no risk," be skeptical.

MONEY MARKET FUNDS

As soon as you have enough money in the bank to get free checking, you're ready to learn about a particular type of mutual fund called a **money market fund**. Also known simply as money funds, these offer a good way for first-time investors to get their feet wet. They're the safest, most stable type of mutual fund, and they tend to pay returns that are about one to two percentage points higher than the rates paid on bank savings accounts.

Why Invest in a Money Market Fund?

Don't let the name confuse you; money market funds are very different from bank money market accounts, which you learned about in Chapter 4. For one thing, money funds are not federally insured like bank accounts. But they are considered nearly as safe. Since money funds pay a higher rate than bank accounts, you can view them as a smarter type of bank account. Aim to save at least three months' worth of living expenses in a money fund before you even think about branching out into stock funds and bond funds. This money fund savings stash will serve as an excellent emergency financial cushion in case of a temporary job loss or illness.

What Are Money Market Instruments?

To better understand what money funds are, you'll need a crash course in money market instruments, the securities that money funds invest in. When large companies or governments need money for very short periods, they issue money market instruments in exchange for the cash they need. These **money market instruments** are basically IOUs. Money market fund managers invest mainly in money market instruments issued by reliable institutions such as the federal government, various state governments, and big-name corporations.

Since money market funds invest primarily in large, financially stable institutions that promise to repay their money market debts very quickly, they are considered quite safe. On those relatively rare occasions when an institution hasn't made good on its obligations, the money fund manager has generally been willing to reimburse the fund, thus protecting the fund's investors from any loss. Over the last 15 years, just one money fund has lost money for its investors, and even then it lost only 4% of their investment. Practically speaking, this probably isn't worth losing much sleep over.

How Your Money Grows in a Money Market Fund

As with any mutual fund, when you invest in a money fund, you're actually purchasing shares of that fund. Money fund managers try to keep the price (or NAV) of each share equal to a dollar at all times by investing in short-term debt securities they believe to be very safe. So when you invest $250 in a money fund, what you're really doing is buying 250 shares of the fund. The fund manager then lends your $250 (together with the money it collects from other investors) to various governments and/or corporations, receiving IOUs (money market instruments) in return.

In addition to repaying their debts, these governments and corporations must pay the money fund interest on the money they're borrowing from it. Now here's the good part: The fund then passes these interest payments on to you in the form of **dividends,** which are typically credited to your account every business day. If you like, most money market funds will wire these dividends into your bank account or mail them to you (usually once a month). Many investors, however, choose to have their dividends automatically **reinvested** in the money fund. In this case, their dividends are used to buy more shares in the fund. This is a smart thing to do; in addition to avoiding the hassle of depositing an additional 12 checks each year, it's a relatively painless way to increase the size of your account and keep yourself from spending your monthly dividend checks.

The **yield** of a money fund is analogous to the interest rate paid on a savings account. You can calculate the yield by dividing the fund's **dividends per share** by its share price (which is generally a dollar). The yield of each money fund fluctuates from day to day. Since money funds all calculate their yields in the same way, though, you can compare the yields of several money funds before selecting one. Call the fund company's 800 number and ask for the money fund's **SEC seven-day yield,** which is the average yield for the past seven days.

Some money funds send out statements monthly; others mail them out quarterly. Your statement will indicate the number and value of the shares you own; the two figures are usually the same because the price per share is almost always a dollar.

Different Types of Money Market Funds

There's not just one kind of money fund but a variety of types to choose from. Your choice of fund type may be influenced by your tax bracket and the state you live in. In addition, some types of money funds are, at least in theory, slightly riskier than others. Because money market funds hardly ever lose money, though, many sophisticated investors treat them all as essentially risk-free; they go for the highest-yielding fund they can find (subject only to tax considerations), regardless of the variety.

The choices are listed below. They can be divided into two basic categories—taxable money funds and tax-exempt money funds. Although you don't need to memorize all the details, you'll want to refer to this information when you're actually choosing a money fund. Here's a brief rundown:

- **Taxable money market funds.** With a taxable money market fund, you are required to pay federal taxes on the dividends you earn (although in some cases, you may be exempt from certain state or local taxes on those dividends). Here are the major subcategories of taxable money funds.

    —*U.S. Treasury money funds* invest in short-term federal government IOUs called Treasury bills. These money funds are the closest in terms of safety to bank accounts since Treasury bills are issued by Uncle Sam and are said to be backed by the "full faith and credit" of the U.S. government. (This basically means that the government crosses its heart and promises to pay you everything you're entitled to even if it has to raise taxes or print more money to do so.) Although the dividends you receive will be taxed by the federal government, they may be free from state and local taxes, depending on which state you live in.

—*U.S. government money funds* invest in various types of money market instruments issued by the U.S. government itself and/or by federal agencies such as the Small Business Administration or "quasi-federal" agencies such as the Federal National Mortgage Association. Because U.S. government agency securities are backed only by the "moral obligation" of the federal government and not by its "full faith and credit," they are considered just a little bit riskier than U.S. Treasury bills. To compensate investors for this slight degree of additional risk, the yield on government money funds is generally slightly higher than that of money funds that invest exclusively in Treasuries. Some of the dividends may be free from state and local taxes in certain states.

—*Corporate money funds* invest in money market securities issued by private companies in the United States and abroad. Because the risk that a corporation will fail to repay its debts is considered higher than the risk of default by the federal government or a federal agency, and because the dividends paid by a corporate money fund are not exempt from state tax, corporate money funds tend to offer somewhat higher yields than money funds that invest in government instruments. Neither the additional risk nor the additional yield is very large, however.

• **Tax-exempt money market funds.** When people refer to a money market fund as tax-exempt, they generally mean only that its dividends are exempt from *federal* tax. The dividends of tax-exempt funds are sometimes exempt from state (and, in certain cases, local) tax, but this is not the case for all such funds. In either case, the yield on tax-exempt money funds is lower than the yield of taxable funds, but since the dividends aren't subject to federal income tax, you may end up earning more money in the end with a tax-exempt fund. Here are your choices:

—*Federal tax-exempt money funds* (sometimes referred to simply as tax-exempt money funds) invest in money market instruments issued by various states, counties, cities and towns, along with tax-exempt entities such as turnpike authorities and utilities. The dividends paid by these funds are not subject to federal tax, but if you live where there's a state or local income tax, you'll have to pay these taxes on all or most of your dividend income. In most cases, federal tax-exempt funds invest in the securities of a number of issuers in a number of different regions, in an effort to reduce risk through diversification.

—*Double tax-exempt money funds* invest in money market instruments issued by a single state (or by counties, cities, towns, or tax-exempt authorities located within that state) and pay dividends that are exempt from both federal *and* state income taxes, as long as you're a resident of that state. Because such funds are not able to invest in the securities of as many issuers in as many regions, they may be somewhat riskier than multistate federal tax-exempt money funds.

—*Triple tax-exempt money funds* may be of interest to you if you live in a city like New York, where residents pay income tax not only to the IRS but to the state and city as well. These funds are similar to double tax-exempt money funds but restrict their investments to a single city, and not just a single state. Although they offer a triple tax break (federal, state and local) for residents of that city, such funds are even less diversified (and thus a bit riskier) than double tax-exempt money funds.

Tax Considerations When Choosing a Money Fund

With the possible exception of the double and triple tax-exempt funds, risk should probably not be a big factor in your choice of a money fund since all money funds are comparatively safe. The main thing you'll want to focus on is the yield—or to be more precise, what's left of the yield after you pay your income taxes. For this reason your choice of a money fund may be influenced by your federal income tax bracket, and if you live in an area where you're required to pay state and city income taxes, by your state and city tax brackets as well. (To figure out your tax bracket, see Chapter 9.)

Say you're considering investing in a corporate money fund that pays 5%. Assuming that there's no state or city income tax where you live and that you're in the 28% federal tax bracket, 28% of that 5%, or 1.4%, will go to Uncle Sam, leaving you with an after-tax yield of only 3.6%. That means you need to earn more than 3.6%

CHECK WRITING AND MONEY FUNDS

Whether you get your money fund at a mutual fund company (my recommendation), a brokerage firm, or a bank, chances are you'll be offered some sort of check-writing privileges. But before you dump your ordinary checking account, understand the limitations of writing checks against your money fund accounts at these institutions:

- *Mutual fund companies.* Many fund companies won't permit you to write checks for amounts less than $100, and those that do typically require a large minimum balance. They also don't provide you with an ATM card to access your money fund.
- *Brokerage firms.* Many brokerages offer asset management accounts that enable you to write an unlimited number of checks in any amount against your money fund account. But asset management accounts usually have hefty minimum requirements (often $10,000), and you may be required to purchase stocks or bonds through the firm at least once a year in order to avoid account maintenance fees. Furthermore, although you

from a tax-exempt money fund in order to beat the return you'd get on the taxable fund. In this case, a tax-exempt fund paying 4%, for example, would be a better deal for you than the 5% taxable fund. Since the yields on money market funds fluctuate, you should repeat this comparison every few months.

If you're subject to state and/or city income tax, do the above calculation using your combined federal, state and local tax rates. You can then decide whether a double or triple tax-exempt money fund would give you enough additional after-tax yield to make it worth taking a bit more risk.

may get an ATM card, you might have to pay a fee (typically a dollar) each time you make a withdrawal or deposit, no matter how much money you have in your account.

- *Banks.* Most banks won't allow you to write checks against your money fund account for amounts less than $100. Some waive the monthly charges on standard checking accounts if you keep a specified minimum balance (typically several thousand dollars) in your money fund and checking account combined. However, you may not want to get your money fund at a bank, since banks tend to charge higher fees on money funds than are charged by low-cost mutual fund companies.

All things considered, you're probably best off investing in a money fund offered by a low-cost mutual fund company, and using a bank to meet your checking needs. Find a bank that has a low minimum balance requirement for free checking, and after you've met that minimum, invest the rest in your money fund.

Where to Find a Money Market Fund

Although you can invest in money funds at brokerage firms and many banks, your best bet usually is to get your money fund at a low-cost mutual fund company. (For recommendations on specific mutual fund companies that might satisfy all your fund needs, see the section "Choosing a Mutual Fund Company" later in this chapter.) If you're interested in investing in money funds right now, you may also want to check out the recent issues of personal finance magazines such as *Money* and *Kiplinger's*. They include the names of money funds that have the lowest fees, and thus the most attractive yields. (For a discussion of how fees affect yields, see the section "Mutual Fund Expenses" later in this chapter.)

A WORD ABOUT INFLATION

You may wonder why people don't keep all their money in nice, secure money market funds. After all, even if your money won't grow quite as fast in a money fund as it might in some other, riskier investment, at least it will be growing, right?

Well, maybe not, at least in the way that matters most. After you finish paying any taxes due on your earnings from a money fund, you'll probably have a hard time even keeping up with **inflation**— the tendency of prices to increase steadily over the years. If you earn, say, a 5% yield on a taxable money fund one year but are in the 30% (combined federal, state, and local) tax bracket, you'll be left with only 3.5% at the end of the year. While this doesn't *sound* so bad, if everything you want to buy costs 3.5% more on average at the end of the year than it did at the beginning, you may *look* richer on paper but are actually right back where you started.

It's easy to forget about the effects of inflation when you think about how your money will grow over the years. To help put things into perspective, it's worth taking a look at the way inflation has weakened the "purchasing power" of the dollar over the past few decades. Say your parents bought a new car for $3,000 in 1966. If you bought a comparable auto today, you'd pay about $20,000. Put another way: $3,000 today buys only about one-seventh of what it bought in the mid-1960s. Amazing.

Inflation has bounced around a lot over the years—it was about 12% in 1980, for example, and only about 1% in 1986—and it's hard to predict how high it will be in the future. One thing that seems pretty likely, though, is that inflation will continue to erode the value of the dollar over the next few decades, just as it has in the last few. If you put $20,000 under your mattress and inflation increases at, say, an average of 4% a year, after 30 years your $20,000 will have reduced in value to the point where it buys only what you can now buy for $6,166.

The rate of return you receive on an investment (known as the **nominal rate of return**) minus the rate of inflation is called the **real rate of return**. So if an investment is paying 5% and the inflation rate is 4%, your real rate of return is 1%. Take a look at Figure 5-1. It shows the nominal and real rates of return (without considering the effect of taxes) associated with various categories of securities over the period from 1926 to 1994. Don't worry for now about the exact definitions of these different securities; they'll be explained later. For now, the thing to notice is that stocks and bonds (and although they're not shown in this table, the mutual funds that invest in them) have done a much better job of overcoming the effects of inflation over this period than Treasury bills (which are often found in money funds).

It's clear from the table that if you'd kept your money in a money market fund that invests in Treasury bills, you would barely have kept pace with inflation. Although Treasury bills had a *nominal* return of 3.7%, the real rate of return, after accounting for inflation, was a pitiful 0.5%. And things look even worse when you take taxes into consideration. Although after-tax returns vary depending on an investor's tax bracket, most investors would actually have *lost* money by investing in Treasury bills over this period, after accounting for taxes and inflation. By investing in stocks and bonds they would have done considerably better.

As mentioned at the beginning of this chapter, the fact that a particular stock has done better historically than most other stocks tells us little or nothing about how well it's likely to do from now on. Still, it's the best guess of many financial analysts that over the long term, stocks and bonds *as a whole* will continue to offer rates of return that are significantly higher than the rate of inflation. Although there's no guarantee that this will actually happen (or even that you won't lose money by investing in the stock and bond markets over the years), my guess is that these analysts are guessing right.

So although the safety of money funds makes them a good place to keep your three-month emergency savings cushion, if you want a fighting chance at keeping up with inflation and can tolerate a bit

Figure 5-1
HOW VARIOUS INVESTMENTS
HAVE FARED OVER TIME

Type of Investment	Average Return[1] (Nominal)	Average Return[1] (Real)	Highest Return[2] (Nominal)	Lowest Return[2] (Nominal)
U.S. Treasury Bills	3.7%	0.5%	14.7%	2.9%
Government Bonds (Long-Term)	4.8%	1.7%	40.4%	-7.8%
Government Bonds (Intermediate-Term)	5.1%	1.9%	29.1%	-5.1%
Corporate Bonds (Long-Term)	5.4%	2.2%	42.6%	-5.8%
Large Company Stocks	10.2%	6.9%	37.2%	-7.2%
Small Company Stocks	12.2%	8.8%	57.4%	-21.6%

[1] Compound annual total return, 1926-1994
[2] Best and worst years, 1975-1994

Source: Ibbotson Associates, Chicago

more risk, your next step should be to consider two more aggressive types of investments: stock mutual funds and bond mutual funds.

STOCK
FUNDS

Just as money market mutual funds invest in money market instruments, **stock mutual funds** invest in—you guessed it—stocks. The appeal of a stock fund is that your return over the long term may be significantly higher than the return you'd get with a money market fund. The downside is that with a stock fund you risk losing money. (See Figure 5-1 for a look at how stocks performed in their best and worst years over the past two decades.)

What Is Stock?

To understand stock mutual funds, you must first understand stocks. Stock is sold in units known as shares. A **share of stock** represents a small piece of a company; if you buy stock in a company, you become the owner of a fraction of that company. The more shares you buy, the more of the company you own. The amount of money paid for one share is called the **stock price** or the **price per share**.

A stock's price rises and falls depending on supply and demand. When a lot of people want to buy a stock, they'll tend to "bid up" its price, the same way that rival bidders at an art auction might bid up the price of a painting. If, on the other hand, there are more sellers than buyers, the price tends to fall. Anything that might influence investors to buy or sell a company's stock may thus affect the share price. New information that might lead investors to believe that a company will make more money than previously expected, for example, will generally cause its share price to rise. Unanticipated bad news, on the other hand, typically leads to a decrease in price.

In some cases a company's stock price moves up or down for reasons that have nothing to do with changes in the firm's expected profitability. A stock may fall, for example, because a large investor decided to sell lots of shares to raise money for some other purpose and had to settle for a lower price in order to cash in quickly. And in many cases, stock prices may go up or down for what appears to be no particular reason at all.

Stocks do not pay interest like a savings account. The most common way to make money from stocks is to sell your shares for more than you paid for them. The difference between the price you sell them for and the price you paid for them is called a **capital gain.** Certain types of stocks pay **dividends,** which are regular cash payouts that companies make to keep shareholders happy. Typically, older, well-established firms pay dividends on their stocks, while newer firms do not. Some stock fund managers invest in stocks they believe will reap hefty capital gains; others focus on companies that have historically paid substantial dividends on a regular basis even if they're unlikely to increase much in price.

What Is the Stock Market?

You've probably heard reports on television that the stock market was up or down. Loosely speaking, the stock market is said to have gone up if the prices of most stocks have risen. The barometers most people use to keep track of "the market," though, are not based on *all* of the thousands of stocks that people trade but on some sort of more-or-less representative sample. The prices of all stocks in the sample are generally averaged in some way (the details of which may vary) to calculate what is known as an **index.**

The most widely known index is probably the **Dow Jones Industrial Average,** which despite its fame is actually based on the stock prices of only 30 large companies and for that reason doesn't provide an especially accurate reading of the direction of the market as a whole. Another closely followed indicator is **Standard & Poor's Index of 500 Stocks.** The "S&P 500," as it is more commonly called, is a more representative index that tracks changes in the stock prices of 500 large companies. When someone tells you that "the market" has gone up, they're usually referring to one of these two indexes.

Different Types of Stock Funds

Stock mutual funds can be divided into two basic categories. The vast majority are **actively managed funds,** which means a fund manager uses his own judgment to pick and choose among the thousands of stocks available. The other major type of stock fund is an **index fund,** which invests in nearly all the stocks that make up a particular index, such as the S&P 500. Some people refer to index funds as **unmanaged** or passively managed since the fund manager exercises little discretion over which stocks go into the fund. With an index fund, the manager's job is simply to come as close as possible to replicating the performance of the index it tracks.

Which type should you choose? I recommend that you go with an index fund. Although it might seem surprising, a number of academic studies suggest that stock portfolios managed actively by "expert" fund managers actually do no better on average than the passively managed portfolio of an index fund. (In his extensive research on this topic, for example, Princeton economics professor Burton Malkiel has found that over long periods most active managers have underperformed the S&P 500.) What is different about an actively managed fund, though, is that the fund manager usually charges a lot more for his services than the manager of an index fund. Most index funds provide the same or better diversification and allow you to participate in the (historically attractive) returns associated with the stock market without paying too much for the privilege.

But don't expect to hear this from a salesperson at a brokerage firm or mutual fund company. Higher expenses may be bad for you, but they're great for the companies that offer actively managed funds. (I'll say more about fund expenses later in this chapter.)

Questions and Answers on Stock Funds

Q: *Wouldn't I be better off choosing a top-performing managed stock fund?*

A: That would be true if you knew which funds were going to perform well in the future. After all, it would be well worth paying a bit more in expenses if the fund manager could deliver high enough returns to more than pay for them. Researchers have found, though, that funds whose returns have been unusually high in the past don't perform substantially better on average than funds that have performed poorly. If there's any advantage at all to betting on past winners, it's probably not large enough to justify paying the higher fees charged by active managers.

Q: *But what about those few fund managers who have done well year after year?*

A: Maybe they're brilliant, and maybe they're not. But before jumping to conclusions, it's worth remembering that given the number of stock funds that have been formed over the years, it would be surprising if some of them didn't do better than average for a number of years by sheer chance.

Let's talk odds for a minute. Suppose all fund managers choose their stocks completely at random. The chance that a particular fund will perform better than average (that is, better than half of all the funds that are out there) during any given year is 50%, or one chance in two. There is one chance in four (two times two) that this fund will do better than average for two successive years, and one chance in eight (two times two times two) that it will be in the top half of its class for three years in a row. Do this ten times, and you'll discover that there's one chance in 1,024 that a given fund will beat the average for ten years running through sheer luck. These may sound like pretty slim odds, but with more than 5,000 fund managers out there picking stocks, we should expect something like five of them to do better than average ten years in a row—enough to convince almost anyone that they're financial geniuses even if they're in fact choosing their stocks at random.

To be fair, this doesn't prove that there aren't any mutual funds whose managers are genuine stock-picking geniuses. But even if there are, how are you going to distinguish them from the ones who have just been lucky? My advice: Don't try.

Q: *What kind of stock index fund should I invest in?*

A: Later on in this chapter I'll list some of the competing mutual fund companies that offer funds based on various stock market indexes. First, though, you need to know a little about the indexes themselves. Here are a few of the better-known ones:

- **The S&P 500 Index.** The most popular index funds by far are those designed to replicate (or "track") the S&P 500 Index, which is based on 500 large companies whose stock is traded on the New York Stock Exchange—the world's largest forum for buying and selling securities. There are a lot of S&P 500 funds out there, some of which have very modest fees and are willing to accept a relatively small initial investment. While this is a fine place to get started, especially if you don't have much money to invest, a possible drawback of the S&P 500 is that it includes only the stocks of large firms. For more diversification you might ideally want to invest in an index that includes the stocks of small and medium-size firms as well.

- **The Wilshire 5000 Equity Index.** Despite its name, the Wilshire 5000 is actually based on more than 6,800 stocks, including those of a wide range of small, medium, and large companies. While I personally like the Wilshire 5000 because it offers some serious diversification, at the time of this writing only one major mutual fund company offers a fund that tracks this entire index, and this company requires an initial investment of at least $3,000. (For details, see below.)

- **The Morgan Stanley International EAFE Index.** If you're the adventurous type, you may want to consider investing at least a small portion of your money in the stock markets of other countries. Morgan Stanley Capital International, a division of the New York investment bank Morgan Stanley &

Co., has designed an index that tracks the performance of about 1,100 companies based in Europe, Australia, and the Far East (hence the acronym EAFE). Investing in a mutual fund that mirrors this index provides a convenient way of achieving some degree of international diversification. Foreign stock markets are sometimes quite volatile, though, and the fees charged by international fund managers tend to be higher on average than those of U.S. funds. So if you decide to buy American and pass on the exotics, there's no need to feel guilty about it.

BOND
FUNDS

Bond mutual funds invest in bonds, which will be discussed in a minute. First, though, you should know where bond funds fall on the risk/return spectrum. While the exact answer depends on the type of fund, bond funds are generally riskier than money market funds but less risky than stock funds. Not surprisingly, the returns of bond funds have historically been somewhere between those of stock funds and money market funds.

What Is a Bond?

Like a money market instrument, a bond is an IOU issued by a company, government, or some other institution. The main difference is that in the case of a bond, the issuer has more time to repay its debt.

When you buy a bond, you're basically lending a sum of money (the **principal**) to the issuer for a fixed period of time (the **term**). In return for the loan, the issuer pays you interest, computed at a fixed rate called the **coupon rate**. Interest is generally paid monthly or quarterly, but in the case of a **zero coupon bond**, you won't receive any interest at all until the end of the bond's term. (The bonds you received as graduation or Bar Mitzvah gifts may have been zero coupon bonds.) When a bond reaches **maturity** at the end of its term, you're entitled (at least in theory) to get back your full initial investment.

So What's Risky About a Bond?

The risks associated with buying a bond can be divided into two categories. The first, which is often referred to as **default risk** or **credit risk,** is the possibility that the issuer may fall on hard times and be unable to pay you interest or repay your principal.

The second, which is somewhat more complicated, is known as **interest rate risk.** Here's one way to think about this kind of risk: If interest rates rise unexpectedly fast during the period in which you own the bond, you won't be able to take advantage of them. You'll be stuck with the same fixed coupon rate, which will start to look worse and worse by comparison with prevailing market rates. And since inflation tends to rise along with interest rates, the dollars you receive when the issuer finally pays you back probably won't buy as much as you'd originally thought they would.

So why not simply sell your bond if interest rates rise unexpectedly and buy another one with a higher coupon rate? Unfortunately, you're not the only one who has thought of this. Nobody is going to buy your low-coupon bond if a new, high-coupon bond can be had for the same price. Since the bond market, like the stock market, obeys the law of supply and demand, the price you'll be able to get for your bond will drop as soon as interest rates rise. The higher interest rates climb, the less your bond will be worth.

A bond that doesn't have much time left until its final payback date, though, won't drop in value all that much when interest rates rise. This is because its holder won't have to put up with a lower-than-market coupon rate for very long and because inflation won't have much time to erode the value of the principal. A bond with many years left until its final payback, on the other hand, will fall much further when interest rates go up by the same amount.

So far the discussion has been only about how interest rate risk can hurt you when interest rates increase. The other side of the coin is that when interest rates *fall* more than the market expects, bonds tend to *rise* in value. Before you quit your job to become a bond trader, though, you should review the exact wording of the previous sentence. It's not enough to know that interest rates are likely to fall if everyone else knows that, too, since those expectations will almost certainly already be reflected in the price you'll have to pay to buy bonds. To "beat the market" you'd have to outguess thousands of experts who spend their time thinking of little else.

My recommendation: Don't even try. The point of this discussion is not to teach you how to make extraordinary profits by predicting the future direction of interest rates but simply to help you understand the two major factors—default risk and interest rate risk—that contribute to the uncertainty surrounding a bond's future performance.

Different Types of Bond Funds

Bond funds differ according to the type of bonds they invest in. There are two key variables to look at. The first is who is issuing the bond. This may affect not only the degree of default risk you're exposed to but also whether the income you receive from the bond is taxable or tax-exempt. As in the case of money market funds, there are bond funds that invest in bonds issued by the U.S. Treasury, by various federal agencies, by cities, states, and counties, and by corporations of varying degrees of creditworthiness.

From a tax perspective, these different types of bond funds work in pretty much the same way as the corresponding types of money market funds. This is true of default risk as well, except that the stakes are higher: Even a somewhat shaky corporation may be able to stay afloat long enough to repay a three-month money market instrument, but whether it will last long enough to make good on a 20-year bond may be another story.

But that doesn't mean that shaky corporations don't issue bonds. In fact, there's a whole class of bonds (most commonly known as "junk bonds," though brokers prefer the term "high-yield") that are issued by financially troubled firms. Because such bonds are issued by relatively unstable companies, they have to pay higher coupon rates to attract investors. Since a junk bond fund typically invests in the bonds of a *number* of "junky" companies, the failure of any one of them may not be a disaster for the fund's investors. If many of these companies were to fail and therefore default on their bonds, though, investors could earn a much lower return and might even lose a substantial part of the money they originally invested.

The second variable is the average number of years before the bonds in the fund come due, or "mature." **Short-term bond funds** typically invest in bonds that will mature in fewer than four years; **intermediate-term bond funds** in instruments with maturities of between four and ten years; and **long-term bond funds** in bonds that won't mature for at least ten years.

Because changes in both market interest rates and the financial stability of the issuing companies exert a larger effect on bonds with a long time left until maturity than on those with less time remaining, long-term bond funds are generally riskier than short-term funds. As might be expected, the relative safety of short-term bond funds comes at a price: Historically, they haven't performed as well as intermediate- and long-term bond funds.

The type of bond fund you select will depend in part on how much risk you're willing to take. As we've just seen, funds that invest in the bonds of less creditworthy companies are generally riskier than those that invest in otherwise comparable high-quality bonds; funds that invest in long-term bonds are riskier than funds that invest in the short-term bonds of similar companies. Only you can decide how much risk you're willing to accept for the possibility of a higher return.

That said, I'm willing to stick my neck out and recommend a middle-of-the-road approach that may represent a reasonable compromise if you want to choose a single bond fund and have a more-or-less average tolerance for risk: a fund that invests entirely or primarily in intermediate-term bonds issued by "highly rated" corporations. While there's no guarantee that this will prove to be your best move, there's a good chance that such a fund will provide you with a bit more income than, say, a short-term U.S. Treasury or government bond fund, without subjecting you to a huge amount of default or interest rate risk.

If you have the patience to evaluate and keep track of more than one bond fund, another alternative you might want to consider is spreading your money among several types of funds that fall at different points on the risk/return spectrum. If not, though, don't worry; the guidelines in the next section will allow you to "hedge your bets" reasonably well even if you choose to follow the simpler, single-bond-fund approach.

Questions and Answers on Bond Funds

Q: *Where can I get information about the types of bonds in a bond fund?*

A: Details about the types of bonds a fund invests in are contained in the fund's **prospectus,** a document you can get by

Figure 5-2
BOND RATINGS

	S&P	Moody's	Description
Investment Grade	AAA	Aaa	Highest quality
	AA	Aa	High quality
	A	A	Good quality
	BBB	Baa	Medium quality
High-Yield (Junk Bonds)	BB	Ba	Risky elements
	B	B	Risky
	CCC	Caa	Riskier
	CC	Ca	Highly risky
	C	C	Extremely poor prospects
	D	–	In default

Source: Standard & Poor's. Moody's, and the Investment Company Institute

calling the fund company. While it's not always easy to decipher a prospectus, you should be able to find enough comprehensible information about the issuers and maturities of the bonds that the fund invests in to help you make an informed decision. You may also want to ask for a copy of the fund's most recent **shareholder report,** which gives a breakdown of the **credit ratings** of the bonds that the fund recently held. These ratings are assigned by one of several rating agencies, the best known of which are Standard & Poor's and Moody's. (See Figure 5-2 for the meaning of various ratings.)

Q: *Within a given category of bond fund, how should I pick a particular fund?*

A: Although it might seem like a good idea to compare the historical returns of various bond funds or do research on various fund managers, my advice would be to concentrate primarily on one thing: fees. Studies have shown that bond fund managers have little effect on the performance of bond funds, so there's no point in paying extra for someone who claims to be better than average.

Q: *Are there bond index funds?*

A: Yes, although not many mutual fund companies offer them. For details, see the section below on choosing a mutual fund company.

THE RIGHT MIX OF INVESTMENTS

As I've said, your first investing move should be to save three months' worth of expenses in a money fund. But what happens after that? If you're ready to start investing more aggressively, how much money should go into stock funds and bond funds, and how much should stay in a money market fund?

Unfortunately, there's little agreement even among "experts" about the right answer to this question. Once again, you'll have to decide for yourself how much risk you're willing to take in pursuit of higher returns. A fairly typical decision, though, might be to allocate roughly 50% of your assets to stock funds and 30% to bond funds, while keeping 20% in "cash" (meaning money market funds and bank accounts). This type of breakdown would put a lot of your money into those investments that have historically had the highest returns, while keeping some of it in safer places, just in case. Most important, you avoid putting all your eggs in one basket, taking advantage once again of the benefits of diversification.

Some financial advisors maintain that young people should put even more of their assets—say, 75% to 80%—in stock funds since they have much more time to ride out the downturns of the stock market. But others (including Paul Samuelson, winner of the Nobel Prize in economics) have questioned whether it really makes sense to allocate assets based on your age.

To help determine the right mix for you, consider these questions:

- **What's your risk tolerance?** Are you a risk taker by nature? Do you like to gamble? Are you willing to lose $10 for the chance of earning $30? If so, you might be willing to put a lot of your money in stocks. But if you're afraid of risk and sickened by the thought of losing any money, a large percentage of your investment portfolio should probably be in a money market fund.

- **Are you diversified?** As mentioned above, to reduce the overall risk in your portfolio you will want to have a mix of different types of investments. Before you make any decisions, examine the types of investments in your company retirement plan. If you invested your company 401(k) plan mainly in stocks, for example, you will probably want your non-retirement holdings to include some bond and money market funds. (For details on 401(k)s, see Chapter 6.)

- **What are your goals?** If you have $10,000 that you'll need to use in the next year or two for a down payment on a home, you may not want to invest it in a stock fund or a long-term bond fund where you could lose a lot of it if the market were to "crash" or interest rates were to soar. But if you're just trying to build up your savings over the next 10 or 20 years without a fixed goal in sight, you might want to take some risk in the hope of getting bigger returns.

One final note: Don't be discouraged if you can't create the perfect investment mix immediately. If you don't yet have enough money to meet the minimums required for separate investments in both a stock fund and a bond fund, it's important not to use that as an excuse to postpone investing. Start with a stock index fund, then begin investing in a bond fund after you've accumulated some more savings.

MUTUAL FUND EXPENSES

Because there's little evidence that one mutual fund manager is any more likely to beat the market than another, it makes sense to focus on the one thing that will definitely affect your investment results: the fund's **expense ratio**. This ratio is computed by dividing the fund's **total annual operating expenses** (which will be discussed in a minute) by the value of all securities held by the fund. The fund's operating expenses are generally passed on to its investors, so the higher the expense ratio, the less you'll earn on your investment. If, for example, you invest in a fund that earns a 10% annual return on the securities it holds but has a 2% expense ratio, your investment will grow at a rate of only 8% a year.

One component of a fund's total annual operating expenses is the **management fee** paid to the fund manager (or fund company) for investing and managing the fund's money. Management fees typically range between 0.5% and 1% of the fund's assets per year. Other expenses include legal fees and administrative charges. Some fund companies also charge investors what's known as a **12b-1 fee**, which is used to cover the fund's marketing costs. Why should you pay for these? You shouldn't. Find a fund without 12b-1 fees.

As of this writing, expense ratios average about 1.5% a year for stock funds, just under 1% for bond funds, and around 0.6% for money market funds. As you'll see in the next section, though, the expense ratios of some funds are much lower, and there's no reason to believe that low-expense funds will perform any worse than high expense ones. The moral of this story is simple: Invest in funds with the lowest expense ratios you can find, and ignore anything a broker, financial advisor, or bank employee might try to tell you about the great track record or bright prospects of the high-expense fund he's trying to push.

One other trap you should look out for: **loads**. Loads are typically one-time fees paid at the time you buy and/or sell shares in certain mutual funds (which are often referred to as **load funds**). They aren't included in the fund's expense ratio, so you'll have to look out for them separately. Loads typically range between 3% and 4% but can be as high as 8.5%. Studies show that load funds perform no better on average than **no-load funds**, so why does anyone pay a load? Because they've been talked into a load fund by an aggressive salesperson. Loads are commonly used to provide generous compensation to the people who sell them, so they're highly motivated to convince you that the fund's performance will justify the load. Just say no. What you want is a no-load fund with a low expense ratio. The salesperson will get over it.

To get the scoop on a fund's fees and expenses, read the prospectus. It will spell them all out in detail.

CHOOSING A MUTUAL FUND COMPANY

Today there are more than 400 mutual fund companies in the United States alone, many of which offer a number of funds. Fortunately, you should be able to meet all your fund needs with just one or two of these companies. The main advantage of getting all your funds from a single mutual fund company (sometimes called a "fund family") is convenience. You'll get a single statement covering all your holdings and will generally be able to move your money from one of its funds to another with little hassle. Depending on your financial circumstances, though, you may be able to get a slightly better deal if you're willing to go to the trouble of splitting your money between two fund families.

So how do you choose a fund family? If you follow my advice, you'll find it surprisingly simple. What you're looking for is a company that offers no-load funds with low expense ratios and initial minimum investment requirements that you're able to meet. In this section you'll be directed to four companies that currently fit the bill. (If things have changed radically by the time you read this, you may have to look through one of the lists that appear from time to time in the personal finance magazines—*Money, Smart Money,* or *Kiplinger's,* for example—to find other companies that satisfy the simple criteria outlined in this paragraph.) Although others might tell you differently, I don't believe it's necessary for you to hook up with a stockbroker, subscribe to *Institutional Investor,* or spend your evenings doing research in the local business school library. Just pick a fund family that fits your current financial situation (a process that should take all of five minutes), then call them up and ask them to send you the forms needed to open an account.

One company that is definitely worth considering is the Vanguard Group (800-662-7447). (Just for the record, I don't get any kickbacks, discounts, or free slide rules from Vanguard or any of the other firms mentioned in this book.) Vanguard is a no-load firm that has some of the lowest expenses in the business. As of this writing, Vanguard's stock index funds have an average expense ratio of 0.2%—about half of the industry average for stock index funds. Vanguard also has the largest range of index funds to choose from, including international index funds, bond index funds, and broad-based U.S. stock index funds such as the Total Stock Market Portfolio, which tracks the entire Wilshire 5000 Index. The only problem with Vanguard is that it has a minimum initial investment requirement of $3,000 per fund (except in the case of IRAs, for which the minimum is $500.) If you can afford it, great. If not, you'll have to invest elsewhere for now.

One possibility might be Charles Schwab & Co. (800-2NO-LOAD), which has several no-load stock index funds with a minimum investment of $1,000. If that's still too steep for you, T. Rowe Price (800-638-5660) offers an S&P 500 index fund and will let you start investing with just $50 as long as you commit to setting aside at least $50 a month through its automatic investment plan. (For details on automatic investment plans, see the box below.)

Unfortunately, you may have trouble finding a fund family that offers bond index funds with low minimum initial investment requirements. For this reason you may have to settle for a managed bond fund if you can't meet the $3,000 minimum for Vanguard's bond index fund. Again, the key is to focus on no-load funds with low expenses. One company to look at is USAA (800-531-8181), a no-load firm that *Money* magazine cited in the summer of 1994 as offering the lowest expense bond funds after Vanguard. The minimum required for USAA's taxable bond funds is $1,000.

START WITH JUST $50 A MONTH IN AN AUTOMATIC INVESTMENT PLAN

Many no-load mutual fund companies will waive or lower their minimum initial investment requirement if you sign up for their automatic investment plan. With these plans you can have a fixed amount—the minimum is usually $50 or $100—siphoned off once or twice a month from either your paycheck or your bank checking account and funneled into the mutual fund of your choice. If your employer will allow you to have the money deducted from your paycheck and your mutual fund company can accommodate this, you're in luck; this is the most hassle-free arrangement. Otherwise, have the mutual fund company withdraw the money from your bank. When you choose a fund family, simply indicate on the application that you want your money invested automatically and specify where you want the money to come from. After that, you won't have to do much except sit back and watch the money accumulate in your mutual fund account (though you may also want to check your investment mix occasionally to make sure it's still in the proportion you want).

All the companies mentioned above have several money market funds to choose from, so that shouldn't be a problem. If you can find a money fund somewhere else with lower expenses, though, go for it.

SOCIALLY RESPONSIBLE INVESTING

People often ask me to recommend "socially responsible" investments. There are more than two dozen mutual funds that fall into this category, and each has a different idea of what it means to be socially responsible. Some funds that consider themselves socially responsible don't invest in tobacco or liquor companies. Others invest in companies that have good records on energy conservation and pollution control, and shun those that don't. Still others zero in on firms that treat employees well by providing child-care services, promoting women and minorities, and offering generous benefit packages.

Are do-good firms also good investments? Nobody knows for sure. There are those who believe that the securities of a socially minded company should perform about the same as the market as a whole, and some even argue that they should do better since they may be the targets of fewer lawsuits (for everything from pollution to discrimination). Others say that by restricting the universe of qualified companies, the ethically aware fund manager is limiting his ability to take advantage of attractive investment opportunities and is likely to underperform the market.

Whether you choose to invest in a socially responsible fund or stay with an ordinary index fund (and perhaps set aside some money for tax-deductible contributions to your own favorite charities) is a personal decision. If you choose the former route, though, steer clear of any fund that charges a load or that has an unusually high expense ratio. For a free list of socially responsible mutual funds, you can call the Franklin Research and Development Corp. (617-423-6655), an investment firm that publishes a newsletter on socially responsible investing.

FINANCIAL CRAMMING

- The first phase of your investment plan should be to build up an emergency savings cushion equal to at least three months' worth of living expenses. Put these savings in a money market fund.

- Your next move is to begin investing in stock and bond mutual funds. Your best bet is probably index funds since actively managed funds tend to charge higher fees and on average have not performed any better historically.

- Invest only in no-load funds. There's no point in paying hefty fees to invest in a load fund since there's no evidence that they're better investments than no-load funds.

- Don't invest in a mutual fund that charges investors high expenses. As of this writing, "expense ratios" average about 1.5% a year for stock funds, just under 1% for bond funds, and around 0.6% for money market funds. Find a fund that charges you lower expenses.

- Sign up for an automatic investment plan. These plans allow you to have small amounts of money—say, $50 each month—withdrawn from your bank account or paycheck and funneled into a mutual fund. If you invest automatically, some funds will waive the minimum initial investment requirements.

6

LIVING THE GOOD
LIFE IN 2030

Think It's Crazy to Worry Now About Retirement Then? It's Crazy Not To

GET THIS. Suppose you set aside $1,000 a year (about $19 a week) from age 25 to 34 in a retirement account earning 8% a year, and never invest a penny more. By the time you turn 65, your $10,000 investment will have grown to $168,627.

But if you don't start saving until you're 35 and then invest $1,000 a year for the next 30 years—a total investment of $30,000—you'll have only $125,228 by age 65.

You might want to read this example over again, slowly.

The moral of this story (a depressing one if you're 35) and the focus of this chapter: If you don't start saving in a tax-favored retirement account while you're young, you'll miss out on perhaps the best investment opportunity of your life. That's because retirement plans offer terrific tax advantages that allow your savings to grow rapidly. In order to maximize the benefit, though, you should get started right away. The government limits the amount you can set aside each year, so if you fail to contribute now, you won't be able to make it up when you're older (and perhaps wiser).

But there's more at stake here than losing out on a juicy tax shelter: You could actually end up living out your golden years in *poverty*. The Social Security Administration currently predicts that by the year 2013 it will be paying out more than it is taking in, and unless Congress somehow finds the money for a complete overhaul by about 2030, there won't be enough money in the fund to pay out full benefits. Even if the system doesn't completely collapse, we certainly can't rely on Social Security to support us adequately in our later years.

A less publicized but even more pressing problem is the quiet revolution now taking place in the private pension world. In our parents' era, employees stayed with the same company for 20 or 30 years, and many were rewarded with pensions that were paid by their employers. Old-fashioned pensions, known as **defined benefit plans,** are rapidly becoming the spotted owls of the employee benefits world as fewer and fewer companies offer them to new employees. By the time most of us retire, traditional pensions may well be nearing extinction.

And because high-tech medical advancements promise to keep us alive anywhere from ten to twenty years longer than our grandparents, we need to stash away even more cash for our old age. Most Americans who reach the traditional retirement age of 65 today can expect to live beyond the age of 80. By the time our generation retires, the figure could well be closer to 90.

Before I go any further, I have a confession to make. Although I was eligible to start contributing to my company's retirement savings plan in 1989 when I was 24, I waited until the end of 1991— simply because I didn't get around to it. And I paid dearly. I currently have $14,150 in my 401(k) retirement plan but would have had more than $30,000 if I had started saving when I was supposed to. Learn from my mistake.

This chapter will teach you everything you need to know about retirement accounts but have been too apathetic to ask. You'll be happy to learn that you don't have to be rich or financially savvy to put money into an individual retirement account (IRA) or a company plan. And unless you have a massive trust fund or are expecting a giant inheritance from a wealthy old relative, you'd be wise to start doing exactly that—right now.

WHAT ARE RETIREMENT
SAVINGS PLANS, ANYWAY?

Back in the days when Sonny and Cher were still a couple, Congress decided to give savers a break by creating tax-subsidized retirement savings programs. And although the Bonos have long since split up and Sonny is now a member of Congress, Americans are still blessed with these tax-favored plans, called 401(k)s, 403(b)s, and IRAs.

Here's a rundown:

- **401(k)s** are retirement savings plans available to employees of most major companies and many small ones.

- **403(b)s** are offered to employees of public schools and certain religious, charitable or educational tax-exempt organizations. (Since 403(b)s are similar to 401(k)s, I will refer only to 401(k)s throughout this chapter except when noted.)

- **IRAs** are available to all working Americans but are especially attractive for those who work for companies that do not offer retirement savings plans.

The tax-saving principle behind all these plans is simple: You agree to contribute a certain portion of your income, and Uncle Sam allows you to delay paying taxes on that money. So if you earn $20,000 in a year and put $1,000 into a 401(k), you'll pay taxes on only $19,000 that year. That could mean several hundred extra dollars in your pocket each year. What's more, you get to delay paying taxes on the interest (or other earnings) your retirement account generates over the years. When you withdraw the money at the time of your retirement, you will pay taxes on the whole sum—the amount you contributed plus your earnings. But because the money is able to grow tax-free for many years, paying taxes later rather than sooner could result in thousands of dollars more for you over your lifetime. The effect of your interest earning interest without being taxed is known as **tax-free compounding.** When money compounds tax-free for, say, 40 years rather than 30, it not only grows for a longer period of time but also grows more quickly, as the example at the beginning of this chapter shows.

CONTRIBUTING TO YOUR COMPANY PLAN

Most companies allow employees to decide what percentage of their salaries they want to contribute to a company retirement plan. In 1996 the maximum an employee could contribute to a 401(k) was $9,500. (Actually, the maximum you're permitted to contribute may be less, depending on factors such as your salary and the amount, if any, contributed by your employer on your behalf.) The rules for 403(b) plans are similar. This limit may increase with inflation.

One of the biggest benefits of a 401(k) is that many employers match a portion of the amount you contribute with a contribution of their own. Many companies contribute fifty cents for every dollar you put in, up to a fixed maximum (often 3% to 6% of your salary). That's the equivalent of a 50% return on your investment. To take full advantage of this amazing deal, try to contribute at least the maximum amount for which you are eligible to receive matching funds.

Contributions to 401(k)s and 403(b)s are deducted from your paycheck. After a while, most people don't even miss the money that's being skimmed off and discover that they're saving money faster than they ever thought possible.

CONTRIBUTING TO AN IRA

The maximum amount you can contribute to an IRA is $2,000 a year, plus an additional $250 to your spouse's IRA if he or she doesn't earn any income. If you and your spouse both work, you can each contribute up to $2,000 a year to an IRA.

There are certain circumstances under which IRA contributions cannot be subtracted or "deducted" from your taxable income. These circumstances depend on what your "adjusted gross income" is and whether you're covered by an employer retirement plan. (For details on what your adjusted gross income is, see Chapter 9.)

So here are the rules. You can't deduct your *full* IRA contribution if you (or your spouse) are covered by an employer-sponsored retirement plan and

- you're single, and your adjusted gross income is more than $25,000;

- you're married, you file a joint tax return, and together your adjusted gross income is more than $40,000 combined;

- you're married but file separately.

Even if you're not eligible to deduct the full contribution you make to an IRA, you may be able to deduct part of it. In the examples above, the single person could deduct a portion of her IRA if her adjusted gross income is less than $35,000; the married person filing jointly could deduct a portion of his IRA if his adjusted gross income is less than $50,000; and the married person filing separately could deduct a portion of her IRA if her adjusted gross income is less than $10,000. Even if you don't qualify for any deduction, you can still take advantage of the fact that the *earnings* on IRAs are not taxed until you withdraw the money.

HOW YOUR RETIREMENT SAVINGS GROW

The money in your retirement plan doesn't just sit there; it's channeled into investments so it can grow. When you sign up for a plan, you're given a choice of investment options. You pick the ones you want and decide how to divide your money among your selections.

Your options will depend on the kind of plan you enroll in. With a 401(k), the employer narrows down the investment options for you. Many plans offer you a "menu" of about four alternatives, which might include shares of your company's own stock, a stock mutual fund, a bond mutual fund, a balanced mutual fund (which has a mix of stocks and bonds), and a money market fund. Every time you contribute, the money is automatically divided according to your initial specifications. You may not get to choose how your employer's matching contribution gets divided, however.

IRAs are slightly more complicated because they involve more choices. First you have to decide where to open one. Although IRAs are offered by banks and brokerage firms, your best bet is probably a large, no-load mutual fund company.

A LESSON IN HOW A LITTLE BIT ADDS UP TO A LOT

Although he has never earned more than $24,000 a year, Peter, 35, has more than $74,000 in retirement savings. How did he do it? Peter works at a company that allows him to sock away 15% of his salary each year into a 401(k). His starting salary in 1982 was just $10,000 a year, but he immediately began contributing the maximum he could to his company plan (even though his company offered no matching program) and has continued to do so ever since. For the three years he lived with his parents after college (he moved out at age 25), Peter also deposited an additional $2,000 into an IRA each year. Although it's true that Peter profited by the fact that stock and bond funds did very well throughout the 1980s and early 1990s—he averaged a 9% annual return for the years he invested—his real achievement has been his determination to contribute to his 401(k) every year. If he continues to save the maximum in his plan, gets a 4% cost-of-living salary increase each year, and earns 8% a year on his investments, he will have more than $395,000 by the time he turns 50. Amazing.

Here's why: When you open an IRA at a bank, your options may be limited to ultra-safe investments like certificates of deposit (CDs) and money market accounts—neither of which typically offers a high enough rate of return to keep you comfortably ahead of inflation over the long term. While more and more banks also offer the option of putting mutual funds in your IRA, there's a good chance you will pay a load on these funds. A full-service brokerage firm may also charge a hefty commission. A no-load, low-expense mutual fund, such as the ones listed in Chapter 5, does not charge loads or commissions.

Since retirement plans allow your money to grow tax-deferred, you may want to consider the tax advantages (and disadvantages) of putting certain investments in them. For instance, it doesn't make sense to put tax-free bond funds into a retirement plan; stick with taxable investments only. (For a discussion of different investment options and suggestions on the pros and cons of each, see Chapter 5.)

SOME DRAWBACKS (AND WHY THEY DON'T MATTER)

On the surface, IRAs and 401(k)s have a major downside for young people. Once you put money into these accounts, you must wait until you reach the age of 59½ to withdraw your money without paying a penalty. If you tap into your IRA before then, you'll have to pay a stiff 10% penalty (plus income tax on the amount you withdraw). The tax and penalty rules are the same for 401(k)s, but withdrawing your money early is even more difficult: You must prove to your employer that you need the money for something important, such as paying medical bills, and that you have nowhere else to turn.

These tough rules are meant to prevent savers from raiding their retirement plans, but they aren't as rigid as they seem. Many 401(k)s, for instance, offer an escape hatch: They allow you to *borrow* the money at rates that are sometimes more favorable than a bank's. When you borrow from your 401(k), you are essentially borrowing money from yourself, and the payments you make—including interest—go right back into your own account.

Borrowing rules vary from company to company, so check the details with your employer. In general, you can borrow half the amount you contributed to your 401(k) plus earnings. Depending on how long you've worked for the company, you may be able to borrow up to half of your employer's contributions, too. Some employers do not permit loans of less than $1,000. Loans usually must be paid back within five years. If you use the money to buy your primary home, you may be able to pay it back over a longer period.

IRAs offer borrowing options that are far less generous, but if you need your IRA money, you can withdraw it once a year without penalty as long as you pay it all back within 60 days. As of this writing, Congress is considering changes to the IRA rules so savers can borrow from their IRAs for medical emergencies and first homes. But even if your retirement plan doesn't allow you to borrow, it usually still makes sense to invest in an IRA or a 401(k). The advantage of tax-free compounding is so great that over many years its benefit could outweigh the 10% penalty you'd have to pay for making early withdrawals.

A WORD ABOUT INFLATION AND TAXATION

Personal finance articles and books often offer dramatic examples of the rewards of saving without ever mentioning inflation. So far in this chapter I haven't done much better. It's time for me to come clean.

Although saving over a long period of time really is a good idea, the fact is that it won't make you as rich as it might seem from the examples given so far. As you may remember from Chapter 5, inflation can drastically reduce the purchasing power of the dollar over time. Consider, for example, the scenario outlined at the beginning of this chapter; the $168,627 you'd have 40 years from now would not buy nearly as much as $168,627 can buy today.*

This doesn't mean you shouldn't save. As the numbers show, you still come out way ahead if you start saving in a retirement account while you're young—even after inflation. As I said before, when money is allowed to grow for decades without being taxed, the results are extraordinary.

Consider the following example. Suppose you put $2,000 into each of two accounts—an IRA and a taxable account—in 1996. Let's also assume that each account earns 8% a year, you're in the 33% tax bracket, and the annual inflation rate is 4%. After adjusting for inflation and the taxes you'd have to pay upon withdrawal, the $2,000 in the IRA will have grown to approximately $4,150 (in 1996 dollars) after 30 years. The $2,000 in the taxable account, on the other hand, will have increased only to about $2,950 (again in 1996 dollars). The bottom line: You will have earned more than twice as much ($2,360 versus $955) by keeping your money in a tax-favored account than by putting it in a taxable one.

ANSWERS TO SOME COMMON QUESTIONS

Okay. Now you've got the point: You don't want to miss out on the benefits of saving in a retirement plan when you're young. This next section will help you determine which type of account you can sign up for and what you need to know before you get started.

---

* There's a less obvious way that inflation comes into play in this example. If you decided to save for ten years starting at age 25, you'd be making your ten annual $1,000 deposits many years earlier than if you waited until you turned 35 and then invested $1,000 a year for 30 years. Because $1,000 buys more today than it will many years from now, each of the $1,000 deposits you'd make from age 25 to 34 would buy more than each of the $1,000 deposits you'd make if you waited ten years and saved from age 35 to 65. Thus the benefits of saving early are offset somewhat by inflation.

The Facts on 401(k)s

Q. *Am I eligible for a 401(k)?*

A: Ask your employer. You may be required to work for your
employer for a year or reach age 21 before you can contribute.

Q: *One of my 401(k) investment options is stock in my company. Should I bite?*

A: Probably not. When you work for a company, you already
have a huge "investment" in it. If the business runs into difficult
times, you are at risk twice: Not only could you lose your job, but
you could also see your retirement portfolio plummet. What's more,
many employers match employee contributions with shares of company stock, so you may already be heavily invested in your firm.

Q: *My plan allows me to invest in a GIC. What's that?*

A: A **guaranteed investment contract,** or **GIC,** is an investment
that's similar to a CD (certificate of deposit) but is guaranteed by an
insurance company instead of the federal government. While GICs
are generally considered relatively safe investments, several major insurance companies have failed in recent years, leaving GIC holders,
in some cases, waiting for years before they were able to get their
money. Before choosing the GIC option you may want to ask your
employee benefits or human resources officer what the rating is for the
insurance company offering the GIC. Standard & Poor's, Moody's,
and A.M. Best are all in the business of evaluating the financial stability of insurance companies. (For details, see Chapter 8.)

Q: *What happens if I change jobs?*

A: The good news is that you can transfer your 401(k) money
into an IRA or into your new employer plan if your new boss allows
it. But you must be aware of a few annoying rules. It's important that
you tell your old employer that you want a **direct rollover** into your
new company's 401(k) or into an IRA. Although the rules say your
old employer can pay out or "distribute" the 401(k) money directly
to you, there are several reasons to avoid this method. If your
employer gives the money directly to you, he must withhold 20% of

the amount you are due and send it to the IRS. You are then responsible for replacing that 20% from your other savings when you make the transfer into your new plan. If you can't come up with the money in 60 days, you will have to pay tax on that 20% plus a penalty. (I told you these rules were annoying.)

Another option you may have is to leave your 401(k) money with your old firm. Once you leave a company, you're no longer eligible to contribute to its 401(k), but your account will continue to grow if your investments do well.

No matter what you do, resist the temptation to simply cash in your 401(k). You will have to pay tax on the money, plus the 10% penalty.

Q: *What happens if I have an outstanding loan against my 401(k), and I quit or am fired?*
A: You should try to avoid this situation. Most companies will ask you to pay the entire loan back in one lump sum when you leave the firm. If you can't, the amount you owe may be treated as money withdrawn (instead of borrowed) from the plan, and you may therefore owe taxes plus the 10% penalty.

Q: *They tell me I'm vested. What does that mean?*
A: To be **vested** is to have a nonforfeitable right to the money your employer contributed to your retirement plan on your behalf. Most company retirement plans require you to work for the firm for a certain number of years before you become fully vested, meaning you can get 100% of the money your employer contributed for you. Typically it takes about five years. Some companies have a gradual vesting policy: You might be 20% vested after two years, 40% after three years, and so on. Once you become vested, however, it doesn't mean you may withdraw your money without paying the 10% penalty and taxes on your earnings. If you're not vested and need to get your money when you leave the firm, you can withdraw the money you contributed (plus earnings on those contributions), but you can't keep any of the money your employer contributed (or the earnings on those employer contributions). If you're partially vested, you'll get to keep a portion of the money your employer

HOW SAFE IS YOUR 401(K)?

If the company you work for is facing rough financial times, you may worry whether your boss can dip into the 401(k) to pay his bills. The answer is no. Your employer is not legally allowed to use the 401(k) money for business purposes. What's more, if your employer files for bankruptcy, the 401(k) money is protected, and none of the employer's creditors can touch your account. The person (or company) who is legally responsible for ensuring that no one tampers with your 401(k) is called the trustee. The trustee might be, for example, a bank or the president of your company. And what if your employer decides to end the plan? You'll still be okay because you'll receive all the money you put in plus any contributions made by your employer on your behalf.

contributed, plus earnings. Knowing your company's vesting schedule can help you time a career move. Keep in mind that what some companies consider a "year of service" might be less than a full calendar year (for instance, five months and a day). That's why you should consult your company's employee benefits or human resources department to find out the exact date you'll be vested.

The Scoop on IRAs

Q: *Where should I open my IRA?*
A: Find a no-load mutual fund company that offers you the option of investing your IRA in funds with low expense ratios. (See Chapter 5 for details on finding such a company.) At the very least, the company should have a stock fund, a bond fund, and a money market fund.

Also, research the company's rules. Some require IRA customers to make an initial contribution of only $250, while others demand $1,000 or more to open an account. And choose a firm that can establish an automatic savings program linked to your paycheck or your savings or checking account.

Q: *Are there any IRA fees I should watch out for?*
A: Yes. One common practice is to tack on an IRA maintenance fee of between $10 and $30 a year. Sometimes the fund company will waive the fee if you maintain a given minimum amount in your account.

Q: *What's the deadline for contributing to an IRA?*
A: The deadline is April 15 of the *following* year. If, for example, you suddenly realize on January 1, 1998, that you forgot to make your 1997 IRA contribution, you're still okay; you have until April 15, 1998, to contribute and have it be deductible on your 1997 tax return.

Q: *Can my parents give me the money to open an IRA?*
A: Yes. But you must be a U.S. citizen and have a job to open one.

IF YOU'RE SELF-EMPLOYED

If you're your own boss, consider opening one of two basic types of retirement savings plans for self-employed people. The advantage of these plans is that they allow you to contribute (and deduct) much more than you might be allowed to in an IRA. The first type is called a **simplified employee pension,** or **SEP,** sometimes also referred to as a **SEP-IRA.** SEPs work pretty much like IRAs. The main difference is the amount of money you can contribute. You can contribute 15% of your first $150,000 of **net earnings from self-employment** to a SEP. (To figure out your net earnings you subtract your business deductions, half your self-employment tax, and your SEP contribution from your gross income. Consult an accountant to help you figure this out.) So, depending upon how much you earn, you can contribute as much as $22,500 annually to a SEP—clearly a more attractive option than a standard IRA. If you don't have employees, a SEP-IRA is the easiest self-employed retirement plan to set up; if you do have people working for you, however, you may have to contribute for them, too. (For details see Chapter 9.)

Another option is a retirement plan known as a **Keogh**. A Keogh requires somewhat more paperwork, but it also has advantages. For starters, you may not have to make contributions for your part-time employees. There are several different types of Keogh plans to choose from; the most popular is called a **profit-sharing plan**. You can contribute up to 15% of your first $150,000 of net earnings (again, for a maximum of $22,500 each year) to a profit-sharing Keogh. With this type of Keogh you can vary your contributions annually, meaning you're not required to contribute a set amount each year. Other types of Keogh plans generally allow you to contribute more money (up to $30,000 a year), but you're locked into contributing a set percentage of your earnings each year. For more details, contact a no-load, low-cost mutual fund company.

FINANCIAL CRAMMING

- Enroll in your company retirement savings plan or open an individual retirement account (IRA) at a no-load mutual fund company—right now.

- Looking for easy money? If your company offers a 401(k), contribute at least as much as your employer will match. A fifty cent match for every dollar you put in is the same as earning a 50% return on your investment.

- If you're thinking of changing jobs, check your vesting schedule to see whether you've worked long enough to take all your 401(k) money with you when you quit. Staying an extra few months could mean thousands of extra dollars in your pocket.

- If you work for yourself, check out SEP-IRAs and Keoghs. These plans may permit you to sock away much more money for your retirement than you could with an IRA.

OH, GIVE ME A HOME

Advice on Getting an Apartment or House of Your Own

IF YOU FEAR you're destined to be a renter forever, you're not alone. The fact is that it's tougher for us to buy homes than it was for our parents' generation. And though homes are currently more affordable for first-time buyers than they were in the '80s, many young people are still priced out of the market.

Depressed yet?

Don't be. There are a growing number of programs that make it easier for first-time buyers to purchase homes. Most of this chapter explains these options and discusses everything you need to know about buying a place of your own.

And even if you're nowhere near the point where you can consider buying, you can benefit from this chapter. The first section offers tips on being a smart renter.

WHAT EVERY RENTER
NEEDS TO KNOW

Okay. So the odds of your purchasing a home are about as good as your chances of being offered your own talk show. For now you're a tenant, so be a wise one. Here are steps you can take to reduce the cost of renting and eliminate the headaches you're likely to encounter as a tenant. Keep them in mind before, during, and after you sign a lease:

- **Try to negotiate the rent.** I know a lot of twentysomethings who feel squeamish about doing this, but force yourself. When you find a place you like, tell the landlord you're very interested but you hadn't planned to spend as much as he's asking for. Ask if there's any way you can get a break—say, $25 a month. If you're a desirable candidate (that is, you have a good credit record and have been working at the same job for at least a year), there's a decent chance the landlord will make some reduction. If he doesn't, nothing lost.

- **Negotiate the terms of the lease.** Though it isn't exciting, it's important that you read your lease, which might be two or three pages long. Look for provisions that seem unfair; they may be illegal. In some states, for example, a landlord can't include clauses banning water beds or demanding excessive penalties for late rent. To find out the rules in your area, call your state or county housing office or office of consumer affairs. These government agencies may also be able to supply you with brochures that answer your questions about tenants' rights.

  Also look for clauses that, although legal, may be burdensome to you. You may be able to negotiate them out of the lease *before* you sign. Beware of provisions that give your landlord the right to enter your apartment without your permission or the right to raise your rent if his taxes or operating costs increase. Watch out for provisions that say no one but you can live in the apartment. Look for bans on pets; although

you may not have one now, you might want to get one in the
future. And think twice before agreeing to any unreasonable
stipulation the landlord may have added to the standard lease
agreement. I know of one couple who had to agree to wash
their landlord's plants every week with soap and water! That
meant they couldn't go away for more than a week without
getting someone to take over this ridiculous chore.

- **Negotiate with the real estate broker if you're dealing with
  one.** In most cities if you use a broker to help you find an
  apartment to rent, you don't pay him or her a commission.
  But in a few places, such as New York City and certain parts
  of Boston, renters are sometimes expected to pay brokers as
  much as 15% of the year's rent to secure a place. If possible,
  try to avoid dealing with brokers by combing newspaper ads
  for rentals offered directly by the owner. If you must use a
  broker, explain up front that you're a serious customer but
  are willing to pay only a commission of say, 5%. If you hunt
  around, you may find a broker willing to cut a deal.

- **List all your roommates on the lease and have them all sign
  it.** Although some landlords won't allow this, it's worth
  asking about. Having all your roommates listed on the lease
  ensures that you will all share legal responsibility in case of a
  problem. It also protects you if one of your roommates
  suddenly changes his or her mind and decides to move out
  before the lease is up.

- **Get everything in writing.** In general, ask for a written lease
  instead of a verbal agreement. Also, get any additional promises the landlord makes (such as guarantees to paint walls or
  fix leaky faucets) included in the lease before you sign.

- **Understand how the security deposit works.** A security deposit is money you give to a landlord to protect him in case
  you damage the apartment or house. If you don't cause any
  damage, the security deposit will be returned to you when
  the lease is up. Most states limit the size of security deposits
  to one or two months' rent, and many also restrict the ways

in which they can be used. In general, the landlord can use the money to fix damages you caused or to cover your rent if you break the lease early, but not for basic maintenance on the apartment or house.

Get a receipt for the security deposit from the landlord. In some states the landlord is required to put the money in an interest-bearing account and pay you the interest at the end of the tenancy. (Even in states that don't require a landlord to pay you interest, many landlords will.) Call your state or local housing office for the rules. When your lease is up and you move out, the landlord must refund your deposit if you did not cause any damage. If you don't trust your landlord, take pictures of how you left the place and have a neighbor (or, if possible, your landlord) sign a statement saying that you left the apartment in good condition.

- **If you plan to renew your lease, contact your landlord two months before the lease is up and try to negotiate.** If you live in an area where there is an abundance of available rentals, your landlord may agree to keep the rent the same or even lower it. But don't wait too long to bring up the subject; start the negotiations a couple of months before your lease is up. If you wait until the week before the lease ends, the landlord will assume you're bluffing when you say you're thinking of moving out.

- **Know your rights.** The law protects renters in many ways. Here are a few:
  - —Federal law prohibits a landlord from refusing to rent to you based on your race, color, religion, sex, or familial status (meaning, for example, whether you're single, married, or have kids).
  - —In many states, you must be told of an impending rent increase before your lease is up. The amount of time you must be given varies from state to state.
  - —In most states, if you disobey a provision in your lease and your landlord knows but accepts your rent anyway, the landlord cannot kick you out for violating that provision.

For example, if your lease forbids overnight guests but your landlord knows you had a friend stay over and accepts your rent check anyway, he cannot evict you later based on the fact that you had a friend stay over.

—In some states you can withhold rent if there has been negligence on the part of the landlord, but the rules are very specific about how to go about this. Again, call your county or state housing office or office of consumer affairs to find out the rules in your area. If you don't receive adequate help from these offices, call the office of the attorney general in your state. For additional assistance, try contacting local branches of consumer groups such as the Public Interest Research Group (PIRG) or the Legal Aid Society.

SHOULD YOU RENT OR BUY?

Many people believe that, given the choice, renting is a bad idea. They think it's the equivalent of "throwing money away." But when you're young, it's often smarter to rent than to buy.

Unfortunately, making the decision involves a lot more than simply comparing your monthly rent with the monthly mortgage you'd pay as an owner. A variety of factors must be taken into account, including how long you plan to own the home, how much you think the home will increase in value, or *appreciate,* the tax break you will get for buying, the fees you'll have to pay when you buy, and the rate of return you think you can earn by investing the cash you would save by *not* buying (this is called the **opportunity cost**). (Of course, plenty of emotional factors go into this decision, too, but I'll leave those for you to think about.) In all, more than a dozen different financial factors affect the rent-versus-buy decision, but you can get a rough idea of what to do by looking at the two graphs in Figure 7-1. Also consider these tips:

- **If you can't see yourself in the same place for several years, you should probably rent.** Like I said, there are many financial factors (more than a dozen) that can determine whether it makes sense for you to buy or rent. One very important factor is the thousands of dollars in up-front fees you'll pay when you purchase a home. These charges are called **closing costs** because they're paid when you close the deal and sign the final paperwork on a new home. Then when you sell your home, you can expect to pay thousands more to a real estate broker. If you remain in your new home for many years, these costs won't make much difference, at least in theory; the hope is that your home's selling price will increase by more than enough to cover them. But if you move after a couple of years and your home's value did not appreciate significantly, you may not be able to sell your home for a profit that would cover these costs. In general, our lives change so much when we're in our twenties and thirties that buying is not always smart. This is important to keep in mind. I know many people who purchased studio apartments when they graduated from college and then two or three years later got married and had to sell their places at huge losses.

- **If you have an amazing deal on a rental, it may make more sense to rent and invest your savings elsewhere.** In some cities there are still low-cost apartment deals to be had. If you're lucky enough to have found a **rent-controlled apartment** (one for which the landlord cannot charge more than a fixed rent and fixed increases) that is substantially below the going rental rate, you may be better off holding on to it and putting the money you save in your company retirement plan or some other investment.

- **Don't assume you always get a tax break for buying.** Most of us have at least one relative who prattles on about how buying a home is the best tax break around. That's because the federal government allows homeowners to deduct the mortgage interest they pay, meaning they get to subtract it from their taxable income. If you're buying a low-priced home, however, the tax break may be worth very little.

Consider this example. Say you paid $10,000 in mort-

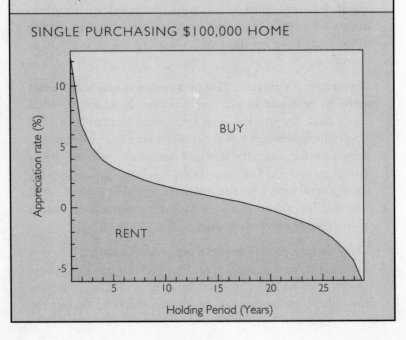

Figure 7-1
SHOULD YOU BUY
OR SHOULD YOU RENT?

Deciding whether to rent or buy a home can be a complicated and confusing process. In the end, it pays to sit down and consider all the variables that enter into the decision. For example: Let's say you're thinking of buying a $100,000 home. The down payment on the home is $10,000, the interest rate on the mortgage is 8% and the opportunity cost is 6%. You're currently paying $800 a month in rent. Does it make sense for you to buy a home, or should you just go on renting?

The following graphs may help you get a feeling for whether you should rent or buy. Here's what to do: Estimate how much the price of the home

SINGLE PURCHASING $100,000 HOME

gage interest and had an income of $50,000. You would be able to subtract, or *deduct,* the $10,000 worth of interest and bring your taxable income down to $40,000. Assuming your tax rate is 33%, that would translate into a savings of

you want to purchase will rise each year (the appreciation rate). Next, estimate how many years you will own the home. Select the graph that matches your marital status and make a dot corresponding to your estimated appreciation rate and estimated holding period. If the dot is above the line, you should buy. If the dot is below the line, you should rent.

Keep in mind that if the assumptions we started with do not fit your own situation, these graphs may not be applicable to you. If you have access to a computer with a Lotus-compatible spreadsheet program, however, you may want to order a spreadsheet application called BUY-RENT.WK1, which could help you come up with an answer tailored to your personal circumstances. For information, send a self-addressed stamped envelope to Ed Chang at 1616 NE 16th Way, #215, Gresham, OR 97030. Write BUY-RENT in the lower left-hand corner of the SASE. Cost: about $20.

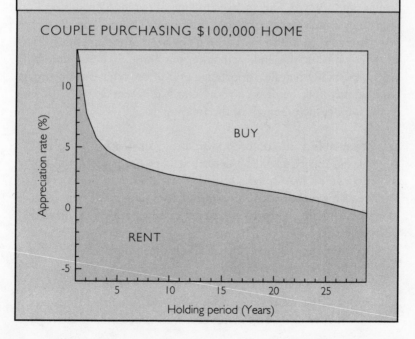

COUPLE PURCHASING $100,000 HOME

$3,300. But if you have a very small mortgage, you may not get a tax benefit at all. That's because all taxpayers get a break known as the **standard deduction**. In 1996 the standard deduction is $4,000 for single taxpayers and $6,700 for married taxpayers filing joint returns. In order to reap a tax advantage from buying, the annual interest you pay on your mortgage (plus other deductions you get) must be *greater* than the standard deduction. If you're buying a low-priced home, this may not be the case. If you don't qualify for a tax break, there's much less of an incentive for you to buy. (For details on other tax breaks that homeowners can receive, see Chapter 9.)

WHAT LENDERS LOOK FOR

The first question most prospective home buyers ask is, what price home can I afford? The answer, to a great extent, depends on how big a **mortgage** you can obtain. A mortgage is a loan you use to pay for a home. It is said to be "secured" by your home, meaning if you don't pay it back, the lender can take your home. To determine if you can responsibly handle a mortgage and, if so, what size mortgage you qualify for, lenders look at many different aspects of your financial life, including all of the following:

- **Your ability to come up with the cash.** With a couple of exceptions that will be described later on, lenders will not give you a loan for the full purchase price of a home. They require you to contribute some of your own money up front; this is called a **down payment**. Lenders tend to require a down payment of 3% to 20% of the price of the home. Coming up with this kind of cash is the number one obstacle for first-time home buyers.

  The typical home buyer also has to pay about 5% of a home's price in closing costs, which include fees for inspections, appraisals, title insurance, credit checks, land surveys, and legal services. This can add another $5,000 on a $100,000 home. Also, some lenders want buyers to have two to three months' cash reserve.

- **Your income.** Lenders want to make sure you earn enough to pay the costs of owning a home. To do this they compare your future monthly housing costs (also known as your **PITI,** which stands for Principal, Interest, property Taxes, and Insurance) to your pre-tax monthly income. They use the following guideline: Your PITI costs should not exceed 28% of your pre-tax monthly income. (If you buy a condominium or cooperative, the condo or co-op fees are also considered part of the basic monthly housing costs. Thus, the acronym should actually be PITIC.) Figure 7-2 gives you an idea as to what price home you can qualify for based on your income.

- **Your debt.** Lenders also want to make sure that you aren't already burdened with lots of loans. That's why they look at your current monthly debt commitments, such as auto loan payments, student loan payments, and minimum credit card payments, *plus* your future monthly housing costs, and calculate what portion of your monthly income before taxes will be devoted to these expenses. The percentage they come up with is called your debt-to-income ratio. Lenders like to see a debt-to-income ratio that doesn't exceed 36%.

- **Your credit record.** Lenders want to make sure you have a history of paying back your loans. To do this they will obtain a copy of your credit report, which is the long-term record of your financial behavior. (See Chapter 3 for details on credit reports.) If you've defaulted on a loan in recent years, been 60 days late on a loan or bill payment within the last two years, or been repeatedly late by 30 days during that time, you may have trouble getting a bank to give you a mortgage. And even if you've paid all your bills on time, a lender may consider you too inexperienced to handle a mortgage if you haven't had a credit card or a car loan for at least two years.

- **Your job history.** Lenders like to see that borrowers have a secure job. In general, if you've worked in the same industry for at least two years, they view you more favorably than if you've changed your occupation during that time.

COSTS OF OWNING A HOME

As mentioned earlier, when you become a homeowner, you will incur a variety of expenses that you may never even have heard of as a renter. Here's a description of each:

- **Principal and interest.** Your monthly mortgage payment consists of two parts—principal and interest. The amount you borrow from the lender is known as the principal. The fee the bank charges to lend you money is called interest, and it is expressed as an annual percentage. Suppose you get a mortgage of $100,000 and you're expected to pay it back over 30 years (that's standard). If the lender charges you an interest rate of 10%, after 30 years you would have paid the lender back the $100,000 in principal plus a total of $215,925 in interest. (Shocking, isn't it?) In the early years of your loan, you're paying back mostly interest and very little principal. As time goes on, you start to pay back the principal. To soften the blow somewhat, you do get to deduct your interest payments if you itemize.

  To get a feel for what your monthly mortgage payment would be, check out Figure 7-3.

- **Property tax.** This is an expense you pay to your town, city, or county. It is based on where you live and on the official

Figure 7-2
HOW MUCH HOME CAN YOU BUY?

One of the key factors that will determine how expensive a home you can purchase is your income. To get a ballpark idea of what you can afford, use this table. First, to find out what current home loan interest rates are, call your local bank and ask for the rate on the "fixed, 30-year mortgage with two points," since that's a typical combination. (For a full discussion of points, see page 166.) Then look in the left column and find your before-tax income. Locate the point where your income and the current rate meet. That figure represents the cost of the home you are likely to qualify for.

This table assumes that you have a good job and a good credit report, and that you can make a 10% down payment. It also assumes that 25% of your income is devoted to principal and interest payments, 3% to property tax and insurance, and 8% to other debt such as student loans.

| | INTEREST RATE YOU PAY | | | | | |
	7%	8%	9%	10%	11%	12%
$ 20,000	$ 69,587	$ 63,094	$ 57,538	$ 52,755	$ 48,614	$ 45,008
30,000	104,380	94,641	86,307	79,133	72,921	67,513
40,000	139,174	126,188	115,076	105,510	97,228	90,017
50,000	173,967	157,736	143,845	131,888	121,535	112,521
75,000	260,951	236,603	215,767	197,831	182,303	168,782
100,000	347,934	315,471	287,690	263,775	243,070	225,042
150,000	521,901	473,207	431,534	395,663	364,605	337,564

(Left axis label: Income (Before Taxes))

Source: National Association of Home Builders, Mortgage Finance Department

appraised value of your home and the land on which it is built. To get a sense of the property taxes charged for various homes in neighborhoods you're interested in, ask a real estate broker. You can also call the town hall or city hall and ask for the tax assessor's office. One bit of consolation: If you itemize your deductions, you can deduct property taxes. (See Chapter 9 for details.)

- **Insurance.** Most lenders require you to get **homeowners insurance** so that the insurance company will pay the cost of replacing your home in case it is destroyed in a disaster, such as a fire. That's because your home is the lender's collateral. If it's completely ruined and you walk away from it (and your loan obligation), the lender is protected by your homeowners insurance. Depending on where you live, you may be required to buy flood insurance also. (For tips on buying insurance, including renters coverage, see Chapter 8.)

  Another type of insurance you may be required to buy if you make a down payment of less than 20% is **private mortgage insurance (PMI).** PMI protects the lender if you default on your mortgage. There are two basic ways you are charged for PMI. With one type of PMI, you are asked to pay an up-front fee of about 0.5% of the loan amount. (On a $100,000 mortgage, you would pay $500.) After that you will generally be charged a fee of one-third of 1% per year. With another type of PMI, you don't pay anything up front, but your monthly payment will be higher. Once you've paid off 20% of the loan's principal, many lenders will allow you to discontinue PMI coverage. (It's important to ask your lender about this when you obtain the mortgage.)

- **Condominium and cooperative fees. Condos** and **co-ops** are housing units (usually apartment buildings) that are jointly owned. Each resident owns his or her own unit or apartment, while the common spaces (stairwells, elevators, hallways, lobbies) are owned collectively by all the residents. To pay for the upkeep of these common spaces, residents pay extra fees. These fees are also known as maintenance fees or common charges.

  The main difference between a co-op and a condo is the way in which the units are owned. In a co-op, residents do not technically own the apartments; instead they own

Figure 7-3

GETTING A HANDLE ON
MONTHLY MORTGAGE PAYMENTS

Based on what you learned from Figure 7-2, locate your house cost in the left-hand column. Now find the current interest rate being charged for 30-year fixed-rate mortgages. As you can see, you'd have a lower monthly payment with a 20% down payment than with 10% down.

Note that this table includes only principal and interest payments, and not property taxes, homeowners insurance, or PMI. Use the following rules of thumb to (very roughly) estimate these costs: Annual property taxes are typically between 1% and 3% of the cost of your home; PMI amounts to about 0.4% of your mortgage per year; and homeowners insurance can range from $200 to $1,000 per year. These extra costs can vary dramatically, though, depending on where you live and the amount of your mortgage. For more precise estimates, ask a lender or a local real estate agent.

Cost of Home	Down Payment %	Down Payment $	Monthly Mortgage Payment With Interest Rate Of 6%	8%	10%	12%
$ 50,000	10%	$ 5,000	$ 270	$ 330	$ 395	$ 463
	20%	10,000	240	294	351	411
100,000	10%	10,000	540	660	790	926
	20%	20,000	480	587	702	823
150,000	10%	15,000	809	991	1,185	1,389
	20%	30,000	719	881	1,053	1,234
200,000	10%	20,000	1,079	1,321	1,580	1,852
	20%	40,000	959	1,174	1,404	1,646
300,000	10%	30,000	1,619	1,981	2,369	2,777
	20%	60,000	1,439	1,761	2,106	2,469
400,000	10%	40,000	2,158	2,642	3,159	3,703
	20%	80,000	1,919	2,348	2,808	3,292

Source: Federal National Mortgage Association

shares, or units of ownership, in the cooperative. The cooperative owns all the units in the building. In order to buy or sell units in a co-op, residents usually must get approval from the co-op board, which is a group comprised of co-op residents. With a condo, residents have more autonomy;

the apartment and can usually buy and sell the place without getting permission from any board.

SPECIAL PROGRAMS FOR NEW HOME BUYERS

Even if you're having trouble qualifying for a mortgage at your local bank, you may still be able to get one. You just have to know where to look. There are several options especially appealing to people in their twenties and thirties:

- **Get a mortgage from your state or local housing agency.** One of the best-kept secrets of home buying is the special mortgage deals offered by state and local housing agencies to first-time home buyers. The reason you've probably never heard of these programs is that they don't advertise the way banks do. The interest rates on the mortgages offered by these programs tend to be anywhere from one to four percentage points lower than the rates offered by banks. That could mean savings of hundreds of dollars a month on your mortgage payments, and tens of thousands of dollars over the life of your loan. Another major plus: These programs allow you to make very low down payments, ranging from "no money down" to 5% of a home's price.

  Details vary from state to state, and many states have a variety of programs to choose from. Typically, you can participate in the program if your income is no more than the county or state's median household income and the home you want to purchase costs slightly less than the area's average purchase price. However, some states have low-rate loan programs for buyers whose incomes exceed the state's median income level or who are buying homes that cost more than the local average. For the phone number of your state housing agency, see Figure 7-4. When you call, say that you're a first-time home buyer looking for a mortgage.

- **Get a "Fannie Mae" or "Freddie Mac" loan for first-time home buyers.** If you earn too much money to qualify for a state-sponsored mortgage but can't qualify for a standard mortgage, don't despair. Special mortgage programs for first-time home buyers created by the Federal National Mortgage Association (Fannie Mae) and the Federal Home Loan Mortgage Corporation (Freddie Mac) may make it possible for you to afford a home. Fannie Mae and Freddie Mac are two private companies created by the federal government to help banks and mortgage companies expand their mortgage offerings to all types of borrowers. These companies do not offer loans directly to borrowers; instead, they design new mortgage programs that are offered to consumers by thousands of banks and other lenders across the country.

  Lenders often put their own names on these programs. For example, Countrywide Funding Corporation, a giant mortgage company, calls its Fannie Mae program "House America." When you shop around, ask lenders if they participate in Fannie's "Community Home Buyer's Program" and "FannieNeighbors" and in Freddie's "Affordable Gold." They'll know what you mean.

  In general, the criteria for qualifying for these Freddie or Fannie mortgages are less strict than those that bankers use for standard mortgages, with one exception: You must have a good credit record. If you've been habitually late paying back student loans or credit card bills in the last two years, you may not be eligible. In nearly every other way, these loans are easier to qualify for. You need only a 5% down payment for Freddie's program, and Fannie grants loans to borrowers with as little as 3% down. And while you must come up with three-fifths of the down payment from your own savings, the remaining two-fifths can come from gifts (but not loans) from friends, relatives, or community groups. In addition, your debt can be higher and your income lower than with traditional mortgages. You're sometimes allowed to borrow money from friends and relatives to cover the closing costs, which many standard lenders do not permit. You don't have to have had a credit card or car loan for more than two years because other aspects of your financial life—your utility-bill- and rent-paying habits—will be used to determine whether you're reliable.

In most major cities there are no income restrictions for Fannie and Freddie programs. (For a list of these cities call 800-832-2345 for Fannie's program and 800-FREDDIE for Freddie's program.) In 1996, the maximum loan you can get from Fannie is $203,150; from Freddie, it is $207,000. (In Alaska and Hawaii, the maximums are 50% higher.) Con- tact banks and mortgage companies for details. For a free copy of Fannie's publication *Opening the Door to a Home of Your Own,* call 800-688-HOME.

- **Get help through the Federal Housing Administration.** If your credit record isn't spotless, you might not get a Fannie or Freddie loan. One possible option that is somewhat more le- nient is the Federal Housing Administration (FHA) loan pro- gram, which is especially appealing if you're very low on cash.

    FHA mortgages are not government loans; they are loans made by banks, and especially mortgage companies, that are insured by the federal government. The insurance protects the lender in case the borrower defaults. With FHA loans your debt can be higher and your income lower than with traditional mortgages. And FHA loans require only a very small down payment—from 3% to 5%, depending on how much you borrow. The FHA (unlike Fannie or Freddie pro- grams) allows you to add your closing costs to your mort- gage and borrow the entire amount from the bank. And your credit record does not have to be flawless.

    One drawback to FHA loans is that the total cost can be higher than the cost of a Fannie or Freddie loan because the cost of federal mortgage insurance is somewhat higher than the cost of private mortgage insurance. But if an FHA loan is the only kind of mortgage you can qualify for, the additional cost may be worthwhile.

    There are no maximum income limits on FHA borrowers. Maximum loan amounts vary from city to city. In high-cost areas like San Francisco and New York City, the maximum loan you can get in 1996 through the FHA is $155,240. In other areas the maximums are lower. Most banks and mortgage companies offer FHA loans. Contact a lender or your local Housing and Urban Development (HUD) office for more information.

- **Get assistance from the Department of Veterans Affairs.** Another federal insurance program is offered to home buyers who have been in the armed services. Veterans Affairs, or VA, mortgages are not government loans; they are made by lenders—mostly mortgage companies—and are partially guaranteed by the VA. These loans generally do not require any down payment at all, although in some cases the lender may require one. You pay a one-time charge called a **funding fee,** which covers mortgage insurance. As of 1996 the funding fee ranges from 0.5% to 3% of the mortgage, depending on the terms of your loan.

  Eligibility is limited to people who at some point enlisted in active duty or who served at least six years in the Selected Reserves or the National Guard. The maximum VA loan amount is $203,000. There are no maximum income limits on applicants for these loans. For more information call 800-827-1000.

IF YOU DON'T QUALIFY FOR SPECIAL PROGRAMS

Even if you're not eligible to participate in any of the loan alternatives above, you still have some options. Below you'll find some common problems you may face and some possible solutions.

If Your Problem Is the Down Payment

As already mentioned, this is the most common problem new home buyers face. Here are some tips that may help:

Figure 7-4
TELEPHONE NUMBERS OF
STATE HOUSING AGENCIES

Alabama Housing Finance Authority	(334) 244-9200
Alaska Housing Finance Corporation	(907) 561-1900
Arizona Department of Commerce	(602) 280-1365
Arkansas Development Finance Authority	(501) 682-5900
California Housing Finance Agency	(916) 322-3991
Colorado Housing and Finance Authority	(303) 297-2432
Connecticut Housing Finance Authority	(203) 721-9501
Delaware State Housing Authority	(302)-739-4263
District of Columbia Housing Finance Agency	(202) 408-0415
Florida Housing Finance Agency	(904) 488-4197
Georgia Housing and Finance Authority	(404) 679-4840
Hawaii Housing Finance and Development Corporation	(808) 587-0567
Idaho Housing Agency	(208) 331-4883
Illinois Housing Development Authority	(800) 942-8439
Indiana Housing Finance Authority	(317) 232-7777
Iowa Finance Authority	(515) 242-4990
Kansas Department of Commerce and Housing	(913) 296-5865
Kentucky Housing Corporation	(502) 564-7630
Louisiana Housing Finance Agency	(504) 342-1320
Maine State Housing Authority	(207) 626-4600
Maryland Community Development Administration	(410) 514-7514
Massachusetts Housing Finance Agency	(617) 854-1020
Michigan State Housing Development Authority	(517) 373-6840
Minnesota Housing Finance Agency	(612) 296-7613
Mississippi Home Corporation	(601) 354-6062

Missouri Housing Development Commission	(816) 753-6222
Montana Board of Housing	(406) 444-3040
Nebraska Investment Finance Authority	(402) 434-3900
Nevada Housing Division	(702) 687-4258
New Hampshire Housing Finance Authority	(603) 472-8623
New Jersey Housing and Mortgage Finance Agency	(800) 654-6873
New Mexico Mortgage Finance Authority	(505) 843-6880
State of New York Mortgage Agency	(800) 382-4663
North Carolina Housing Finance Agency	(919) 781-6115
North Dakota Housing Finance Agency	(701) 328-9800
Ohio Housing Finance Agency	(614) 466-7970
Oklahoma Housing Finance Agency	(405) 848-1144
Oregon Housing and Community Services Department	(503) 986-2047
Pennsylvania Housing Finance Agency	(717) 780-3800
Rhode Island Housing and Mortgage Finance Corporation	(401) 751-5566
South Carolina Housing Finance and Development Authority	(803) 734-2069
South Dakota Housing Development Authority	(605) 773-3181
Tennessee Housing Development Agency	(615) 741-4968
Texas Department of Housing and Community Affairs	(512) 475-2120
Utah Housing Finance Agency	(801) 521-6950
Vermont Housing Finance Agency	(802) 864-5743
Virginia Housing Development Authority	(804) 782-1986
Washington State Housing Finance Commission	(206) 464-7139
West Virginia Housing Development Fund	(304) 345-6475
Wisconsin Housing and Economic Development Authority	(608) 266-7884
Wyoming Community Development Authority	(307) 265-0603

Source: National Council of State Housing Agencies

- **Find a lender that will allow you to make a down payment of as little as 3% of the price of the home.** If you earn too much to qualify for the Freddie or Fannie programs, you might still find a lender willing to accept just a 3% down payment. Lenders sometimes offer low down payment mortgages to customers who have excellent credit records, good debt-to-income ratios, and incomes large enough to handle the monthly housing payments.

  Of course, the lower your down payment, the larger your loan. That means your monthly mortgage payment will be bigger, and the total cost of the loan will be higher. What's more, with a small down payment you will have to purchase private mortgage insurance. Still, if you're anxious to buy and this is the only way you can do it, get a low down payment loan.

- **Get the down payment (or part of it) as a gift.** About one in four first-time home buyers receive money from friends or relatives to cover their down payment. Some lenders require that your down payment consist at least partially of your own money. Others permit the entire down payment to come from a gift. Some lenders require that the gift come from a relative; others allow it to come from friends. In most cases lenders require a letter from the generous friend or relative stating that the down payment money is a gift, not a loan.

  Keep careful records if you receive a cash gift. Lenders want to be able to verify that the portion of the down payment that you claim is from a gift isn't, in fact, a loan. Some will review your bank records before granting your loan. When they see that a large sum of money was deposited in your account a few months before you tried to get a mortgage, they'll ask you to prove that the money is not a loan. Make copies of any large gift checks you receive (wedding gifts, for instance). Also, if you sell something valuable (like a car), keep receipts of the transaction.

- **Look for special programs that require no down payment.** A few banks and brokerage firms will lend you 100% of the cost of a home (meaning that you don't have to make a down payment) if your relative or employer will put 20% to 30% of the loan amount into the institution's investments. These loan programs are known as **pledged asset mortgages (PAMs)** because they allow relatives and employers to use their assets as collateral for your mortgage. A PAM makes sense, however, only if it enables your relative or employer to make a worthwhile investment. There aren't many companies offering PAMs now, but you can expect to see more in the future.

- **Borrow money from your 401(k) plan.** Most large companies allow employees to borrow for a first-time home purchase. Your bank will allow you to do this, and it will treat the 401(k) money as your own savings. The bad news is that because this money is a loan, it will increase your debt-to-income ratio. (For details on borrowing from a 401(k), see Chapter 6.)

- **Start saving.** Okay, so this is an obvious one. But you should run, not walk, to sign up for an automatic savings program. If you save regularly, your down payment will accumulate sooner than you think.

If Your Problem Is Your Tainted Credit History

If your problematic credit record is your only barrier, try this:

- Find a lender that will overlook your checkered past. With most lenders you need to have a good credit record (generally meaning no payments 60 days or more past due and not more than one or two payments 30 days past due) for at least a year to qualify for a standard mortgage. If you've messed up in the past by being late on student loan or credit card payments, the best thing you can do once you're on track is to stay timely for at least a year. Some lenders will overlook an occasional late payment if you can prove that you've made timely rental payments for at least a year or have been in the same line of work for at least two years. If you absolutely can't wait that long to buy a home, you may want to consider what is called a **non-conforming mortgage,** although I don't recommend it for most first-time home buyers. These special mortgages offered by some lenders require a large down payment (typically 20% to 30%) and have high interest rates that can easily be one to two percentage points higher than the rates on standard mortgages.

- **Consider hiring a mortgage broker.** Mortgage brokers are people who shop for a mortgage for you. Some specialize in getting mortgages for people who have trouble qualifying because of a problematic credit report or lack of credit history. Because people with shaky financial pasts are considered riskier than those with good credit records, the interest rates on these mortgages can be higher—by two percentage points or more—than the standard rates. But be careful. There are a lot of shady operators who promise to get you a mortgage in exchange for a hefty fee. Before you sign up, find out exactly what you'll be charged for the service. To find a reliable broker, ask friends and relatives for referrals. To ensure that a broker is reputable, check with your state banking department or your local mortgage brokers association.

If Your Problem Is Your Income

If you have a stellar credit record but simply don't earn enough to qualify for the mortgage you want, try this: Find a lender that is willing to look at other aspects of your financial life. Increasingly, lenders are more flexible with borrowers who have good credit histories. If, for instance, the monthly housing costs of a home you're interested in exceed 28% of your monthly income, your lender may give you some leeway. If you can show that you have been able to handle a monthly rent of, say, 35% or more of your income, the lender may approve your mortgage application.

SHOPPING FOR
A MORTGAGE

If you were shopping for a stereo or a car, you wouldn't dream of buying the first one you saw. This should be true when you shop for a mortgage as well. If you're able to save just half a percentage point on a mortgage interest rate, you'll save thousands of dollars over the life of the loan.

You can get a mortgage from several different types of lending institutions: One option is a bank. Credit unions also offer mortgages. Then there are mortgage companies—financial institutions whose only business is granting mortgages. There are no overwhelming advantages to dealing with one type of lending institution over another. Your best bet is to compare the offerings of several different kinds of lenders. This section will highlight what you need to look for—and look out for—when shopping for a mortgage.

Fixed Rate Versus Adjustable Rate

All lenders offer two basic types of mortgages. The most common type is a **fixed-rate** mortgage, which is usually paid back over 30 years. (Your parents probably have this type of mortgage.) A 30-year fixed-rate mortgage has an interest rate that stays the same over the 30 years you repay it, so the monthly mortgage payment stays the same for the entire 30 years.

The other general type of mortgage is the **adjustable-rate mortgage (ARM)**, sometimes known as a variable-rate mortgage. The interest rate on an ARM changes based on what happens to interest rates in the economy. If rates go down, your ARM interest rate decreases and so does your monthly payment. If rates go up, your interest rate and monthly payment rise. With most ARMs the lender raises or lowers the interest rate only once a year. And most lenders guarantee that they will not increase (or decrease) an ARM's interest rate more than two percentage points per year or more than six percentage points over the life of the loan.

IF YOU'RE THINKING ABOUT GETTING AN ADJUSTABLE RATE MORTGAGE

When Nicole and Jimmy found their dream house, they were thrilled to find a lender offering an adjustable rate mortgage (ARM) with an initial rate of 5%. They knew that the rate would fluctuate but assumed that if interest rates in the economy held steady, their rate would remain the same. Unfortunately, that's not the way it always works. In fact, even if interest rates fell slightly, their ARM rate would *increase* to 7% the following year. Here's what Nicole, Jimmy, and all prospective ARM customers need to know:

- **The benchmark the ARM rate is pegged to.** Your ARM's rate fluctuates based on ridiculously named benchmarks like the "One-Year Treasury Constant Maturity" and the "11th District Cost of Funds." Know which one your ARM is tied to.
- **The teaser rate.** Sometimes a lender will offer you an extremely low initial interest rate for the first year. Don't let this rate fool you. In the case of Nicole and Jimmy, 5% was a teaser rate. Their ARM was pegged to the One-Year Treasury Con-

Whether you're getting a standard mortgage or a special mortgage from Fannie, Freddie, the FHA, or the Department of Veterans Affairs, you can get either an ARM or a fixed-rate mortgage. Unfortunately, there isn't an easy answer about which one you should opt for. Your choice will depend on your financial situation and your temperament. It will also depend on one factor that no one can predict: the way interest rates will change in the future.

stant Maturity, which was 5.75% when they got their loan. When their ARM adjusts for the first time, the new rate they pay will be based on the current rate of the One-Year Treasury benchmark plus a fixed number of percentage points (typically three) called a **margin**.

- **The cap.** The annual cap is the maximum amount an ARM rate can increase in any one year. Nicole and Jimmy's ARM has an annual cap of two percentage points. Here's why the cap protects them somewhat: If the One-year Treasury benchmark falls to 5.25% at adjustment time, the lender will add three percentage points to it, resulting in a new rate of 8.25%. Since their ARM has an annual cap of two percentage points, the lender will increase their rate to just 7% (the 5% current rate plus the two percentage point cap). In year three, if the Treasury benchmark stays at 5.25%, the lender will raise their 7% rate to 8.25% (that's 5.25% plus the three percentage point margin). In addition to an annual cap, look for an ARM with a lifetime cap of five or six percentage points. That way you'll know exactly how bad it can get.

ARMs are especially appealing to first-time home buyers because the *initial* interest rate is lower than the rate on fixed-rate mortgages. In 1995 the average 30-year fixed-rate loan charged an interest rate of 7.4%; the average ARM charged an initial rate of 5.6%. This lower initial rate can mean lower monthly payments for the first couple of years of the ARM. Because ARMs have lower monthly payments at the beginning, they can be easier to qualify for than fixed-rate mortgages. You could do extremely well with an ARM if interest rates in the economy do not rise. If rates increase, however, after five years or so the total cost of the ARM could exceed the cost of the fixed-rate loan. (For tips on evaluating ARMs, see the box below.)

The benefit of fixed-rate mortgages is that your monthly payments will be steady forever. Some people rest easier knowing that their mortgage payments will always be the same. And if interest rates in the economy take a nosedive, people with fixed-rate mortgages are not locked in to their rate. Lenders allow borrowers to "refinance"—the process of paying off an old mortgage with a new one at a lower rate.

There are many variations on these two basic mortgage types. Some special mortgages, for instance, charge a fixed interest rate for five years and then adjust at the end of the fifth year based on prevailing interest rates. From then on the loan adjusts annually. This is called a 5-1 mortgage. There are also 7-1 and 10-1 mortgages. Another hybrid is called a 5-25 loan, which is fixed for five years and then adjusts just once to a fixed-rate loan for the remaining 25 years. There's also a 7-23 mortgage. Since the initial rates on these loans will be lower than the rates on 30-year fixed-rate mortgages, they can be very appealing if you know you will want to sell your home before the loan starts adjusting. But be careful: It's difficult to be absolutely certain today that you'll move in five, seven, or ten years. If you end up staying longer, you may be hit with a big jump in your monthly payments if interest rates have risen by the time your rate adjusts. No matter what type you get, read all the provisions extremely carefully to make sure you know exactly what you're committing yourself to.

Rates Versus Points

The most important factors contributing to the cost of a mortgage are the interest rate and the **points.** As you know, the interest rate is the fee, expressed as a percentage of your loan, charged by the bank for lending you money. Points are another type of fee a bank gets for lending you money. Unlike interest, which is paid regularly for the life of the loan, points are paid only once, at the time you close the deal. Points are part of your closing costs. One point equals 1% of the loan. So one point on a $100,000 loan, for instance, equals $1,000.

Lenders offer various combinations of rates and points. This is true not only from bank to bank but also within one bank. In general, if you pay more points, you'll pay a lower interest rate. If you pay fewer points, you'll get a higher interest rate.

What combination should you look for? That is determined by how long you plan to live in your home. If you're going to be in your home for many years, it often makes sense to pay more points and get a lower interest rate. The lower monthly payments you get with a lower rate will more than make up for the few thousand dollars you paid in points. If you don't plan to stay in your new home for very long, it makes sense to pay fewer points. Of course, if you're low on cash your only option may be to go with as few points as possible. But if you're planning to live in your new home for a long time, you'll ultimately end up paying more.

No matter which rate/point combination you choose, you will want to go with the lender that offers you the most attractive deal. To make it easier for you to shop, the federal government requires lenders to tell you a mortgage's **annual percentage rate (APR)**. The APR is what you'd get if you took most of the charges you're paying on the mortgage (including the interest, points, private mortgage insurance, and certain fees) and expressed them as an annual interest rate. To help you comparison shop, you can compare APRs of the same types of loans. For instance, you can ask each lender for the APR on a 30-year fixed-rate mortgage for a specific loan amount. Although this is basically a good way to comparison shop, it isn't perfect. That's because the APR doesn't take into account a host of other charges such as appraisal and document preparation fees. What's more, the APR can be affected by a lender's specific policies. For instance, *refundable* application fees are taken into account when calculating the APR, but *nonrefundable* application fees are not. So in addition to asking for the APR, ask each lender for a list of fees that are not included in the APR. Also, if you're interested in an adjustable rate mortgage, don't rely on the APR alone; essential factors such as margins and caps are not taken into account when calculating the APR.

There are services that can help you with your mortgage shopping. One outfit is HSH Associates; it surveys more than 2,000 lenders in 125 major cities and publishes a weekly list of the best deals. To get a copy of the latest list, call 800-UPDATES. You'll get the names of about 25 lenders in your area for $20. Also check the local newspapers, which often print weekly listings of mortgage rates.

Fifteen-Year Versus Thirty-Year Mortgages

By far the most common type of mortgage is a fixed-rate loan that lasts for 30 years. Another type of mortgage you may consider is a 15-year fixed-rate mortgage. This type of loan is more difficult to qualify for than a 30-year mortgage, and it often has a lower interest rate than a 30-year fixed-rate mortgage. Since you pay it off in 15 years rather than 30, you're able to build up **equity,** or ownership, in the home sooner. Although some people view a 15-year mortgage as a disciplined way to pay off their home loans faster, it's not always the best choice. The monthly payments on a 15-year mortgage are higher than those on a 30-year loan. Depending on your situation, it may make more sense to go with the lower monthly payments of a 30-year loan and use the cash you're not pouring into your home for other investments. For example, you may be better off putting the money in a 401(k) in which your employer matches your contributions. Instead of locking into the higher monthly payment of a 15-year mortgage, you may want to get a 30-year loan that allows you to pay it off faster when you want to. For that reason, get a mortgage that does not include **prepayment penalties,** which are fees for paying off your loan early.

Two Mortgages to Avoid

One type of mortgage you probably should stay away from is the **graduated-payment loan**. Although this type of mortgage looks appealing, particularly to young people, it can be dangerous. With a graduated loan you do not pay all the interest you owe each month; instead, the unpaid interest is added to the unpaid balance of your mortgage. It's attractive because it keeps your monthly payments very low in the early years. Of course, that's because you're not paying off all your interest, and you're not paying off any principal—you're just building up more debt. Your monthly payments will gradually increase. Eventually you will end up paying the full interest due each month. At that point you will be in deeper debt than when you first got the mortgage. And if for some reason you have to sell your home at that time, you could find yourself in big trouble.

Another type of mortgage to avoid is a **balloon mortgage**. The way it works is that you make small monthly payments for a fixed number of years—anywhere from one to seven—and then you're required to pay off the remainder of the loan in one large payment. People sometimes opt for balloon mortgages if they anticipate that they will be getting a chunk of cash—maybe a big raise or an inheritance—when the loan comes due. But if something goes wrong and you can't make the final balloon payment, you could default on the loan if you aren't able to refinance with a lower-rate loan.

MAKING THE PROCESS GO SMOOTHLY

If you've gotten this far in the chapter, you have a good basic understanding of what you need to know to get a mortgage. When you're actually ready to begin your search, you're likely to encounter some hassles. Here are steps to take to help you avoid some of them:

- **Before you do anything, get a copy of your credit report.** Even if you've never been late on a payment, you should do this. (See Chapter 3 for details on how.) Credit reporting agencies are notorious for making mistakes.

- **Before you start house hunting, call your local bank or mortgage company and say you want to get "prequalified" for a mortgage.** Prequalification is a shorthand method used by lenders to give prospective buyers a sense of whether they can qualify for a mortgage, and if so, how large a mortgage they can get. Prequalification does not mean you have a guarantee of a mortgage from the lender. It's an informational service for you. It gives you a lender's firsthand impression of what you can afford. A growing number of lenders are willing to perform this service via telephone. For a list of personal information you need to have handy when you call, see Figure 7-5.

- **Once you've shopped on your own, consider enlisting the help of a mortgage broker.** As mentioned above, mortgage brokers are people who shop for a mortgage for you. Al-

A WORD ABOUT REAL ESTATE AGENTS

First-time buyers tend to trust real estate agents (also known as real estate brokers) a little too much. An agent's goal is to get you to buy the house or apartment he or she shows you, not to get you a great deal. He gets a commission of as much as 6% of the home's selling price from the seller. On a $100,000 house, the agent can make $6,000. And the more you pay, the more he gets.

If you live in a state that requires an attorney to be present during the closing, use a lawyer you find on your own—not one

though some deal only with clients who have bad credit records, others offer home buyers with good credit records another shopping alternative. Brokers can sometimes get you a discount on a mortgage because of their relationship with certain lenders. First you should shop around on your own to find the best deal you can, and then see if a broker can beat it. The broker may charge you (or the lender) a fee for his service—often 1% to 2% of the loan amount. So use a broker only if the mortgage he finds you, minus any fee you have to pay, is a better deal than the best mortgage you found on your own. Again, you need to be especially careful that the broker you're dealing with isn't part of a fly-by-night operation. Ask friends and relatives for referrals, and check with your state banking department or your local mortgage brokers association.

- **If you find a lender offering a good deal, consider getting a "preapproved" mortgage.** Although "prequalify" and "pre-approval" sound similar, their meanings are very different. Preapproval is a process by which the lender does a thorough analysis of your financial situation and commits to offering you a mortgage before you find a home you want to buy. You

recommended by the agent. When you're looking for a mortgage, don't ask the advice of your real estate agent; some mortgage companies offer incentives to real estate brokers who steer business to them.

One final suggestion: Comb the real estate listings on your own without an agent. If you don't use an agent, you may be able to get the seller to accept a lower price.

will be asked to submit all the necessary paperwork, and the
lender will look at your credit report and verify your employment information. If everything checks out, the lender
will give you a commitment letter that says you are entitled
to a loan. The only major snafu can occur if the bank's
appraisers deem the home you choose too high priced relative to its true value. Otherwise, you'll usually be able to sail
smoothly through the mortgage process.

Lenders sometimes charge $100 or so for this service, but
you should try to dispute it. Once you've done your homework and are convinced a lender is offering a good mortgage
deal, get preapproved. A preapproved loan can even be used
as a bargaining chip with a homeowner who is anxious to
sell. The seller may be willing to knock the price down a bit
when he discovers that you have a mortgage commitment
because that means the deal can take place immediately.

• **Find out if you can lock in a rate.** Some lending institutions
offer programs that allow you to lock in an interest rate
while you shop for a home. There is often a lock-in fee of 1%
of the loan amount, but this money will go toward your
closing costs when you close on the deal. Some lenders
charge as much as $250 to lock in a rate and won't refund
the fee; others do not charge at all. These programs protect
you if rates soar. (If rates fall, some lenders will not force you
to go with the locked-in rate. Try to find a lender who offers
this flexibility.) Before you lock in a rate, you should get
preapproved by the lender. Also, before you pay extra for a
lock-in loan, find out all the details. Ask how long the lock is
good for. It often takes at least 45 days to do all the paperwork associated with a home loan, so a 30-day lock would
be useless. Try to find a minimum 60-day lock.

• **Cozy up to your loan officer (or at least shake his hand).** The
process of actually getting your mortgage can be time con-
suming and frustrating. You can't just fill out your application and keep your fingers crossed. You have to stay on top
of it. The basic rule is, be assertive but polite. Call once a

Figure 7-5

INFORMATION YOU NEED
IN ORDER TO APPLY FOR
MORTGAGE PREQUALIFICATION

GENERAL INFORMATION

Name and co-borrowers' names	Number of kids
Age	Address
Marital status	Telephone Number

INCOME

Employer's name and address	Salary
Job title	Bonuses
Date hired	Average overtime or commissions

ASSETS
Total sums in:

Bank (including savings, checking, money market accounts)	Automobile, including year bought and current value
CDs	Retirement accounts
Mutual funds	Cash-value life insurance
Bonds	Value of furniture
Other investments, including real estate	Gifts expected from friends or relatives

DEBTS
Current balances and monthly payments on:

Credit cards	Car loans
Student loans	Other loans

EXPENSES
Monthly cost of:

Rent	Renters Insurance
Utilities	

week to see how the process is going, and always ask the name of the person you're speaking with. Try to meet the people working on your loan. This might make them less likely to throw your application into a pile and forget about it. If you get your mortgage from your own bank and you maintain a hefty balance in your accounts (usually at least $3,000), you may be able to get a quarter percentage point off the mortgage interest rate. Ask your loan officer.

FINANCIAL CRAMMING

- If you're about to rent an apartment, read the lease carefully. There may be a condition you don't like, such as a provision that allows your landlord to enter your apartment without your permission or a prohibition against overnight guests. Try to negotiate unwanted conditions out of the lease before you sign.

- If you can't come up with the cash to qualify for a mortgage, don't despair. Try your state's housing agency (see Figure 7-4 for a phone number). Also, ask your local lender about Fannie Mae, Freddie Mac, and FHA mortgages.

- Before you go hunting for a home to purchase, get "prequalified" for a mortgage by your local bank. Doing so will not guarantee you a home loan, but it will give you an idea of how large a mortgage you can afford. See Figure 7-5 for the information you'll need to give the bank to get prequalified.

- Check with several banks and mortgage companies before you get a mortgage. Call HSH Associates at 800-UPDATES and request a list of lenders in your area offering good deals (cost: $20). Also check the local newspapers, which often print weekly listings of mortgage rates. Careful shopping can save you thousands of dollars in the long run.

8

INSURANCE: WHAT YOU NEED AND WHAT YOU DON'T

Finding the Right Policies and Forgoing Coverage You Can Do Without

F OR MOST OF US, there are two classes of insurance: insurance we have too much of, and insurance we have too little of. Into the first category goes the life insurance policy you were talked into buying when you graduated from college and the credit unemployment protection you signed up for when you got your Visa or MasterCard. Into the second group goes the renters insurance you never even thought about purchasing and the health insurance you figure you can get by without. This chapter will help you decide how much protection you should have, if any, in each of the basic categories: health, auto, disability, home, and life. It will alert you to types of policies to avoid, show you how to maximize insurance-related benefits you get from your employer, and offer you advice on how to find the least expensive comprehensive policies on your own.

No matter what type of insurance you think you need, begin by reading the first three sections—"Shopping for Insurance," "Checking Out Credentials," and "Making the Most of Your Employer Plan." Then you can skip around and read only the sections on the type of insurance you need.

SHOPPING FOR
INSURANCE

The point of insurance is to protect you and your family from financial loss due to illness, accident, or natural disaster. The charge you pay for all types of insurance is called the **premium**. Remember this term. You'll hear it a lot.

Premiums can vary tremendously from one insurance company to the next. Take the case of auto insurance. Studies have shown that insurers in the same city often sell the same policies at premiums that differ by thousands of dollars. The Illinois Department of Insurance found that a 20-year-old male living on the West Side of Chicago could pay as little as $456 or as much as $6,115 for the same amount of auto liability protection! The point is clear: Shop around before you select any kind of insurance policy.

Before I get into the details of the various types of coverage, here are some general tips that will help you save money when you buy insurance:

- **Get the highest deductible you can afford.** With certain types of coverage—health insurance, home insurance, and some auto insurance—you must pay a fixed dollar amount of the costs yourself before the insurance kicks in. This fixed amount is known as a **deductible.** For example, on a health insurance policy with a $200 annual deductible, you must pay the first $200 worth of medical bills you incur each year with your own money. Any expenses you incur above $200 will be paid, at least in part, by the insurance company.

  One way to reduce your premium (there's that term again) is to increase your deductible. For example, say you're a 30-year-old single resident of Los Angeles who purchased a health insurance policy from Blue Shield of California. If you opted for a $200 deductible, you'd pay a premium of $184 a month. If you chose a $1,000 deductible, you'd pay just $95 a month—resulting in a 48% decrease in your premium. The same basic principle applies to renters insurance, homeowners insurance, and auto insurance.

This rule isn't right for everyone, of course. It makes sense to choose a lower premium only if you have enough savings to cover the higher deductible. Also, with a higher deductible you'll end up regularly covering certain costs yourself—for example, routine medical checkups and minor car and home repairs. If you tend to go to the doctor a lot or you're prone to car accidents, a lower deductible might make more sense for you. Otherwise, a higher deductible is probably a smart option.

- **Check with a couple of insurance agents.** There are two categories of agents: **Life and health insurance agents** sell life, health, and disability insurance; **property and casualty insurance agents** sell homeowners, renters, and automobile insurance. In general, insurance agents make their money through commissions, so they're understandably eager to make a sale. But don't be shy about shopping around. If an agent is impatient and doesn't want to answer your questions, find another one. And don't feel obliged to buy from an agent just because he did some research for you. That's his job.

  In theory, agents known as **independent agents** or brokers shop among a handful of insurance companies to find the best deal for you. In practice, if you don't do your homework, you may end up with the policy that pays the highest commission, or **load,** to the agent. Still, it's certainly worth it to give one of these agents a call. To find one, ask your relatives and friends for recommendations. Another type of agent, known as a **captive agent,** tends to sell only the products of one particular company. Why, you may wonder, would you ever go to a captive agent? Well, sometimes the companies they sell for offer very attractive policies. Find the section on the kind of insurance you need for the names and numbers of some captive agents to consider.

- **Contact companies that sell directly to consumers.** Some insurance companies sell directly to consumers rather than through agents. These firms can often charge less because they don't have to pay the salaries and expenses for hundreds of agents. The service reps who answer the phones at these companies may not be able to advise you on what to buy, but they can answer basic questions. If you have confidence in your ability to choose a policy (and you should, after you read this chapter), get a price quote from such a firm, typically known as a **low-load** company. See the section on the type of insurance you're looking for to get names and numbers of companies that sell direct.

- **Call a few services that will shop for you.** There are several 800-number services that will scan their multicompany databases and send you a free list of the least expensive life, health, or disability policies. (At the time of this writing there aren't any firms that do this for auto and homeowners insurance.) If you purchase a policy through one of these 800-number outfits, you pay no more than you would have had you purchased the policy from an insurance agent; these services make their money by keeping the commission the agent would have received. One advantage to these firms is that they have access to many more policies than ordinary insurance agents do. Locate the section on the type of insurance you're interested in to get the names and numbers of the appropriate services to call.

- **Try the Consumer Reports Buying Guide.** This guide sometimes has ratings of companies that sell auto, health, homeowners, or life insurance. The 1995 guide, for example, rates auto insurers.

AUTO INSURANCE:
YOU'D BETTER SHOP AROUND

Sam, 29, was about to move from New York City to Washington, D.C., and had to purchase auto insurance for the 1987 Nissan Maxima his parents would be giving him. After making just three phone calls to insurance companies, he reaped the rewards of shopping around. He gave each company representative the same information: He wanted a $500 deductible; he had a spotless driving record; he wouldn't be using the car to commute to work; and he would be driving only about 2,000 miles a year. One firm quoted Sam an annual rate of $1,700; the premium was especially high because he was previously uninsured. (It didn't matter that he hadn't previously owned a car.) Another firm said it charged $1,253 a year. The third firm quoted Sam an annual rate of just $958. An added bonus: When Sam mentioned he was about to turn 30, the agent at the last firm said he should call back a month before his 30th birthday, and he'd get a $60 discount on the annual rate. The bottom line: In just 20 minutes Sam saved more than $700 by comparison shopping.

CHECKING OUT
CREDENTIALS

You're not going to spend your life (or even several days of your life) investigating every detail of a particular insurance company or agent, but it does pay to do some legwork. The following tips can at the very least help you avoid disaster:

- **If you use an agent, ask about qualifications.** When you're buying life, health, or disability insurance, you may want to look for an agent who has the letters "CLU" after his or her name. This stands for Chartered Life Underwriter. If you're looking for auto or homeowners coverage, the designation to look for is "CPCU" (Chartered Property and Casualty Underwriter). Although these credentials offer no guarantee of good service, they do tell you that the agent has taken tough insurance courses and has a certain amount of basic insurance knowledge.

- **Contact your state insurance department.** Figure 8-1 lists the phone numbers of every state insurance department. You should call to make sure the agent you're dealing with is licensed in your state. Some state insurance departments will tell you whether there have been any complaints filed against an agent. You can also call to see if there have been any complaints filed against the insurance company you're considering doing business with.

- **Check on the insurer's financial health.** It's a good idea to do business with a financially sound company. Even though states have "guarantee funds," which are supposed to protect consumers (up to certain limits) if insurance companies go bankrupt, you could wait a long time before you collect on a claim.

  There are four major rating agencies that judge the safety and soundness of insurance companies: A.M. Best, Duff & Phelps, Moody's, and Standard & Poor's. It doesn't hurt to stay with an insurer that gets high grades from two of these firms. But even then, you won't be guaranteed that a company is sound. For instance, A.M. Best gave one insurer an A+ rating just two weeks before it failed. Nevertheless, you may want to make sure that a company you're interested in hasn't received a really low grade from one of these agencies.

  If you're dealing with an agent, ask him or her to send you the ratings and the full reports on the companies whose policies you're interested in. If you're not dealing with an agent, a

local library or nearby university library should have the
ratings books published by these companies. The following
firms will give you at least three ratings on the phone for free:
Duff & Phelps (312-368-3157), Moody's (212-553-0377),

Figure 8-1
TELEPHONE NUMBERS OF
STATE INSURANCE DEPARTMENTS

Alabama	(334) 269-3550
Alaska	(907) 465-2515
Arizona	(602) 912-8444
Arkansas	(501) 686-2945
California (number valid in CA only)	(800) 927-4357
Colorado	(303) 894-7499
Connecticut	(203) 297-3900
Delaware	(302)-739-4251
District of Columbia	(202) 727-7424
Florida (number valid in FL only)	(800) 342-2762
Georgia	(404) 656-2056
Hawaii	(808) 586-2790
Idaho	(208) 334-2250
Illinois	(217) 782-4515
Indiana	(317) 232-2385
Iowa	(515) 281-5705
Kansas	(913) 296-7801
Kentucky	(502) 564-3630
Louisiana	(504) 342-5900
Maine	(207) 624-8475
Maryland	(410) 333-6300
Massachusetts	(617) 521-7794
Michigan	(517) 373-9273

and S&P (212-208-1527). A.M. Best (800-424-BEST) charges for inquiries. When you call, it's essential to ask what each rating means. For example, a company that gets a "B" from Moody's is considered to be in poor financial health.

Minnesota	(612) 296-6848
Mississippi	(601) 359-3569
Missouri	(314) 340-6830
Montana	(406) 444-2040
Nebraska	(402) 471-2201
Nevada	(702) 687-4270
New Hampshire	(603) 271-2261
New Jersey	(609) 292-5360
New Mexico	(505) 827-4500
New York	(212) 602-0429
North Carolina	(919) 733-7343
North Dakota	(701) 328-2440
Ohio	(614) 644-2658
Oklahoma	(405) 521-2828
Oregon	(503) 378-4271
Pennsylvania	(717) 787-5173
Rhode Island	(401) 277-2223
South Carolina	(803) 737-6160
South Dakota	(605) 773-3563
Tennessee	(615) 741-2241
Texas	(512) 463-6464
Utah	(801) 538-3800
Vermont	(802) 828-3301
Virginia	(804) 371-9185
Washington	(360) 753-7301
West Virginia	(304) 558-3386
Wisconsin	(608) 266-0102
Wyoming	(307) 777-7401
Source: Insurance Information Institute	

MAKING THE MOST OF YOUR EMPLOYER PLAN

Most large employers pay for a portion of your health insurance premium. And many purchase a fixed amount of life insurance and disability insurance for employees. The type and amount of insurance employees get vary tremendously from company to company. The best way to learn about your plan is to read the information your employer provides. (I know, I know—this is about as much fun as doing your taxes. But the time you spend will be worth it.) Then make an appointment with whoever is in charge of benefits at your company so you can ask questions about your coverage.

In the health, disability and life insurance sections below, I've listed specific steps that will help you evaluate your employer's offerings. Meanwhile, here are some general rules to keep in mind:

- **If your company has a "flexible benefits plan," make the most of it.** A flexible benefits plan (also known as a **flex plan** or a **cafeteria plan**) is a program that gives employees the opportunity to choose among a variety of benefits. Options often include health insurance, life insurance, and disability insurance. (With some flex plans you may also be given a choice of non-insurance benefits, such as extra vacation days or additional employer contributions to a 401(k) plan.)

  Under a flex plan the employer gives you a fixed number of "credits" to spend on benefits. You get to decide how to use the credits. For instance, you may opt for a top-of-the-line health insurance plan but forgo life insurance because you don't need it. Or if your spouse has a terrific employer-sponsored health insurance plan that covers you, you could forgo your own company's health insurance and opt for extra disability insurance. These plans can be extremely beneficial if you study your choices carefully and spend your credits wisely.

- **If possible, purchase health insurance on a before-tax basis.**

If your employer offers this option, it means that you will not have to pay taxes on the portion of your salary that goes toward your premium. This little perk can save you hundreds of dollars a year.

- **If your company offers a flexible spending account (FSA), use it.** An FSA is a special tax-favored account offered by some employers. Don't let the similar names confuse you: A flexible spending account is different from a flexible benefits plan. (Clearly, employee benefits personnel could use a little help coming up with more creative names.) An FSA is an account in which you can put a fixed amount of your own money—typically anywhere from $100 to $5,000—to pay for specific medical expenses that aren't covered by health insurance. What makes an FSA different from a savings account is that you can put the money into the FSA on a before-tax basis, and that money will never be taxed. FSA money is commonly used to pay for eyeglasses, contact lenses, allergy shots, dental care, prescription drugs, and chiropractic sessions. You can also use the money to pay the deductibles on your medical and dental plans. You can't use FSA money to pay for things like cosmetic surgery, electrolysis, or health club memberships. Rules vary from company to company, so educate yourself before you sign up.

  There is one drawback to an FSA: If you don't use the money you put into the account during the year, you'll lose it. That's why you should put in only an amount you're certain you will spend.

HEALTH INSURANCE

Everyone should have health insurance. If you're lucky, you're covered through your job. Although you probably have to cover some portion of the annual cost, the amount you pay is much less than what you'd pay if you had to purchase insurance on your own. If you don't have an employer who provides coverage for you—if you freelance, run your own business, work for a small company that doesn't provide insurance, or are unemployed—you're responsible for your own coverage. Because individual coverage is so expensive, it may be tempting to go without it. (One in four people in their twenties do just that.) Don't. If you get into an accident and you're hit with thousands of dollars in medical bills, you could lose every penny you have and find yourself in deep debt.

The Two Basic Types of Health Insurance

The jargon used in the health insurance industry is so confusing, it's enough to make anyone feel sick. But you need to learn the essential terms even if you have group coverage through your employer. The two main types of health insurance are called **fee-for-service** and **managed care.**

Fee-for-service offers freedom at a price. It allows you to see any physician you choose. That means you can stay with your current doctor (or choose another) and visit specialists you select when necessary. But fee-for-service plans are typically expensive. In addition to the annual premium, you are required to pay a deductible that can be anywhere from $100 to $2,500 a year. Once your medical bills exceed the annual deductible, the insurer will start chipping in. Usually, the insurer will pay 80% of your medical expenses that exceed the deductible, and you'll pay the remaining 20%, known as a **co-payment.** There are often annual caps on the total amount you have to pay yourself, and lifetime ceilings on the amount the insurer will pay for you.

The second health insurance option is managed care. This kind of coverage costs less, but it can limit your choices. Under a managed-care plan you are given a list of participating doctors. If you stick with these doctors, your costs will be much lower than if you use a doctor outside the managed-care plan. Compared to fee-for-service plans, managed-care plans have lower premiums, smaller co-payments (sometimes as low as $5 per doctor's visit), and usually no deductibles.

There are two main types of managed-care programs. The more restrictive type is the **health maintenance organization (HMO)**. In an HMO you usually have to get permission from your primary doctor every time you want to see a specialist within the HMO network. With another type of managed-care plan, called a **preferred provider organization (PPO)**, you usually don't need permission to see a specialist.

If Your Employer Offers Health Insurance

A growing number of companies allow employees to choose between a fee-for-service plan and a managed-care program. Here are some suggestions that will help you make an informed decision:

- **Ask about waiting periods or exclusions when you start a new job.** If you have any chronic medical problems, known as **pre-existing conditions**, find out if your company insurance plan will cover you for these ailments immediately. Some fee-for-service plans have a waiting period of six months before they cover pre-existing conditions. In general, HMOs do not have such a waiting time.

- **Evaluate the managed-care option carefully.** Although managed-care plans can be less expensive, there are some serious trade-offs to consider. You may have to wait several days to see a doctor because he or she has limited hours. You may find that your doctor is less apt to prescribe expensive lab tests than doctors you have visited in the past. As mentioned earlier, you may have to get permission from your primary physician before you can see a specialist such as an allergist or dermatologist. And if you ever want to see an out-of-plan physician, you will have to cover all or most of the cost yourself.

Before you sign up for a managed-care plan, compare its premium and benefits with those of your company's fee-for-service plan. Speak to a few coworkers who are using the managed-care plan and ask if they feel it's a good one. Before you dismiss it, find out if your current doctor participates in your company's managed plan; you may find that he or she does.

- **Know what is covered by your fee-for-service plan.** Some plans cover everything from therapy sessions to chiropractic adjustments; others cover a more limited range of services. You'll want to know the details. Ask, for example, whether you are covered for prescription drugs. For about six months I didn't know that all I had to do was show my company insurance card at the drugstore to get my prescription medication for just $5. Not too swift.

BEFORE YOU LEAVE YOUR JOB, ASK ABOUT HEALTH COVERAGE

If you work for an employer with 20 or more employees, in most cases your company must offer you the option of continuing your health coverage for 18 months—whether you're fired or you quit. (Actually, if you're fired for doing something truly heinous, like embezzling company funds, you probably won't be eligible for this extension.) Under federal rules, your employer must offer you the same health insurance you had as an employee, but you will have to pay for this coverage. The law says the employer can charge you 102% of the cost. (If your employer pays $200 a month to cover you, you will pay $204 a month.) Still, this will probably be less expensive than the rate you would pay for a policy of your own with the same type of coverage.

You'll also need to understand your fee-for-service plan's reimbursement policies. Most fee-for-service plans cover 80% of what they consider "reasonable and customary" charges. If your doctor charges $100 for a checkup but your plan specifies that $60 is the reasonable and customary charge for a doctor in your area, the plan will reimburse you for $48 (80% of $60), leaving you to pay the remaining $52. If you know this in advance, you can explain the situation to your doctor and ask for a discount. (You'd be surprised how flexible some doctors can be.)

- **See if you can get a higher deductible and pay a lower premium on the fee-for-service plan.** Some companies have a fixed deductible for all employees. Others base the deductible on your income. No matter how your employer sets your deductible, you should find out if you can raise it to keep your premium costs down.

- **Find out the cost of covering pregnancy.** If you and your spouse are considering having a baby, find out about maternity benefits and pediatric care. Many managed-care plans offer excellent deals. Usually, you get a package that covers the cost of prenatal doctor visits, delivery, hospital stay, and well-baby care for a very small fee. (I know someone who paid just $5 for all her pregnancy needs!) Set up an appointment with your health benefits officer and get the details. Before you sign up for a managed-care plan, ask if you (or your spouse) can meet with the obstetrician in the HMO.

What to Look For in an Individual Health Policy

If you don't have coverage through a group plan, you'll have to purchase insurance on your own. An individual policy is often expensive, but if you know what you're looking for and you do some research, you can find a decent deal. Your goal is to find coverage that will help you pay for a major medical problem. Policies that cover anything more may be prohibitively expensive, depending on where you live. You may find it necessary to pay for routine medical services with your own money and rely on your health insurance only to protect you in case of a medical catastrophe.

Of course, you don't want a policy which offers such skimpy protection that it is worthless. Try to find a policy that meets these conditions:

- **It covers at least 80% of your hospital, surgery, and in-hospital doctor bills once you meet the deductible.** Ideally, you'd be able to find a policy that covers 100%, but unfortunately this type of coverage may be prohibitively expensive. With a policy that covers 80% of these costs, you'll have to pay the remaining 20% out of your own pocket. To avoid getting hit with tremendous medical expenses, look for a policy that caps your annual co-payments at $1,000 to $2,000.

- **It has a maximum lifetime benefit of at least $1 million.** A lifetime cap is the dollar limit the insurance company will pay over the course of the policy. Anything substantially less than $1 million isn't enough.

- **It's guaranteed renewable.** With a guaranteed renewable policy, the insurer can't discontinue coverage or raise your premiums simply because you get sick. Your insurance premiums can go up over time but only according to the schedule governing other similar policies. And you can renew your policy as many times as you like.

- **It isn't riddled with exclusions and limits.** Some individual policies limit coverage to $25,000 for AIDS or fail to cover pre-existing conditions like asthma or recurring knee problems. Others won't cover these ailments for the first year or so of the policy. Pay attention to these kinds of details.

Before You Buy an Individual Health Policy

Depending on your current situation, you may have some alternatives to buying an expensive individual policy. Here are a few to consider:

- **See if you're covered by your parents' plan.** If you're a student, you may still be covered by your parents' policy. Some employer-sponsored plans allow children of employees to be covered until age 26 if the children are still in school. If you're not in school, chances are your coverage has stopped already. If it hasn't, there is a way to extend it. Under COBRA (the Consolidated Omnibus Budget Reconciliation Act of 1985), you can continue to receive your parents' coverage for 18 months if your parents make the request soon after they receive notice that your coverage is about to lapse. You will have to pay for this coverage, but the price will probably be less than the price of a similar policy you could get on your own.

- **Join a group plan.** Groups get better deals than individuals. See if there's a professional association, religious organization, or another group that will offer you coverage. If you're a lawyer, try your local bar association. If you're a real estate or travel agent, call your local trade association. If you're an artist, contact a community artists league. If you're currently doing temp work, look for a temp agency that offers health benefits; some agencies offer employees the chance to purchase group coverage.

- **Get temporary coverage.** If you're out of work but seriously hunting for a job, look into a temporary insurance policy. This type of policy lasts up to four months and can be renewed once. After eight months you will have found a job with health benefits (God willing). The good side to these policies is that they are cheap. The bad side is that you won't be covered for any pre-existing conditions. You should also consider a temporary policy if you start a new job and your employer requires you to be with the firm for several months before you receive any health insurance.

How to Find an Affordable Individual Health Policy

Unfortunately, locating a low-cost individual health insurance policy isn't easy. Here are some tips that may help you in your search.

- **Consider an HMO.** Only about 25% of HMOs in the country allow individuals to sign up. What's more, the premiums on an individual HMO membership may be higher than those of individual fee-for-service policies. Still, if you think you'll be needing many visits to the doctor and you like the particular HMO, this is a worthwhile option. To find one, call your state insurance department.

- **Try Blue Cross and Blue Shield.** These are the largest fee-for-service providers in the United States. In some states Blue Cross and Blue Shield companies have open enrollment policies; that means they provide coverage to everyone who applies. As a result, the premiums may be higher; as a young, healthy person you may do better with a company that picks and chooses its customers. Still, it's worth a call to find out about rates.

- **Contact your state insurance department.** If you have a pre-existing condition that makes it difficult for you to get insurance, call your state insurance department and ask about "high risk" insurance policies. Some states sponsor such policies. If yours doesn't, it may be able to point you toward a private insurer that does.

- **Ask about special deals for people with good health.** Some insurers and HMOs offer small discounts to people with healthy lifestyles. If you're in great shape, ask whether you can get a discount. Keep in mind that smokers pay about twice as much as nonsmokers for health insurance.

- **Call these firms for quotes.** Try USAA (800-531-8000), an insurance company that sells directly to consumers rather than through agents. Also call Quotesmith (800-556-9393), a service that will scan its multicompany database and send you a free list of its least expensive offerings.

AUTO INSURANCE

Auto insurance covers harm done to you, your car, other people, and other people's property. The total amount of coverage you need depends on the health insurance you have, the condition of your car, the value of the assets you must protect in case you're held responsible for an accident, and the rules in your state. Unfortunately, this coverage is especially expensive for young people. Single men under 25 years old often pay two or three times what men over 25 pay; single women under 25 might pay one and a half to two times more than women over 25. For married people, the rates are lower.

Three Basic Auto Coverages

Auto insurance consists of three separate kinds of protection. Here's a rundown of each:

- **Auto liability coverage.** If you cause an accident with your car and injure someone or damage something, auto liability insurance will pay the injured person's medical and repair expenses. Auto liability, which is technically known as **bodily injury liability** and **property damage liability,** will protect you in case you are held responsible for an accident. Of the three major components of auto insurance, auto liability can make up more than half your auto premium.

  Some states, known as **no-fault states,** require drivers

(and their insurance companies) to pay for their own costs in a car accident, regardless of who was responsible for the accident. But even if you live in a no-fault state, you still need liability insurance. That's because each no-fault state has a threshold above which a person who causes an accident can be sued. For example, in some no-fault states a driver can be sued if he causes severe physical injury to another driver.

Most states require car owners to purchase some liability protection. You probably should buy more auto liability insurance than your state requires. Even if you don't have many assets, you need liability protection in case a court decides to garnish your future wages. Insurance analysts are hesitant to say what the "right" amount of liability protection is, but here's a reasonable guideline to use: If you don't have much savings and you don't own a home, get coverage of at least $100,000 per person, $300,000 per accident, and $100,000 for property. If you own a home and have some money saved, consider purchasing an umbrella liability policy, which is coverage above and beyond any auto or home owner's liability protection you have. (For details, see the home insurance section.)

• **Medical Payments Coverage.** This insurance covers your medical and hospital bills (up to a certain dollar amount) if you are injured in a car accident. It also covers the medical bills (again, up to specific limits) of any passengers in your car. If you live in a no-fault state, you probably will be required to buy a minimum amount of medical payments coverage, typically called **personal injury insurance** or **no-fault insurance.** No-fault insurance covers your medical bills (and in some cases your loss of income if you are disabled) regardless of who is to blame for an accident.

If you live in a "fault" state, you are usually not required to purchase medical payments coverage, but you may want to anyway. Accidents in which no one can be proven negligent won't be covered by liability insurance, and liability insurance will not cover your own injuries in accidents that you have caused. If you already have good general health insurance, you won't need medical payments insurance to cover your own medical bills, but you may want to consider purchasing it if you often have passengers in your car.

- **Collision and comprehensive coverage.** Collision insurance pays for damage to your car caused in a traffic accident. Comprehensive insurance covers damage caused by fire, flood, theft, tornado, and just about any other physical damage that is not covered by collision. In all states both of these coverages are optional. However, if you took out a loan to buy your car or if you're leasing, the lender or dealer will require that you purchase collision and comprehensive coverage.

  The maximum amount an insurance company will pay under a collision or comprehensive policy is, at least in theory, the cost of replacing the automobile with a comparable used car. (Unfortunately, some insurers aren't this generous.) After your car is about five years old or you've paid off your loan, you may want to consider dropping the collision and comprehensive coverage. To determine whether it makes sense for you to continue this coverage, consider the value of the car minus the deductible. Compare the answer to your annual premium.

An additional type of insurance you may decide to pur-

BABY, YOU CAN'T DRIVE MY CAR

You may think we're a sharing, caring generation, but when someone asks to borrow your car, you should think twice before you say yes. If you permit someone to drive your car and he or she has an accident, *your* insurer is likely to pay for the damage (less any deductible you have to pay). That means your insurance company may raise your premium just as if you had caused the accident.

chase is **uninsured motorists coverage**. This coverage, which is required in some states, protects you if an uninsured driver crashes into your car and you're injured. You may also want to consider getting **underinsured motorists coverage,** which will protect you if the driver who crashes into your car has some but not enough insurance.

If You Rent a Car, Cover Your Assets

One type of coverage you'll want to have when you rent a car is liability protection. If you own an automobile, your standard auto liability coverage may cover you when you rent a car. Check to make sure this is the case. If you don't own a car but you do rent cars, purchase car renter's liability insurance at the car rental counter. If you rent often, it may be cheaper to purchase a car renter's liability policy from an insurance company.

How to Reduce Your Auto Insurance Costs

Your premiums are based on factors such as your age, where you live, the type of car you drive, your gender, your driving record, and how much driving you do. The following suggestions can reduce your premiums by as much as 25%:

- **Drive safely.** Some insurance companies give discounts to drivers who have no violations or accidents. If you have a clean record, point it out when you are pricing policies.

- **Don't drive much.** Some insurance companies charge you less if you drive less. For instance, one major insurer charges lower premiums for customers who drive fewer than 30 miles a week. If you join a car pool or start taking public transportation, alert your agent.

- **Get a heavy, stodgy car.** Certain types of cars are harder to damage or are stolen less often than others. Insurers use this information when setting rates. You can reduce your collision and comprehensive coverage by as much as 45% if you buy a new or used car that is a low-risk model. Ask your agent for a list of such cars.

- **If you buy a new car, get airbags.** Having a driver's airbag could reduce your premiums on your medical payments coverage by 10%. A passenger-side airbag can take off another 10%.

- **Get good grades.** If you're currently a student with a B average or better, in the top 20% of your class, or on the dean's list, tell the insurance agent. Good grades can reduce your premium by up to 25%. College graduates are eligible for discounts based on their grades until they either reach age 25 or get married.

- **Grow up.** Many insurers consider a single female to be an adult once she reaches age 25. A single male is considered an adult at 30. A married female of any age is considered an adult; a married male is considered an adult at 25. As long as you have a good driving record, most insurance companies will reduce your rates when you hit these landmark birthdays. Call your agent to remind him.

- **See if you're entitled to a household discount.** If you're married and you and your spouse both have cars, see if you can save money by getting auto coverage from one company. Insurers often offer discounts of up to 15% if both of your cars are insured on the same policy. If you live at home with your parents, you may be able to get a similar discount if your car is insured under your folks' policy.

- **Check with your state's insurance department.** Some state insurance departments publish lists of companies and prices for residents looking for auto insurance. (See Figure 8-1 for phone numbers.)

- **Call these firms for quotes.** In addition to shopping around

on your own, try Geico (800-841-3000) and Amica
(800-992-6422), two firms that sell directly to consumers.
One note: These two companies can be very picky, and you
may not find their prices attractive if you have a less-than-
perfect driving record or you're under 25 years old. (One 21-
year-old I know was told that in order to get coverage from
Amica, he needed to get a recommendation from a current
Amica customer!) USAA (800-531-8080) offers auto insurance to anyone who is either an active-duty or retired military officer, or a dependent of one. Also contact State Farm
and Allstate, which sell policies through captive agents and
are two of the country's largest auto insurance providers.

DISABILITY
INSURANCE

What would happen if you had a horrible skiing accident and you
couldn't work for ten months?

At the time of this writing, only Puerto Rico and five states—
California, Hawaii, New Jersey, New York and Rhode Island—
require employers to provide income to disabled employees who get
hurt off the job. And federal disability benefits from Social Security
are extremely difficult to get; the majority of people who apply are
rejected.

Your only real protection, therefore, is likely to be private disability insurance. Although you may never have heard of it, it is
something you should have. Ideally, you should have coverage that
would pay you about 60% to 70% of your income following an
cident that leaves you unable to work. For many young people,
disability coverage is more important than life insurance.

If you work for a large company, you may already have some
disability insurance under a group policy. If you do, it may be all you
need. If you don't work for a company that offers disability protection, consider buying an individual disability policy. Unfortunately,
disability insurance can be very expensive, and there are also limita-

tions on who is eligible. For instance, most insurance companies will not sell policies to people who have physically risky jobs, like construction workers or firefighters.

If Your Employer Offers Disability Insurance

Disability protection is different from workers compensation. **Workers comp,** as it is known, protects you if you are injured while performing your job. Disability insurance covers you for any injury or illness, whether it happens at home, on vacation, or on the job. If you're lucky enough to work for an employer who provides you with disability insurance, you should assess exactly how much you're protected. Here are some tips to help you understand your coverage:

- **Find out what percentage of your income you'll receive if you're disabled.** Large companies with more than 500 employees often provide disability insurance that will pay 60% of your income—usually up to $5,000 a month—if you suffer a long-term disability.

- **Ask about waiting periods and benefit periods.** Typically you will start receiving benefits three to six months after you become disabled. This period is known as the waiting period or **elimination period.** (I guess that's because during it any savings you have are eliminated!) The period of time during which you receive disability payouts is known as the benefits period. Should you ever become disabled, you will not continue to pay premiums. Many companies pay disability benefits until the employee reaches 65.

- **Take advantage of your flexible benefits plan.** If you have a choice, opt for disability protection rather than life insurance if you're single and have no dependents.

What to Look for in an Individual Disability Policy

Insurance companies offer all kinds of confusing extras attached to their disability policies. Below are the basics you will need:

- **Illness and accident coverage.** Most disability policies provide both. Make sure the one you're considering does.

- **Guaranteed renewable.** With a guaranteed renewable policy, you can renew your policy each year without undergoing a medical exam, and the insurer can't single you out for a rate increase just because you've made a lot of claims. Only general rate increases will affect you. This is an important feature.

- **Non-cancelable policy.** With a non-cancelable policy, the insurer generally can't cancel your current policy or raise your premium for *any reason*. This attractive feature is being phased out by many insurers, however.

- **Residual benefit protection.** If you're partially disabled, some policies will pay you a portion of your disability benefits, known as residual benefits. This is extremely important coverage in case you become partially disabled and can work only part-time.

How to Reduce Your Disability Insurance Costs

The problem with individual disability coverage is that it's not cheap. For example, a 27-year-old computer programmer who earns an annual salary of $30,000 would pay about $800 a year for a top-of-the-line policy that protects him for about 70% of his income. Here are three ways to keep your costs down:

- **Consider a step-up, or gradual-payment, policy.** This type of policy allows you to pay lower premiums when you're young and higher ones when you're older. With this plan, the computer programmer would pay only about $500 a year for the first five years, and $900 or so from then on.

• **Increase your elimination period.** As mentioned earlier, the elimination period (typically four months) is the time you must wait to receive benefits after becoming disabled. One way to reduce your annual premium is to increase the elimination period to, say, six months. This option makes sense only if you have enough savings to tide you over during the additional delay, if your employer is likely to continue paying you a salary in the early months of your disability, or if it's the only way you can afford coverage.

• **Try these firms for quotes.** A handful of insurance companies specialize in disability coverage. Some of the largest are Unum Life Insurance (800-227-8138), Paul Revere (800-843-3426), Provident Life and Accident (615-755-1011), and Northwestern Mutual Life Insurance (800-822-6582). For companies that sell directly to consumers, try the Wholesale Insurance Network (WIN) (800-808-5810), a service that sells low-load disability policies of several companies. Also try USAA (800-531-8000). Another shopping service, Termquote (800-444-8376), will search its multicompany database of policies and send you a free list of its least expensive offerings.

HOME
INSURANCE

If you own a home, you probably have some homeowners insurance; you were required to get coverage on the building by the lender that gave you a mortgage. But if you're like a lot of homeowners, you don't have enough coverage or you're paying too much. And if you rent, you've probably never even thought about buying any coverage.

Three Basic Coverages if You Own a Home

Homeowners insurance covers the cost of rebuilding or repairing your home (and surrounding structures such as the garage) if it's destroyed or damaged by disasters such as fire, theft, snow, or windstorm. It covers the *contents* of your home up to a fixed dollar amount in the event of many of these same disasters. And it can also protect you if you are held liable for injuring people or damaging property. Here's a more detailed rundown of each type of protection:

- **Your home's structure.** You need to buy enough insurance to cover the full cost of rebuilding your home. To figure out approximately how much it would cost to rebuild, contact a mortgage lender or insurance agent and find out the building cost per square foot in your area. (These professionals will not charge you for this information. A real estate appraiser can also answer the question, but he may charge a fee.) Multiply the number of square feet in your home by the local square foot building cost. This will give you an idea of how much it would cost to rebuild your home, also known as your home's **replacement cost.**

- **The contents of your home.** Standard homeowners policies usually cover the contents of your home—your "personal property"—for 50% of the amount you insured your home's structure for. So if you insured the structure for $100,000, your home's contents would be insured for $50,000. You can increase the amount of coverage you have for a fee. Make sure your **personal property insurance** covers you for **replacement cost,** not **actual cash value** of your home's contents. Replacement cost gives you enough money to buy new comparable items to replace your belongings. Actual cash value pays you the amount of money you could get to repair or replace the items, *minus* the depreciation on the items.

  To figure out how much personal property insurance you need, make a list of everything you own and estimate how much it would cost to replace these items. This is a hassle, but it's worth doing. Write down the purchase date and purchase price of all your belongings, including furniture, rugs, televisions, VCRs, stereos, CD players, computers, dishes, pots and pans, glasses, artwork, and major appliances. Also list your suits, dresses, shoes, and coats. (Don't forget the expensive stuff like a wedding dress or a tuxedo.) Gather as many receipts as you can to back up your list. Write down the serial or model numbers for appliances. When you make major purchases, save the receipts. Take pictures of your more valuable belongings. This inventory will come in handy if you ever need to file a claim. Keep a copy of the list, along with the receipts and photos, at work in a safe place. Also give a copy to a trusted friend or relative. (Don't leave a copy lying around your apartment. It's a great road map for a burglar. For the same reason, don't give the list a revealing file name on your home computer.) You may never get around to doing this exhaustive inventory, but at the very least, take pictures or a videotape of your valuables and store the photos or tape in a safe place.

- **Damage you do to other people and other people's property.** Homeowners policies include liability protection that covers you for damage you cause inside or outside your home. If you leave a pair of boots in the middle of your kitchen floor, and your neighbor trips on them and breaks her leg, your liability insurance will cover her medical bills and other costs if you're held responsible for her injury. If you run a shopping cart over someone's foot in a supermarket, your liability coverage will pay for his or her medical expenses if you're found liable. If you have a pet, your policy will often cover the damage the pet does to people or property.

Many homeowners policies come with a standard amount of liability insurance of about $100,000 per accident. In these litigious times, this may not be enough. There is no perfect way to figure out how much you need. To get a rough idea, tally up all your major assets including your home, your car, your possessions, and your investments (don't forget about your retirement savings). The amount of liability insurance you get should exceed this amount.

Choose a Policy That Covers the Most Disasters

Your possessions and your home's structure are protected against losses caused by **perils**. The types of peril covered by homeowners insurance can include fire, lightning, windstorm, riots, vandalism, and even civil commotion. Various types of homeowners insurance cover you for different types of peril. Your options here are vaguely reminiscent of high school chemistry—you can choose HO-1, HO-2, or HO-3. (This odd code is used in nearly all states.) Insurance agents sometimes refer to these three classifications as basic (HO-1), broad (HO-2), and special (HO-3) coverage. If you can afford it, buy HO-3. It doesn't cost much more than the others, and it covers a much wider range of perils.

Certain perils, such as earthquakes and floods, aren't covered by any of the standard homeowners policies—not even by HO-3. If you live in a region threatened by earthquakes, consider buying earthquake insurance. If your area is prone to flooding, get adequate flood insurance; call the National Flood Insurance Program at 800-638-6620.

If you live in a co-op or condo, you will need to purchase a special policy known as HO-6. If you rent, the policy you need has the designation HO-4.

What's Covered and What's Not

Though policies vary, there are limits on what most homeowners policies cover. For example, many policies protect jewelry for about $1,000 and computers for around $5,000. If this isn't enough to replace your jewelry and computer equipment, purchase extra protection by adding an **endorsement**, sometimes referred to as a

floater. This is simply an amendment to your insurance policy to protect a specific item. With an endorsement you can, for example, increase the coverage on your computer from $5,000 to $10,000 if the computer is worth that much. The cost for this increase in coverage would range from $50 to $100 per year.

Many homeowners policies include **off-premise** protection, which covers your possessions outside your home—whether you're robbed while on vacation or mugged on your block. If, for example, your portable computer or luggage is lost or stolen when you're trekking around Europe, your homeowners insurance should cover the loss. Check your policy carefully. If you live in a high-crime area, you may have to pay extra for it.

Most policies include some **loss of use** protection. If your home is damaged and you're forced to live elsewhere for a while, this coverage will pay the cost of your motel bills, meals, and other basic living expenses minus your usual daily living expenses. Don't expect the policy to pay for lavish hotels or restaurants. A typical amount of coverage is 20% of the total amount of insurance you bought for your home's structure.

If you work at home, your home office equipment is usually not covered by your homeowners policy. If the business is small, you can get additional coverage by purchasing an endorsement. For larger businesses you will have to purchase a separate policy. Ask an insurance agent for details.

If You Rent, Insure Your Belongings

If you rent an apartment or house, the idea of buying **renters insurance,** also known as **tenants insurance,** may not have crossed your mind. You may figure that because you have few valuables and little or no savings, you don't need it. But you're wrong. The first and most obvious reason to buy it is to protect your personal property. If all your possessions were stolen or ruined in a fire, including your clothes, jewelry, stereo equipment, television, VCR, computer, camera, sofa, and bike, a renters policy would cover you up to a fixed dollar amount.

In addition to protecting your possessions, a renters policy offers you some liability protection inside and outside your home. If someone slips and falls in your apartment, your renters policy will cover that person's medical bills if you're held liable. If you accidentally leave the tap running when you go to work, ruin the floor, and are held responsible, your renters insurance will pay for the cost of repairs. And if you knock over a sculpture in an art gallery, your renters policy will cover the expense, up to a set maximum.

How to Reduce Your Homeowners or Renters Insurance Costs

The first step (as with health insurance) is to get a high deductible so you can keep your annual premiums low. Remember, this makes sense only if you have enough savings to cover the higher deductible. Here are some other suggestions that apply whether you own a home or rent.

- **Ask if you're eligible for any discounts.** If you have dead-bolt locks on your doors or live in a doorman apartment building, you may be able to get a discount of as much as 10% on your premium. If you have a security alarm, a fire extinguisher, and/or a smoke detector, you can often get a discount of anywhere from 2% to 20%, depending on the type of system you have.

- **Look into federal crime insurance.** If you live in one of the following areas, you may be eligible for inexpensive burglary and robbery coverage: California, Florida, Illinois, Kansas, Louisiana, Maryland, New Jersey, New York, Pennsylvania, Tennessee, and Washington, D.C. For $126 a year you can insure $10,000 worth of possessions. If your home has an alarm, the premium is $120. Call 800-638-8780 for more information.

- **Consider moving your automobile coverage and homeowners or renters coverage to the same insurance company.** Some companies will offer you a dual-policy discount of up to 15%.

- **Check with your state's insurance department.** State insurance departments sometimes publish lists of companies and the premiums they charge for homeowners insurance. (See Figure 8-1 for phone numbers.) This can help you shop around.

- **Call these firms for quotes.** Try Amica (800-992-6422), which sells directly to consumers. USAA (800-531-8080) offers home insurance to anyone who is either an active-duty or retired military officer or a dependent of one. Also contact State Farm and Allstate, which are sold through captive agents and are two of the largest home insurance providers.

CONSIDER AN UMBRELLA LIABILITY POLICY

If you have a lot of assets—or the potential to earn a lot—you should consider getting an **umbrella liability policy.** This special type of policy offers additional liability protection beyond your auto liability and homeowners liability coverage. It also protects you in case you're sued for something unrelated to your car or home, such as slander. The cost for a $1 million umbrella liability policy in 1995 was about $200. Umbrella policies are usually a better deal than purchasing more auto liability and home liability coverage separately.

LIFE
INSURANCE

If you've never received a friendly letter from a life insurance agent, just wait. In the next few years you'll probably get at least half a dozen trying to sell you life insurance. Throw them out. There's a good chance you don't need it.

The purpose of life insurance is simple: If you die, it protects the people who rely on your income. The rules are easy. If you have kids (or anyone else financially dependent on you), you need it. If you're married without kids and your spouse could handle the basic housing and living expenses without you, you don't need it. If you're single and aren't financially responsible for anyone but yourself, you don't need it. (Of course, there are always exceptions, but these are good guidelines for most people.)

Two Types of Life Insurance

The most basic form of life insurance is **term life insurance.** It's called that because it protects you for a specific number of years (a term)—typically from one to twenty years. When the term runs out, you can usually renew the policy and begin another term. If you die, the insurance company will pay out a specified amount of money to your beneficiaries. This payment is called the **death benefit.**

When you're young, the premium you pay for term insurance is very low. For a death benefit of $100,000, a 25-year-old nonsmoker would pay about $150 a year. With most term policies your premium increases slightly each year.

Term life insurance gives you the most coverage for your money when you're young. But don't be surprised if insurance agents discourage you from purchasing it. Agents often don't like to sell term insurance because the commissions on such policies are much lower than the commissions on other types of insurance policies.

Most life insurance agents will urge you to buy a "permanent" insurance policy, often called a **cash value policy.** (For a sampling of some of their best pitches, see the box on page 210.) With a cash value policy, the insurance company takes your annual premium, deducts sales and administrative charges, the cost of death protection, and a margin for profit. The remainder goes into a kind of savings account for you, generally called your cash value. The most common forms of cash value policies are called **whole life, universal life,** and **variable life.** With whole life and universal life policies, the insurance company invests your cash value in bonds and various bond-like investments. With variable life policies, the insurance company provides you with a variety of mutual fund–like investments to choose from, and you decide how to invest the cash value. Because of a quirk in the tax law, the money in the savings account of a cash value life insurance policy grows tax-deferred.

The cost of a cash value policy is usually much higher than that of a term policy for a young person. Even if you can afford it, it probably makes sense to avoid cash value policies and buy term if you need life insurance. That's because the commissions on most cash value policies are very high; they can be more than 100% of your first year's premium, and renewal commissions in subsequent years can be 5% to 8%. You're better off buying term insurance and investing the money you save on premiums in a tax-favored retirement savings plan like an IRA or a 401(k).

There is one set of circumstances under which it may make sense to buy a cash value life insurance policy. If you need life insurance and are already putting the maximum allowable amount into a tax-favored retirement savings plan, you may want to consider a **low-load** cash value policy. Such policies have very low sales and administrative charges. Low-load companies that sell variable life policies are Ameritas (800-552-3553) and American Life of New York (800-872-5963). USAA (800-531-8000) offers low-load whole life and universal life. Also try the Wholesale Insurance Network (800-808-5810), a firm that sells low-load life insurance policies from several different insurers. Keep in mind that not all these insurers sell policies in all states.

How to Shop for Term Insurance

By now it's probably clear that you're better off purchasing term. There are two basic types of term policies to choose from. **Annual renewable term** is coverage that doesn't require you to take a medical exam each year to renew it. Each year when you renew, your premium will usually increase somewhat. A **level premium policy** lasts for a fixed number of years (commonly, 10 or 20 years) and allows you to lock in a premium for that period. After that 10- to 20-

year term is up, you usually have to pass a medical exam in order to renew at attractive rates; otherwise, your premium will increase dramatically. Although the annual renewable term policy will cost you less today, in the long run the 10- or 20-year level premium policy may be less expensive. But level premium policies are increas-

WHY THE PITCHES DON'T MAKE SENSE

Perhaps you've heard the saying that life insurance isn't bought, it's sold. That sentiment comes from the fact that life insurance agents can be very aggressive and extremely persuasive. Who can blame them? The commission an agent gets from selling a cash value policy can be substantial. If you've ever met with a life insurance salesperson, you've probably heard one of the following pitches.

The pitch: "Maybe you don't need life insurance now, but you should buy today when you're young and healthy to protect your 'insurability' in the future."

The reality: The odds of your developing a health problem that renders you unable to qualify for life insurance before you reach age 35 are very low. Since you have limited funds now, why spend your money on insurance you don't need?

The pitch: "Even though you're single, you need life insurance to pay your funeral costs and debts."

The reality: Your parents, other relatives, or friends will probably be willing to pay for your funeral in the unlikely event you die with no assets. As for your debts, unless you cosigned a loan with parents, partners, or friends, no one else will be responsible for paying them. If you have any assets, the creditors will sell them to

ingly difficult to find; a growing number of insurance companies are charging more for them or phasing them out entirely. If you can find one you're able to afford and are fairly certain you won't need life insurance 10 or 20 years from now (if, for instance, you figure your

pay your debts. Otherwise, the creditors will simply take the loss.

The pitch: "If you have a child, you should buy a policy to cover his or her life."

The reality: A child is the last person who needs a life insurance policy. Parents need life insurance. Buying coverage on your kid's life is a waste of money.

The pitch: "Cash value life insurance offers tax-favored growth and is a great forced-savings plan."

The reality: This is true, but you can get the tax-favored benefit plus tax deductibility without paying a commission to an agent if you put your money in a retirement plan like an IRA or a 401(k). (For details, see Chapter 6.)

The pitch: "Buying term insurance is like renting. Buying cash value insurance is like buying. When the term is up, you don't have anything to show for it. But look how much money you'll have in 20 years if you buy a cash value life insurance policy."

The reality: Life insurance companies are notorious for using extremely attractive, overly optimistic future rates of return when selling cash value policies. There's no guarantee that your returns will be as good as an agent says.

kids will be on their own by then), it's worth considering. Otherwise, you may be better off with an annual renewable term policy.

One final tip: Look for a term policy that will allow you to convert to a low-cost cash value policy in the future, regardless of your health. As mentioned above, you may decide when you're older (and maxing out on your retirement plan contributions) that you want to purchase a cash value policy.

You have many options when shopping for term insurance. In addition to getting quotes from agents, try firms that sell low-load policies such as USAA (800-531-8000) and WIN (800-808-5810). Also call Northwestern Mutual (414-271-1444), a firm that sells only through its own agents. And contact SelectQuote (800-343-1985), Termquote (800-444-8376), and Quotesmith (800-556-9393), three services that will search their databases for low-priced offerings.

How Much Death Benefit Do You Need?

You need enough life insurance to provide for your dependents (spouse and kids) so that they can carry on a decent lifestyle if you die prematurely. If you have infants, that means you need to figure out how much they would need to live for at least the next 15 to 20 years. One rough rule of thumb says you should buy a policy that will pay six to eight times your annual before-tax income if you die, but many people need more than that. If you have high aspirations for your kids—say, you want to send them to expensive private schools—or if your spouse doesn't work, you will certainly need more.

If Your Employer Offers Life Insurance

Many large employers provide some life insurance for employees. Your company might pay for a term policy with a death benefit of $50,000. As you know, that's more than enough if you're single and have no dependents. If you need more, you might be better off buying directly from an insurance company rather than through your employer. That's because some employers charge all employees

WHY YOU MAY NEED A WILL

Since we're on the topic of life insurance, this is as good a time as any to discuss the subject of wills. The truth is, I don't know anyone my age who has a will. But that doesn't mean you don't need one.

If you're single, you may want to leave all your possessions (even if that's just a car and a small savings account) to a friend or sibling, but without a will, your property will be distributed to your closest relatives according to state law. If you're married, you might think that your spouse will get everything in the event of your death, but depending on the state in which you live, your parents may be entitled to a share of whatever you leave behind. If you're a parent, you may not want to think about what would happen to your children if you're no longer around, but without a will a probate court will select a guardian for them. You get the picture.

The easiest way to tackle this task is to get a lawyer to draw up a will for you. If you don't have much in the way of assets and your situation is straightforward, this should cost between $100 and $200. If you can't afford the lawyer's fee, but your situation is uncomplicated and you're willing to spend the time, you can write your own will. One book that can help is *Simple Will Book: How to Prepare a Legally Valid Will* (Nolo Press, $17.95). You may also want to check out Nolo Press's WillMaker 6 software, which costs about $40. Keep in mind that once you start earning more money and accumulating more assets, you're going to need to update your will. But having one today is a precaution worth taking.

the same rate for life insurance, regardless of age. If that's the case with your employer, you would be paying the same premium as a 60-year-old, which would be much higher than what you could be paying. Find out about your employer's offerings and also price several term policies on your own.

INSURANCE YOU PROBABLY DON'T NEED

It's very tempting to buy quickie insurance on impulse. After all, it seems so cheap—just $8 a day to get collision coverage at the rental car counter or $25 for $50,000 worth of life insurance at the airport. But before you throw money at this kind of coverage, evaluate it carefully. In most cases you don't need it.

- **Rental car collision insurance.** If you've ever rented a car, you were probably asked if you wanted to buy the **collision damage waiver,** or **CDW.** Next time, do a little research in advance. Review your credit card agreement to see if you are already protected when you charge a car rental on the card. And if you already have collision coverage on your own car, find out if your policy extends to rented cars. Warning: This is different from rental liability insurance, which you may need if you don't own a car or your auto policy doesn't cover rented cars.

- **Flight insurance.** If you need to insure your life, the cheapest way to do it when you're young is to buy a term life insurance policy. If you don't need to, you shouldn't waste money by buying life insurance at a vending machine in the airport. Sure it's tempting (this type of insurance plays on your fear of flying) and it also seems cheap, but it doesn't make sense. Your chances of slipping and killing yourself on the ground are much greater than your chances of dying in an airplane crash. Besides, you may already be covered; some credit card companies give you automatic flight insurance if you charge your tickets on their card.

FINANCIAL CRAMMING

- If you work for a company that offers a flexible benefits plan, evaluate your options carefully. If you're single without any dependents, for instance, it probably makes sense to forgo the life insurance offered by your employer and opt instead for better health insurance or more disability coverage.

- Don't go without health insurance, even if you're healthy. To find affordable coverage, see if there's a group you can join, such as a trade association or religious organization, that offers group insurance. If you're between jobs, purchase low-cost temporary coverage. (For general tips on shopping for an individual policy, see page 189.)

- Check with several agents and the few companies that sell directly to consumers when shopping for auto insurance (see page 198). And think twice before allowing a friend to drive your car. If there's an accident, *your* insurance record will be tainted, not your friend's.

- Get disability insurance to protect yourself in case you can't work due to injury or illness. Ideally, you should have coverage that will pay you 70% of your income if you become disabled. (For advice on reducing the cost of your coverage, see page 200.)

- Purchase renters insurance if you rent a house or an apartment. It protects your possessions if they're ruined in a fire or stolen, and it also offers you some liability coverage inside and outside your home.

- If you own a home, make sure you have adequate insurance for it. Insure your home's structure for the entire cost of rebuilding it.

Catalog the contents of your home and verify that your personal property insurance covers the replacement cost.

• If you have kids or anyone else dependent on your income, buy term life insurance for yourself. If you don't have dependents, you probably don't need any life insurance at all.

9

HOW TO MAKE YOUR LIFE LESS TAXING

Put More Money
in Your Pocket and
Less in Uncle Sam's

Y OU CAN RUN from many financial subjects, but you can't hide from taxes. If you're like most people, you find the rules complex, the forms confusing, and the Internal Revenue Service (IRS) intimidating.

This chapter will help you get over your fear of filing. It describes exactly what kind of taxes you pay, explains how to figure out which tax bracket you're in, and, most important, outlines specific strategies that can save you money. Although exploring the intricacies of the tax code isn't anyone's idea of a good time (except for an accountant I once dated), taking the time to understand the basics could save you hundreds of dollars each year. Whether you do your own taxes—something I recommend you try at least once—or hire someone to do them for you, knowing the rules ensures that you won't miss out on any money-saving tax breaks.

One quick note: Although this chapter will give you a good overview of what you need to know about taxes, you should keep in mind that tax law is constantly changing. And while I've made every effort to provide the most accurate, up-to-date information available, you'll need to check the current rules when you fill out your tax return.

WHY IS YOUR PAYCHECK SO SMALL?

At the point in your life when you received your first paycheck, it became painfully clear that your before-tax salary, also known as your **gross income**, was an illusion. Your after-tax income, or **net income**, was much smaller. The reason, you soon figured out, was that your employer deducted Social Security tax, Medicare tax, and federal, state, and local income taxes from your paycheck.

Your employer deducts or "withholds" tax because the U.S. uses a "pay-as-you-go" system, meaning you pay tax on the money you earn as you earn it. If you're a freelancer or self-employed, you're responsible for making sure you pay enough tax each quarter. If you're an employee, your employer withholds income tax from each paycheck based on your salary and the information you provided on **Form W-4** when you were hired. On a worksheet attached to the W-4, you were asked some basic questions to help you calculate the number of **withholding allowances**. A withholding allowance represents an estimate of the exemptions and deductions you believe you are entitled to in the coming year. (You'll learn more about exemptions and deductions later on.) The more allowances you take, the less income tax your employer withholds from your paycheck; the fewer allowances you take, the more tax is withheld. The number of allowances for which you're eligible can depend on a variety of factors, including whether you're single or married, whether or not you have kids, and whether you own a home.

THE TAXES YOU PAY

Here's a rundown of the major taxes you'll encounter:

- **Income tax.** The federal government, and some state and local governments, require you to pay tax on your **earned**

income, which is the income you receive for work you do. The federal government, and some state and local governments, also require you to pay tax on income you receive from investments. Such **unearned income** includes the interest you get from a savings account and the dividends or capital gains you receive from mutual funds, stocks, and bonds.

- **Social Security and Medicare payroll tax.** Virtually everyone who works must contribute a portion of his or her wages to a fund that provides retirement income for people 65 and older (that's the Social Security part) and health insurance for this same crowd (that's the Medicare part). In 1996, as an employee of a company, the Social Security tax you pay is 6.2% of your income, up to a maximum income of $62,700. The Medicare tax is 1.45%, with no maximum. Your total employee-contribution to Medicare and Social Security is 7.65% of your income, and your employer matches that amount. If you work for yourself, you have to cover the full 15.3% (the 7.65% employee contribution plus the 7.65% employer contribution) to pay for Social Security and Medicare; this 15.3% is also known as the **self-employment tax.** Some states also impose state unemployment and disability insurance taxes.

- **Property tax.** Some state and local governments require residents to pay tax on certain types of property. In Virginia and Connecticut, for example, residents must pay **personal property tax** on the value of their cars each year. And if you own a home, you might owe real estate tax, also known as **real property tax,** to your municipality and/or county based on the value of your home and the land on which it is built.

- **Sales tax.** Most states and many cities and counties impose tax on the items you buy (sofas, potato chips, sneakers) and the services you use (dry cleaning, haircuts, lawn care).

- **Capital gains tax.** Your profit or gain when you sell an investment is subject to a special tax rate called a capital

TAXES AND INHERITANCE

When Rebecca's uncle Al died, she received $13,000 from his estate, which she put in her bank savings account in January. She was thrilled by this windfall, but she worried about whether she would owe tax on the money. Here's how it generally works: You do not owe income tax on money you receive as an inheritance, but if you put that money in a bank account you will have to pay tax on the interest. So Rebecca had to pay tax on the $520 that her uncle's money earned her in interest. (Some states have inheritance taxes, but the executor—the person in charge of sorting through a will and distributing the money to benefactors—is responsible for making sure the applicable inheritance taxes are paid.) If you have any concerns about whether or not your inheritance taxes were paid, check with the executor.

gains tax. Gains from financial assets such as stock mutual funds that are held for more than one year are considered long-term capital gains. Although you pay tax on capital gains in the same way as ordinary income (that is, if you're in the 15% income tax bracket, you will pay 15% on capital gains), the highest possible tax rate for long-term capital gains in 1995 was just 28%—even if you were in a higher tax bracket.

FIGURING OUT YOUR
TAX RATE

When people talk about their tax bracket or tax rate, they're usually referring to their federal income tax bracket or rate. Federal income tax makes up the largest share of your total tax bill. Your federal income tax rate depends on how much income—including wages, bonuses, tips, and earnings from investments—you received over the course of the year. (It also depends on the tax breaks you're eligible for, but more about that later.)

The federal government has a "graduated" tax system that requires people with higher incomes to pay a higher percentage of their income in taxes. A range of income levels is grouped together in what is called a **tax bracket**. A **tax rate** is assigned to each tax bracket. To figure out your tax bracket, you first need to calculate your **taxable income,** which you can do by following the step-by-step instructions on your tax return. For example, if you were single and your taxable income is between $0 and $24,000 in 1996, you would be in the 15% tax bracket. The dollar amounts that fall within each bracket are adjusted for inflation every year. Every few years, the President, with the help of Congress, changes the number of brackets and adjusts the range of incomes in each bracket in order to win friends and influence people. As of this writing, there are five brackets and therefore five rates: 15%, 28%, 31%, 36%, and 39.6%. But figuring out the tax you owe involves more than finding out which rate corresponds to your income.

Take a look at the tables shown in Figure 9-1. Imagine you are single and have a taxable income of $23,950. That would put you in the 15% tax bracket. Simple. But say your income was $30,000. Here's where it gets complicated. Not all your income will fall into the same bracket. The first $24,000 will be taxed at the 15% rate, and the remaining $6,000 will be taxed at the 28% rate.

In this example, 28% is known as the **marginal tax rate,** the rate at which the "last dollar you earn" gets taxed. The marginal rate is the highest rate at which any of your money is taxed. Knowing your marginal rate will help you evaluate the merits of making certain investments.

Depending on where you live, you will probably have to pay state and local income taxes, too. On average, you can expect your state and local tax to be roughly 5%. (Some states charge no state income tax at all, however, and others impose a tax only on certain types of income.) Add 5% to your federal marginal rate to get a

Figure 9-1
1996 TAX RATES

Filing Status	For taxable income that is:	Marginal rate is:
Single	Under $24,000	15%
	Over $24,000, but not over $58,150	28%
	Over $58,150, but not over $121,300	31%
	Over $121,300, but not over $263,750	36%
	Over $263,750	39.6%
Married Couples Filing Jointly	Under $40,100	15%
	Over $40,100, but not over $96,900	28%
	Over $96,900, but not over $147,700	31%
	Over $147,700, but not over $263,750	36%
	Over $263,750	39.6%
Married Couples Filing Separately	Under $20,050	15%
	Over $20,050, but not over $48,450	28%
	Over $48,450, but not over $73,850	31%
	Over $73,850, but not over $131,875	36%
	Over $131,875	39.6%

rough idea of your combined federal, state, and local marginal rate. To calculate your federal, state, and local marginal income tax rate more precisely, consult your state's tax booklet to find out your true state and local marginal rate. You can get a copy by calling your state's department of taxation. Inside the booklet are tables to help you figure out your state and local rates.

Remember, your marginal rate does not indicate what percent of your income will go toward tax. In the example above, if your annual taxable income was $30,000, most of your money would be taxed at a rate of 15% rather than at the marginal rate of 28%. Your overall rate, known as the **effective tax rate,** is a blended, or weighted, average of the tax rates that apply to your income. In this case it's a weighted average of 15% and 28% that results in an effective tax rate of about 18%.

FILING YOUR
TAX RETURN

The term **filing** simply means filling out your tax forms and sending them to the IRS, the government agency responsible for collecting taxes. Although your employer subtracts money for taxes from your paycheck during the year, the amount withheld generally is not the exact amount of tax you actually owe. By filling out tax forms you learn whether you still owe the IRS some money or whether the IRS owes you a refund.

April 15 is usually the last possible day you can file a tax return and pay tax for the previous calendar year without paying a penalty. (If that date falls on a Saturday or Sunday, the IRS allows you to file up until the following Monday.) If you miss the April 15 deadline and owe the IRS money, you may have to pay interest on the money you owe, plus a penalty.

Start getting your paperwork together early in the year. By the end of January your employer will have sent you a **W-2** form that shows your gross income and the amount of tax withheld from your paycheck over the course of the previous year. Your bank and mutual fund company will each send you a **1099** form that lists the interest, dividends or capital gains paid to you during the year. If you've done freelance work, you will probably receive a 1099 from the company you did the work for. Compare your pay stubs and financial statements to your W-2 and 1099s to make sure the figures are accurate. Save these forms in a folder marked "Tax Returns" and create a new folder for each tax year. You'll need them when you fill out your tax return. The remainder of this section will tell you all you need to know about filing.

Who Has to File a Tax Return?

If you're single and are not claimed as a dependent on your parents' tax return, you must file a tax return if your gross income is at least $6,550 (as of 1996). For married couples who file a joint return, the 1996 minimum income for filing is $11,800.

If you're a full-time student and under 24, your parents can claim

A NOTE TO STUDENTS

Scholarships that pay for tuition, course-related fees, books, and supplies are not considered taxable income if you are working toward a degree. But if you received a scholarship to, say, study abroad for a year, and the course work is not related to your getting a degree, you must count the money you receive as income. And whether you're working toward a degree or not, the portion of a scholarship used to pay for room and board is considered taxable income. For details call the IRS at 800-TAX-FORM and ask for its *Scholarships and Fellowships*, Publication 520.

you as a dependent. Even so, you may have to file. If you receive any unearned income and the total of it plus your earned income exceeds $650 in 1996, you will have to file your own tax return. Or if you don't receive any unearned income in 1996 but earn $4,000 or more from a job, you also will have to file your own tax return.

When Should You File?

If you're expecting a refund, send in your tax forms to the IRS as soon after January 1 as possible so that you can get your refund sooner. If you owe money, mail your forms and your check made out to the IRS in early April, so you can hang on to your cash as long as possible. But try not to wait until the last minute.

If you're expecting a big refund or are making a big payment to the IRS, you may want to send your return via certified mail so that you have a record. If the IRS claims it didn't get your return, you will have proof that you mailed it in.

If you simply can't get it together in time, you can file for an automatic four-month extension and send in your tax forms late. But if you think you owe money, you must estimate how much you owe and send in a check to the IRS by April 15. If you have not sent all that you owe by April 15, the IRS will charge you interest on the unpaid amount, plus a penalty if you have paid less than 90% of what you owe.

If You Can't Pay

Even if you don't have enough money to pay the IRS the tax you owe, you should file your return by April 15. If you don't, you will be charged a monthly penalty of 5% of the amount of tax you owe, up to a maximum penalty of 25%. You'll also have to pay interest. To avoid these nasty charges, you can request to pay the IRS in installments by filling out Form 9465 and sending it in with your completed return. Within 30 days the IRS will tell you if you've been accepted for the installment plan. The IRS will still charge you a late fee based on how much you owe and how long you owe it, plus interest and a one-time charge of $43. To get a copy of Form 9465, call 800-TAX-FORM.

If You're Single

If you're not married but have children or dependent relatives living with you, you may be able to file as **head of household.** This status generally allows you to pay less tax than an ordinary single person. To see if you qualify, check the instruction booklet that comes with your tax forms.

IF YOU CHANGE YOUR NAME, TELL SOCIAL SECURITY

If you get married and change your last name, contact the Social Security Administration. The IRS checks to make sure that the name and Social Security number you list on your tax return match the records of the Social Security Administration. If you change your name without alerting the Social Security Administration, the IRS may delay sending you the refund check you are due. What's more, you might not get credit for the money your employer deducts from your paycheck and sends to Social Security. Call 800-772-1213 for a name-change form.

MAXIMIZING YOUR TAX BREAKS

Although the government wants citizens to pay their fair share of taxes, it does offer taxpayers ways to reduce the amount of their income that is subject to tax. This section will discuss the various tax breaks for which you may be eligible.

Exemptions and Deductions

One type of tax break available to all taxpayers is an **exemption,** a specific amount ($2,550 in 1996) that can be subtracted from your taxable income. If you're single and have no children, you are allowed one personal exemption. If you're married and file a joint return, you and your spouse are each entitled to a personal exemption. You also get an additional exemption for each child you have. If you earn a very high income, you may not be entitled to any exemptions.

The other type of tax break is a **deduction.** Deductions are specific expenses that the government allows you to subtract from your income, thus reducing the amount of tax you pay. (For an example of how this works, see the box below.) Uncle Sam offers deductions for certain types of behavior or situations. For instance, to encourage people to buy homes, the government allows taxpayers to deduct the interest they pay on their mortgage.

There are two distinct ways to take advantage of deductions. The simpler way is to take the **standard deduction,** which all taxpayers are permitted to do. The standard deduction is simply a fixed dollar amount that Congress allows all taxpayers to subtract from their income. Even if you don't participate in activities that are deemed deductible by the government, you still get the standard deduction. (Technically, you subtract your standard deduction from a figure known as your **adjusted gross income,** or **AGI.** Your AGI is basically your gross income minus special deductions known as "adjustments." Don't get bogged down in the technical details of how to determine your AGI now; when you fill out your tax form, you'll be able to calculate it.) In 1996 the standard deduction for a single person is $4,000. For a married couple filing a joint return, the standard deduction is $6,700. These figures are adjusted each year for inflation.

A more complicated but potentially more rewarding method is to **itemize** your deductions. Itemizing means listing the specific "items" that are deductible according to current tax rules, and then subtracting their cost from your AGI. If you choose to itemize deductions, you cannot take the standard deduction.

Whether you should itemize or take the standard deduction depends on the specifics of your financial life. The following two sections describe some potential itemized deductions. Once you have read them over, make your own list of the itemized deductions that are relevant to you. If the total of your itemized expenses is greater than the standard deduction, you should itemize. If the standard deduction is greater, you should take the standard deduction. If you do itemize, make sure you can substantiate the amounts you claim. If you are audited, this is the part of your return that the IRS is likely to scrutinize carefully.

FIGURING OUT THE VALUE OF A DEDUCTION

Your tax bracket plays a major role in determining just how much a deduction is worth. Suppose you obtained a mortgage to buy a home. Assume that in the first year the interest payments you made on the mortgage totaled $10,000. You would be able to subtract, or deduct, that $10,000 from your adjusted gross income for that year. If you're in the 15% tax bracket, that would mean a savings of $1,500 (15% of $10,000). But if you are in the 28% tax bracket, the $10,000 tax deduction would be worth $2,800 (28% of $10,000).

But before you read the following lists of possible deductions, I should add a disclaimer: The rules concerning deductions, even the more straightforward ones, can be very tricky. They also change frequently. Use this list only as a starting point. Consult a current tax guide to make sure specific deductions are still valid. Also, if you earn a very high income, you may not be eligible for certain deductions. Remember, you can take the following tax deductions only if you itemize.

Some Straightforward Itemized Deductions

The following list includes some items you may be able to deduct:

- **State and local income taxes.** On your federal tax form you can deduct the state and local taxes you paid (including amounts withheld from your paycheck) during the year. Because most of us pay these taxes, you're likely to be eligible for this tax break.

- **Property taxes.** If you own a home, you may be able to deduct the property taxes (also known as real estate taxes) you pay. If you live in a co-op, it pays property taxes for you as part of your monthly maintenance fee; find out what your share of these taxes is. You may be able to deduct it.

- **Donations to charities.** If you make a contribution to a group that is considered a "qualified tax-exempt organization" by the IRS, you can deduct it. Qualified organizations include most churches, synagogues, charities, and educational organizations. If you're unsure whether a particular organization qualifies, ask to see the document that states that the organization is tax-exempt. Donations you make to your college's alumni association, for instance, may be deductible. If you donate clothes, furniture, or household items to the Salvation Army, you get to deduct their current market value. Write down a description of each item you donate and how much it is worth (basically that means how much you estimate you could get if you sold it at a garage sale). To deduct donations of cash or property of $250 or more, you'll need a receipt from the charity. To deduct donations other than cash worth more than $500 (such as clothing or books), you'll have to fill out a special form (Form 8283) when you file your tax return. If you make a donation worth more than $5,000, you'll need to get a professional appraisal. Also, you can deduct some expenses you incurred when you did volunteer work. If you volunteer at a senior center on weekends, you can deduct some of your transportation costs to and from the center, for example.

If you get some "benefit" (theater tickets, a tote bag, a meal) in exchange for a contribution, you can deduct only the amount of the donation that exceeds the value of the benefit. For example, if you pay $100 to attend a fundraising dinner for the Save the Leapfrogs Society sponsored by the Boy Scouts of America and the actual value of the dinner is $25, you can deduct $75 on your tax return. The receipt you get from your charity should specify any such "benefits" you have received.

- **Housing costs.** If you own a home, you can deduct the interest you pay on your mortgage. (You cannot deduct the portion of your mortgage payment that goes toward paying off the principal.) Also, in the year you buy a home, you may be able to deduct the points even if they were actually paid by the seller of the home. (See Chapter 7 for an explanation of points.) If you live in a co-op building, the co-op may pay interest on a mortgage for the building. If it does, find out what your share of this interest is; you may be able to deduct it.

Some Trickier Itemized Deductions

Certain expenses are deductible only in specific situations. Here are some of those deductions. Again, remember that some are not available to taxpayers with very high incomes. Check a current tax guide for details.

- **Job-related expenses and other miscellaneous deductions.** This broad category includes a variety of expenses. The basic rule is that these expenses must be related to producing income. You can deduct the combined total of these expenses that exceeds 2% of your adjusted gross income (AGI). Here's how that works. Suppose your AGI is $30,000. You cannot deduct the first $600 (2% of $30,000) of your "job-related and miscellaneous expenses," but you can deduct expenses beyond $600. Below are examples of job-related expenses. For more information call 800-TAX-FORM and ask for *Miscellaneous Deductions,* Publication 529.

  —*Work-related home computers, cellular phones, and other equipment.* If your employer requires you to purchase any equipment, you may be permitted to deduct up to $17,500 of the amount you spend each year. You must be able to prove that your employer told you the item is necessary for your job and that you use the equipment more than 50% of the time for business. (Ask your boss to write a letter to that effect, and file it away in case you need to show it to the IRS someday.) Even if you don't meet this "50% rule," you may still be able to deduct the cost of the equipment over several years. For details call 800-TAX-FORM and request *Depreciation,* Publication 534.

  —*Job-search expenses.* The IRS allows you to deduct costs related to a job search as long as you're looking for a job in your *present* occupation. If you're trying to change professions—say, you're a lifeguard looking to break into investment banking—you don't get the deduction. If you're currently out of work, the kind of job you did most recently is considered your occupation. If you're looking for your first job, you don't get the tax break. The expenses you can deduct if you qualify include the fees of career counseling and employment or placement agencies; the cost of preparing, printing, and mailing your resume; phone calls; and transportation costs (and 50% of the cost of meals while traveling) for a long-distance job search.

—*Work-related educational expenses.* If you take a course that helps you maintain or improve the skills you use to perform your current job, you may be able to deduct the tuition expenses. Also, if a course is required either by your employer or by law in order for you to keep your job, you may be able to deduct its cost. If, however, you take a course that will qualify you for a new line of work or that enables you to meet the minimum educational requirements of your profession, you can't deduct the tuition. So a financial analyst who is taking a cooking course can't deduct the cost. A paralegal can't deduct the tuition costs of law school, and an accountant can't deduct the costs associated with taking the CPA exam. However, a financial analyst who goes back to school to get an MBA may be able to deduct tuition expenses.

—*Mandatory uniforms for work.* Suits and ties aren't deductible, but nurses' uniforms, firefighter uniforms, letter carrier uniforms, police officer uniforms, safety shoes and glasses, hard hats, and work gloves are. (If you're a computer programmer who wears a hard hat to work for kicks, it doesn't count.)

—*Business travel and entertainment expenses.* If your employer reimburses you for these expenses, you cannot deduct them. If you pay these costs yourself, there are very specific rules about how much you're allowed to deduct. In general, you must keep a detailed log of your trips and be prepared to explain the business purpose of each expense.

—*Union dues and initiation fees, professional and busi-*

ness association dues, and job-related subscriptions to trade magazines and professional journals. Make sure to deduct these expenses if you are not reimbursed for them by your employer.

— *Tax preparation fees.* Even though these aren't directly related to work, you can deduct the cost of tax-related software and tax publications. You can also deduct money you pay to a tax preparer.

• **Medical expenses.** You can deduct out-of-pocket medical and dental expenses that are greater than 7.5% of your adjusted gross income. You can include premiums you pay for medical insurance, co-payments for doctor visits, the cost of birth control pills, prescription medicines not covered by your health plan, and transportation needed for medical care.

• **Losses due to theft and disaster.** You're allowed to deduct the cost of items you lose in a burglary, fire, or other disaster that exceed 10% of your adjusted gross income. The first $100 of losses above the 10% threshold is not deductible.

THIRTEEN TAX MOVES THAT COULD SAVE YOU MONEY

Here are some additional tips to consider:

1. **Put money into an individual retirement account (IRA) every year.** The money you contribute to an IRA may be deductible if you aren't eligible for an employer-sponsored retirement plan or if your income falls below a certain level. If you're in the 28% tax bracket, a deductible $2,000 IRA contribution will save you $560 on your tax bill. If you're eligible for a deductible IRA, you can take the deduction

even if you don't itemize. There is a place on the tax form that will prompt you to take the deduction. (To find out if you're eligible to open a deductible IRA, see Chapter 6.)

Although you do not have to pay income tax on the money you contribute to an employer-sponsored retirement savings plan like a 401(k), you do not list 401(k) contributions on your tax return. That's because your employer has already subtracted your contribution from your gross salary. Thus, the net salary on your W-2 already reflects this deduction.

2. **See if you can deduct your moving costs.** If you moved to a new place for a full-time job, you may be able to deduct moving expenses, such as transportation, packing, and shipping costs. You don't have to itemize in order to get this deduction. But the rules governing who gets this deduction are tricky, so read the following description of the 1996 rules slowly. The distance between your *new job* and your *old house* must be at least 50 miles more than the distance between your *old job* and your *old house*. (I know. It's outrageously complicated.) You must also stay in your new job at least 39 weeks. If you recently graduated and didn't have a job at school, your moving expenses would be deductible as long as your new job is at least 50 miles from your college residence (on or off campus). You will need to fill out and attach Form 3903 to your tax return to deduct these costs. For details, call 800-TAX-FORM for *Moving Expenses,* Publication 521.

3. **Bunch your deductions into one year.** If you don't have enough deductible expenses to make it worth your while to itemize this year or if you don't meet the minimums for certain deductions, take the standard deduction and put off additional deductible expenditures until next year. For example, make your charitable contributions next January rather than this December.

4. **Consider taxes before you choose a date to get married.** Okay, call me unromantic, but the two of you might save hundreds of dollars if you marry in January rather than December. That's because you may owe more in taxes by

filing a joint return than by filing two single returns. Say you each earn $30,000, and you take the standard deduction. Using figures from 1996, you would each pay $3,518 in taxes for a total of $7,036. As a married couple filing a joint return, you would pay $8,283. So if you put off your nuptials until January, you'll save $1,247—enough to pay for the band. The general rule is that if you and your betrothed earn about the same income, you will probably save money by marrying after the first of the year. If one of you earns much more than the other, it's generally better to get married before the end of the year and file jointly.

5. **Figure out if you'd save money by filing jointly or separately.** If you work and your spouse doesn't, it generally pays to file a joint return. Of course, there are hardly any young married couples who fit this description. If you and your spouse both work, you should figure your tax on both a joint return and on separate married returns to see which way saves you money. Filing separate married returns may make sense, especially if you have many deductible expenses that are subject to an adjusted gross income threshold. For example, say you and your spouse each earn about the same amount of money but you have exceptionally high medical bills. If you file a joint return, your medical bills would have to exceed 7.5% of your *combined* adjusted gross income in order to be deductible. If you file separately, you can deduct medical costs that exceed 7.5% of your *own* adjusted gross income. It may also make sense for you to file your state return separately, so try filling it out both ways.

6. **Check your withholding.** You filled out a W-4 form when you started your job. Changes in your personal life as well as changes in the tax law may result in your having too little or too much tax withheld from your paycheck. If you get married, buy a home, have a baby, or experience any other major financial life change, you should re-evaluate your withholding.

If you receive a big refund from the IRS, you should probably increase the number of withholding allowances you take. Although receiving a cash windfall from the IRS feels great, it isn't a smart financial move. A refund occurs after you've given the IRS too much money during the year. The problem is, the IRS doesn't pay you interest for the additional money withheld from your paycheck during the year. And although some people say that overwithholding is a good "forced savings program," I don't agree. You're better off withholding the right amount and funneling small amounts of cash into an automatic savings program throughout the year. (See Chapter 4 for details.) That way you get forced savings plus earnings.

There are other ways that adjusting your withholding can help you. If you just graduated from college, for instance, and will be working less than 12 months this calendar year, request a special withholding method known as a part-year option. Then your employer will calculate withholding based on the number of months you actually earn money, rather than on your annual salary. This will prevent overwithholding.

A warning: Don't claim more allowances than you deserve. This will result in your employer's withholding too little tax during the year. If you don't pay at least 90% of the tax you owe during the current year or 100% of the tax you paid during the prior year, you may be charged a penalty. Keep in mind that the rules are different if you have a very high income.

7. **Take advantage of state and local deductions.** Read your state's and town's tax instructions carefully. Some states allow you to deduct some of your federal income tax on your state return. Some states allow you to deduct all or a portion of the license fees for your car. And most states give a tax break to homeowners who paid local property taxes.

8. **Consider taxes when you invest.** If your tax rate is 28% or higher, look into investments that offer some tax advantages. While it doesn't make sense to choose an investment solely for the tax break, it is one factor to consider. See Chapter 5 for a simple formula that will help you determine whether tax-free investments are right for you.

9. **Take advantage of tax-favored employee benefits.** If you work for a company that offers you the chance to use a flexible spending account (FSA) to pay for child care or for medical expenses that aren't covered by your insurance, use it. (For details, see Chapter 8.) And, of course, contribute the maximum you can to your 401(k).

10. **If you're eligible, take the "earned income credit."** A tax credit is a special tax break that directly reduces the amount of tax you owe. (That's different from a deduction, which reduces the income that's subject to tax.) According to the 1996 rules, if you're at least 25 and earn less than $9,500 (and no one can claim you as a dependent) you may be eligible for this special tax break. If you have a child, you must earn less than $25,078 to qualify for this credit; if you have two children, you must earn less than $28,495 to qualify. To find out more about the credit, see the instruction booklet that comes with your tax forms.

11. **If you have children, see if you're eligible for the child-care credit.** If you pay someone to take care of your child while you (and your spouse, if you're married) work, you may be a candidate for this credit. Even if you earn a high income, you may be allowed to receive a credit of 20% of your child-care expenses, up to a maximum of $2,400 for one child and $4,800 for two. For details call 800-TAX-FORM and ask for *Child and Dependent Care,* Publication 503. In order to get the credit you will have to make sure that the required employment taxes, such as Medicare and Social Security, are paid for your child-care worker. For details, call 800-TAX-FORM and ask for *Employment Taxes for Household Employers,* Publication 926.

12. **If you're a self-employed performer, see if you're eligible for a special tax break.** Whether you itemize deductions or not, you may get your first big break on your tax form. That's because you're allowed to deduct business-related expenses (the cost of acting classes, headshots, costumes, etc.) if your AGI is $16,000 or less before this deduction. The rules

about who can deduct these expenses are complex, so check the details in *Travel, Entertainment and Gift Expenses,* Publication 463.

13. **Consider refinancing high-rate credit card debt with a home equity loan.** The interest you pay on a home equity loan up to $100,000 is deductible. (For details see Chapter 3.)

IF YOU'RE
SELF-EMPLOYED

If you work for yourself—that includes anyone who has his or her own company or who does freelance work—you have certain responsibilities and are eligible for some special deductions.

If you're self-employed, the companies you do work for probably will not withhold taxes from their payments to you. But you can't simply wait until the end of the year to pay the IRS. Instead, you will have to pay income tax quarterly. Call the IRS and request *Tax Withholding and Estimated Tax,* Publication 505. You must also be sure to pay enough self-employment tax. For details get a copy of *Self-Employment Tax,* Publication 533. Even if you're desperately afraid of tax-related reading, call for these booklets and attempt to read them. After reviewing them, if you still find it difficult to determine your estimated quarterly tax or if you're unsure whether you need to pay self-employment tax at all, seek the help of a tax preparer.

As a self-employed person, you are eligible for many additional deductions. You can deduct half the Social Security and Medicare tax you pay. You can also deduct business travel expenses, whether or not they exceed 2% of your adjusted gross income. And you may be able to deduct the cost of office supplies and equipment. Call 800-TAX-FORM for the *Tax Guide for Small Business,* Publication 334.

You may also be able to deduct your home office expenses. Keep in mind, however, that the IRS has very strict rules regarding home offices. You must use the space that you designate as your home office exclusively for business and on a regular basis. If your desk is in your living room, for example, you will have trouble proving that you use that portion of your home exclusively for work. Consult a tax guide or preparer. Also, call 800-TAX-FORM for the *Tax Guide for Business Use of Your Home,* Publication 587.

As a self-employed person, one of the smartest tax (and savings) moves is to open an IRA. But the most you can contribute to an IRA is $2,000 each year. If you have more money to put aside, consider contributing to a special type of IRA known as a Simplified Employee Pension, or SEP-IRA. You can set aside up to $22,500 each year in these tax-deferred accounts, depending on how much you earn. Another option is to open a retirement plan known as a Keogh, which may allow you to set aside up to $30,000 per year. (For details on IRAs, SEP-IRAs, and Keoghs, see Chapter 6.)

GETTING YOUR TAX LIFE IN ORDER

Probably the most daunting part of the tax process is getting your paperwork in order. This section offers a rundown of the various tax forms. It also includes a checklist to help you avoid drowning in paperwork.

A Rundown of the Tax Forms

Beginning in February most banks and post offices leave stacks of tax forms lying around. You can also get forms from your local IRS office or call 800-TAX-FORM (it generally takes about seven to fifteen business days to receive them). Here are the forms you'll have to choose from:

- **1040 EZ.** The IRS 1040 EZ, which wins in the category of most cleverly named form, is also the easiest to fill out. It's generally for single people, or couples filing jointly, with total taxable income less than $50,000. To use this form you

Figure 9-2
WHAT, ME ITEMIZE?

A lot of young people think they don't earn enough to itemize. But consider the case of Bobby, who recently left his job at a small architecture firm in Denver to work for a design company in New York City. (Moving costs: $700.) His salary is $38,000, and he rents a studio apartment. He just bought a computer ($2,500) and a fax machine ($500) so he can do more work at home; his boss told him to buy them so she could fax him work from her summer house. Bobby uses the computer and fax exclusively for work. Before moving, he donated a couch, a dresser, and a bed to the Salvation Army. He also donated three shopping bags full of old clothes. (Total value of his donations: $2,000.) His only investment is the $2,000 IRA he has opened because his new company doesn't have a pension plan. To see why it makes sense for him to itemize his deductions on the 1040 rather than take the standard deduction on the 1040A or EZ, look at the table below.

	1040EZ	1040A	1040
Total income	$38,000	$38,000	$38,000
(minus) IRA	0	2,000	2,000
(minus) Moving expenses	0	0	700
ADJUSTED GROSS INCOME (AGI)	38,000	36,000	35,300
Personal exemption	2,550	2,550	2,550
Charitable contributions	0	0	2,000
State and local taxes	0	0	3,466
Miscellaneous & business expenses*	0	0	2,294
Other itemized expenses	0	0	0
Total itemized deductions or standard deduction (whichever is greater)	4,000	4,000	7,760
EXEMPTION PLUS DEDUCTIONS	6,550	6,550	10,310
TAXABLE INCOME (AGI minus exemption and deductions)	31,450	29,450	24,990
FEDERAL TAX OWED	5,686	5,126	3,877

*Here's how you get $2,294 in miscellaneous and business expenses in the 1040 column. First, you calculate that 2% of Bobby's AGI ($35,300) is $706. Then you subtract that amount from the $3,000 ($2,500 for the computer and $500 for the fax machine) in total miscellaneous and business expenses.

Source: Ernst & Young LLP

must also earn less than $400 in taxable interest. You can't itemize your deductions on the EZ; it's meant for people who are better off taking the standard deduction. One important reason *not* to use the EZ: You can't deduct your contribution to an IRA.

- **1040A.** This form is almost as simple as the EZ form. To use it, your total taxable income must be less than $50,000, but your taxable interest and dividends can be more than $400. This form does not allow you to itemize, but it does permit you to deduct an IRA contribution and claim the child-care credit.

- **1040.** If you think the value of your itemized deductions is larger than the standard deduction, this form is for you. You'll be *required* to fill out the 1040 if, say, your taxable income is $50,000 or more, or you receive certain types of income such as rent or capital gains. In order to itemize on the 1040, you must fill out an additional form called Schedule A, which will help you figure out the value of your itemized deductions. The tax instruction booklet that you get in the mail or by calling 800-TAX-FORM will tell you which schedules you need. (For an example of how itemizing on the 1040 can work to your advantage, see Figure 9-2.)

What to Keep and What to Chuck

Good record-keeping is important when it comes to filing your taxes. If you use a tax preparer and he or she must spend hours sifting through shoe boxes full of your receipts and documents, you will be charged extra. By keeping neat, accurate records you will save time and money. Below are the names of tax-related file folders you should set up.

- **Tax Returns: 1996, 1997, 1998, etc.** Each year add a new folder to hold your most important tax documents, including a copy of your tax return, income statements from your employers (W-2s), and income statements from your bank and mutual fund company (1099s). Save each year's folder for at least three years; if you are audited, the IRS can request up to three years' worth of tax records. (If you've underreported your income by 25% or more, the IRS can ask for returns from six years back. And if you've committed fraud, there's no time limit.) After three years, throw out your supporting paperwork but hold on to a copy of the return, your attached W-2s and 1099s, and any other IRS forms you filed. If ten years from now the IRS claims you never filed your 1996 return, you'll want to be able to prove that you did.

- **Business-Related Expenses (Unreimbursed).** Include appropriate credit card receipts, entertainment and meal receipts, and receipts for tolls, taxis, parking, gas, car maintenance, tips, union dues, and subscriptions. If you plan to deduct the cost of a computer or cellular phone, in addition to receipts you must keep records that detail when you use the equipment for work and when you use it for leisure activity. If you're self-employed, save all receipts from business-related travel. Also, keep a detailed spending diary when you go on business trips and file it in this folder.

- **Charitable Contributions.** Keep lists of property you've donated and receipts from the organizations you contribute to. If you contribute money, file the canceled checks and receipts from the charity here.

- **Child Care/Dependent Care Expenses.** Hold on to documents indicating the dates and amounts of various fees you paid to an individual or a center to take care of your child or other dependent while you worked. (Sorry, but the money you pay to a babysitter to watch your child so you can go to a movie is not deductible.) Also keep track of the cost of meals and lodging expenses paid to a child-care worker who lives in your home. To be able to claim the child-care credit, you must make certain that the required employment taxes—Social Security, Medicare, and unemployment—are paid for your employee. Keep records that prove these taxes were paid.

- **Home Improvements.** A home improvement, known as a **capital improvement,** is a renovation you make that increases your home's value. If you own a home, save all receipts related to home improvement. Although you can't deduct these expenses now, you can add them to the original purchase price of your home when you're ready to sell; this reduces your reported gain and therefore the amount of tax you pay if you sell the house at a profit. Routine repairs such as painting don't count, but adding a new room, putting on a new roof, installing a new toilet, paneling walls, or adding new tile do. (For details consult a tax book or *Tax Information for First-Time Homeowners,* Publication 530.)

- **Home (Purchase).** Keep the closing statement and any other paperwork related to the purchase of your home. You may need these documents for tax purposes when you sell your home.

- **Individual Retirement Accounts (Deductible and Nondeductible).** Keep papers that indicate when your IRA contributions were made, the amount you invested, the date you opened the IRA, and the source of any money you rolled over from an employer retirement plan into your IRA. This documentation will be useful when you withdraw the money upon retirement. It's especially important to hold on to a copy of IRS Form 8606, which you'll need to file each year if you make nondeductible contributions to an IRA. When you withdraw money from a nondeductible IRA, you won't be taxed on the money you contributed but only on the earnings.

- **Medical Expenses (Unreimbursed).** If you pay any medical costs that your health insurance doesn't reimburse you for, keep the receipts. If at the end of the year these expenses exceed 7.5% of your adjusted gross income, you can deduct the portion that is over the threshold.

- **Miscellaneous Deductions.** This catch-all folder should include receipts for financial publications, tax preparation, job search activities, and certain education expenses.

- **Mortgage Interest Payments.** If you own a home, keep your 1098 form in this folder. A 1098 is an annual statement from your lender indicating how much interest and principal you paid on your mortgage. It may also tell you how much property tax you paid. Co-op owners generally receive a 1098 indicating the amount of interest they paid on the building's mortgage.

- **Mutual Funds.** Many funds provide you with a year-end statement that indicates how many shares you bought and sold during the year (including purchases you made through a reinvestment plan) and the price of those shares. Hold on to these statements. You'll be taxed on any gain you made through selling shares, and you'll get a tax break on any loss. You'll need the statements to figure out what your gain (or loss) was. There are several different methods you can use to calculate your gain—and some are more beneficial than others. In order to weigh the advantages of the various methods, you need to keep careful records of what you paid for the shares. (For details on the different methods used to calculate the tax owed on mutual fund gains, get *Mutual Fund Distributions,* Publication 564.) If your fund doesn't send you a comprehensive statement of your transactions, call and request one.

- **Property and Real Estate Tax.** The monthly mortgage payment you make to your lender generally includes the amount you owe to your local government for property taxes. Lenders typically forward the tax to the local taxing authority. At the end of the year you'll receive a statement from your lender informing you of the amount of property tax you paid for the year. These payments are deductible, so hold on to these statements.

- **Police Reports, Insurance Claims.** With any luck you won't need this file. But if you've been burglarized, save these documents. If you suffered major losses, you may be able to deduct the value of uninsured items.

- **Stocks and Bonds.** If you own individual stocks and bonds, keep the statements you get from the brokerage firm or the company that issued them. Also hang on to any stock or bond certificates, preferably in a bank safety deposit box.

DO YOU NEED A TAX PREPARER?

One of the best ways to learn about your financial life is to prepare your own tax return. If you've never done it, you may be surprised to learn how easy it is—especially if you use a good tax book. But if you're dead set against doing it yourself, at least take the time to find a decent preparer.

If You Don't Use a Preparer

The general instruction book that the IRS produces is quite well written and easy to understand. It's also free. Call 800-TAX-FORM and ask for *Your Federal Income Tax,* Publication 17. This guide, with more than 300 pages, is full of relevant details, including a list of other IRS publications you may want.

If you intend to itemize your deductions, you should also invest in one of the big fat tax guides available in any bookstore. Some good ones are *J. K. Lasser's Your Income Tax, The Money Income Tax Handbook,* and *Consumer Reports Guide to Income Tax.* Make sure you buy the correct book for the current year; you would use the 1998 guides to fill out your 1997 tax forms. These books usually cost less than $20 and are well worth the expense.

You should also consider using your computer to help you do your taxes. For about $35 you can purchase software that provides you with the forms and instructions. The key benefit of tax software is that it does the math for you. If you add or subtract an entry on your tax return, you can press a button and have the entire return recalculated for you. Two popular programs that get high marks from users: TurboTax (or MacInTax for Macs) and TaxCut.

If You Use a Preparer

The most obvious choices are big-name chain tax preparers such as H&R Block and smaller mom-and-pop shops in your neighborhood. The advantage of these services is that they're usually inexpensive. If you're sure you aren't eligible for many deductions and that the standard deduction is for you, a storefront preparer is fine. Keep in mind that the level of knowledge can vary dramatically. Look for a tax preparation business that operates year-round rather than one that is open just a few months a year. Ask friends and family members to recommend specific preparers. Most chain preparers will allow you to request a specific person.

If you have a somewhat more complicated return (for example, if you are self-employed or you have received a large inheritance), you may want to find a preparer with some additional education. One of the top credentials is **CPA**, which stands for **Certified Public Accountant**. CPAs have to meet the toughest requirements to get licensed; they also can be expensive. Another, usually cheaper, option is an **enrolled agent**; the title refers to any preparer who has worked for the IRS as an auditor or in some similar job for five years or who has passed a difficult two-day exam. At the very least find a preparer with a minimum of three years' experience filing returns. **Tax attorneys** are typically the most expensive alternative and are necessary only if you have extremely complicated tax issues to deal with or are in serious trouble with the IRS.

Be sure to ask what the preparer charges; there may be different rates for different preparers at the same company. (You can often find an enrolled agent at a chain preparer such as H&R Block; if possible, ask to work with one.) And finally, if you have someone fill out your forms, look the forms over carefully. *You* are responsible for making sure all the information on your return is true and correct.

FINANCIAL CRAMMING

- Fill out your tax forms as soon after January 1 as possible. If you're owed a refund, file right away; the quicker you mail in your forms, the faster you'll get your check. If you owe money, file in early April so you can hang on to your cash as long as possible.

- If you received a big refund from the IRS, fill out a new W-4 form and readjust your withholding. Since the IRS doesn't pay you interest on the money you overpay during the year, you're better off keeping this money in a bank account or money market fund.

- If you owe the IRS money but can't afford to pay, send in your return by April 15 anyway. You'll have to pay a penalty, but it won't be as stiff as the penalty for late filing.

- Look at the list of deductions beginning on page 229. If you're eligible for some of them, fill out the 1040 form to see if itemizing saves you money.

- If you're taking the standard deduction this year, postpone making charitable donations and home office-related purchases until after January 1. That way you can get credit for the deductions if you itemize next year.

- If you're self-employed, understand that you can't simply wait until the end of the year to pay Uncle Sam. You may be required to pay your taxes quarterly. For details get a copy of *Self-Employment Tax*, Publication 533.

FURTHER READING

If you've read through this entire tome, congratulations! You have all the basic information you need to have a prosperous financial life. If you desire even more information, below are some very selective recommendations. These are the books I would tell my friends to read if they wanted to know more about various topics. Also included are magazines, software, and pamphlets that may interest you. Some of the publications listed here are mentioned in the individual chapters; others are not.

BOOKS

Investing

Malkiel, Burton G. *A Random Walk Down Wall Street*. New York: W.W. Norton, 1991. A must read for anyone who wants to learn more about investing.

Tobias, Andrew. *The Only Investment Guide You'll Ever Need*. San Diego: Harvest Books, 1996. An excellent overview of key investment concepts.

Insurance

Stettner, Morey. *Buyer Beware: An Industry Insider Shows You How to Win the Insurance Game*. Chicago: Probus Publishing Co., 1994. An easy read that can answer some of your basic questions.

Taylor, Barbara. *How to Get Your Money's Worth in Home and Auto Insurance*. New York: McGraw Hill, 1991. A great book for anyone who wants to know more about home and auto coverage.

Taxes

The following three books are excellent tax guides. Make sure to get the most current edition!

Eiss, Eliot. *J. K. Lasser's Your Income Tax*. New York: Macmillan, 1994.

Esanu, Warren H., Barry Dickman, and Elias Zuckerman. *Consumer Reports Guide to Income Tax*. New York: Consumers' Union, 1994.

Sprouse, Mary. *The Money Income Tax Handbook*. New York: Warner Books, 1994.

General Personal Finance

Quinn, Jane Bryant. *Making the Most of Your Money: Smart Ways to Create Wealth and Plan Your Finances in the 90's*. New York: Simon & Schuster, 1991. Although its 900-plus pages may be a bit overwhelming, and some of it will be irrelevant to people in their twenties and thirties, this encyclopedic guide is one of the best.

Miscellaneous

Clifford, Denis. *Nolo's Simple Will Book: How to Prepare a Legally Valid Will*. Berkeley: Nolo Press, 1992. A must read if you're thinking of writing a will.

Maloni, Kelly, Ben Greenman, and Kristin Miller.*Net Money: Your Guide to the Personal Finance Revolution on the Information Highway*. New York: Michael Wolff & Company, Inc., and Random House Electronic Publishing, 1995. A unique book that offers a plethora of information for people who like to roam the net.

PERSONAL FINANCE MAGAZINES

Kiplinger's
Money
Smart Money
Your Future

PAMPHLETS/COMPANY PUBLICATIONS

Debt

Automotive Lease Guide's Residual Percentage Guide, available from Chart Software, 152 Woodcreek Drive North, Safety Harbor, FL 34695. (800) 418-8450.

Choosing and Using Credit Cards, available from the Bureau of Consumer Protection, Office of Consumer and Business Education, Federal Trade Commission, Sixth and Pennsylvania Ave., NW, Washington, DC 20580. (202) 326-3650.

Consumer Handbook to Credit Protection Laws, available from Publication Services, Division of Support Services, Board of Governors of the Federal Reserve System, Washington, DC 20551. (202) 452-3244.

Credit and Divorce, available from the Bureau of Consumer Protection, Office of Consumer and Business Education, Federal Trade Commission, Sixth and Pennsylvania Ave., NW, Washington, DC 20580. (202) 326-3650.

Credit Cards: What You Don't Know Can Cost You, available from Bankcard Holders of America, 524 Branch Dr., Salem, VA 24153. (703) 389-5445.

Equal Credit Opportunity, available from the Bureau of Consumer Protection, Office of Consumer and Business Education, Federal Trade Commission, Sixth and Pennsylvania Ave., NW, Washington, DC 20580. (202) 326-3650.

Exactly How to Get a Low-Interest-Rate Credit Card, available from Bankcard Holders of America, 6862 Elm Street, Suite 300, McLean, VA 22101. (703) 917-9805.

Fair Credit Billing, available from the Bureau of Consumer Protection, Office of Consumer and Business Education, Federal Trade Commission, Sixth and Pennsylvania Ave., NW, Washington, DC 20580. (202) 326-3650.

Fair Debt Collection, available from the Bureau of Consumer Protection,

Office of Consumer and Business Education, Federal Trade Commission, Sixth and Pennsylvania Ave., NW, Washington, DC 20580. (202) 326-3650.

Fix Your Own Credit Problems & Save Money, available from the Bureau of Consumer Protection, Office of Consumer and Business Education, Federal Trade Commission, Sixth and Pennsylvania Ave., NW, Washington, DC 20580. (202) 326-3650.

How to Dispute Credit Report Errors, available from the Bureau of Consumer Protection, Office of Consumer and Business Education, Federal Trade Commission, Sixth and Pennsylvania Ave., NW, Washington, DC 20580. (202) 326-3650.

Solving Credit Problems, available from the Bureau of Consumer Protection, Office of Consumer and Business Education, Federal Trade Commission, Sixth and Pennsylvania Ave., NW, Washington, DC 20580. (202) 326-3650.

Your Legal Guide to Consumer Credit, available from the Public Education Division, American Bar Association, 750 N. Lake Shore Dr., Chicago, IL 60611. (312) 988-5725.

Investing

Planning for College, available from the Investment Company Institute, 1401 H St., NW, Suite 1200, Washington, DC 20005-2148. (202) 326-5800.

Mortgage

Choosing the Mortgage That's Right for You, available from Fannie Mae Consumer Education Group, 3900 Wisconsin Ave., NW, Washington, DC 20016-2899. (800) 688-4663.

The Mortgage Money Guide, available from the Federal Trade Commission, Sixth and Pennsylvania Ave., NW, Washington, DC 20580. (202) 326-2222.

Mortgage Servicing, available from the Bureau of Consumer Protection, Office of Consumer and Business Education, Federal Trade Commission, Sixth and Pennsylvania Ave., NW, Washington, DC 20580. (202) 326-3650.

Opening the Door to a Home of Your Own, available from Fannie Mae

Consumer Education Group, 3900 Wisconsin Ave., NW, Washington, DC 20016-2899. (800) 688-4663.

Retirement

Pension Education Clearinghouse Publication Listing. Send a self-addressed, business-size envelope with 55 cents postage to Pension Education Clearinghouse, P.O. Box 19821, Washington, DC 20036.

Protecting Your Pension Money, Pension and Welfare Benefits Administration. For information, write to: Pension and Welfare Benefits Administration, Department of Labor, 200 Constitution Ave., NW, Room N-5656, Washington, DC 20210.

Tax

Guide to Free Tax Services, available from the Internal Revenue Service. (800) 829-1040.

SOFTWARE

Expert Lease, a program that allows you to do lease-versus-buy analysis for auto costs. Available from Chart Software, 152 Woodcreek Dr.N., Safety Harbor FL 34695, (800) 418-8450.

Managing Your Money, a general personal finance program by MECA Software. Available in computer stores.

BUY-RENT.WK1, a spreadsheet that allows you to figure out whether you should rent or buy a house. Send a self-addressed stamped envelope to Ed Chang, 291 Main St., #3-2, Millburn, NJ 07041. Write BUY-RENT.WK1 in the lower left-hand corner of the SASE.

Quicken, a general personal finance program by Intuit. Available in computer stores.

TurboTax (MacInTax for Macs), a tax-preparation program by Intuit. Available in computer stores.

TaxCut, a tax-preparation program from H&R Block. Available in computer stores.

ACKNOWLEDGMENTS

The following is a list of the hundreds of people who generously gave of their time and expertise to make this book possible. If anyone has inadvertently been left out, I apologize.

INTRODUCTION

Larry Cohen, SRI International; Carmen Denavas, Census Bureau; Neal Fogg, Center for Labor Market Studies at Northeastern University; Stephanie Schlandt, Payment Systems; Andrew Sum, Center for Labor Market Studies at Northeastern University; David Tong, SRI International.

CHAPTER 2: TAKING STOCK OF YOUR FINANCIAL LIFE

Durant Abernethy, National Foundation for Consumer Credit; Kent Allison, Price Waterhouse; Kent Brunette, American Association of Retired Persons; Anthony Burke, Internal Revenue Service; Peg Downey, Money Plans; Steven Enright, Enright Financial Advisors; Wilson Fadely, Internal Revenue Service; Ross Levin, Accredited Investors; Bill Moss, American Express Company; Edward L. Neumann, Furash & Company; Glenn Pape, Ayco Company; John Pfister, Chicago Title and Trust Company; John Rogers, Bureau of Labor Statistics; Steve Sanders, Sanders Investment Advisors; Ken Scott, Ken Scott Communications; William Speciale, David L. Babson & Company; Kristyn Stout, The Ryland Group.

CHAPTER 3: DEBT AND THE MATERIAL WORLD

John Abadie, NationsBank Corporation; Stephanie Babyak, Department of Education; Bill Banks, Chemical Bank; Gary Beanblossom, Department of Education; Ed Block, Automotive Lease Consultants; Elene Cafasso, Oakbrook Bank; Glenn Canner, Federal Reserve Board; Dennis Carroll, National Center for Education Statistics; Tim Christensen, Department of Education; Larry Cohen, SRI International; Paul Combe, Knight College Resource Group; James Daly, Credit Card News; Linda Del Castillo, Student Loan Marketing Association (Sallie Mae); Dr. Richard F. DeMong, McIntire School of Commerce, University of Virginia; Claire Diamond, AT&T Universal Card Services; Rachel Edelstein, Department of Education; Liz Eischeid, Trans Union Corporation; Fritz Elmendorf, Consumer Bankers Association; Brad Fay, Roper Organization; Susan Forman, Visa USA; Gerhard Fries, Federal Reserve Board; Jean Frohlicher, National Council of Higher Education Loan Programs; Luther Gatling, Budget & Credit Counseling Services; Jane Glickman, Department of Education; Linda Lee Goldberg, CarSource; Edward Gonciarz, Goldberg, Gonciarz & Scudieri; David Graubard, Kera & Graubard; Keith Gumbinger, HSH Associates; Robert Hall, Corestates Dealer Services Corporation; Charles Hart, Chart Software; Dayna Hart, General Motors Corporation; Ed Harting, Auto Lease Guide; Paul Havemann, HSH Associates; Robert Heady, Bank Rate Monitor; Stuart Himmelfarb, Roper Organization; Wendy Huntington, Student Loan Marketing Association (Sallie Mae); Dr. Robert Johnson, Credit Research Center, Purdue University; Dr. Jim Jurinski, University of Portland; Jacqueline King, The College Board; Dottie Kingsley, Department of Education; Ross Kleinman, Student Loan Marketing Association (Sallie Mae); Laura Knapp, The College Board; Paula Knepper, National Center for Education Statistics; Janis Lamar, TRW Information Systems & Services; Tony Langan, The Chase Manhattan Bank; Phyllis Laubacher, MasterCard International; Roberta Lazarz, Credit Union National Association; Jean Lesher, American Bankers Association; Gail Liberman, Bank Rate Monitor; Chris Lynn, Oakbrook Bank; John Maciarz, General Motors Corporation; Norm Magnuson, Associated Credit Bureaus; Drew Malizio, National Center for Education Statistics; Garry Marquiss, Bank One Corporation; John Marsh, Wachovia Bank of Georgia; Nancy Mathis, Congressman Joseph Kennedy's Office; Randall McCathren, Bank Lease Consultants; Robert B. McKinley, RAM Research Corporation; David Melancon, Visa USA; Maria Mendler, Citibank; Ed Mierzwinski, U.S. Public Interest Research Group (PIRG); Scott Miller, Student Loan Marketing

Association (Sallie Mae); Bill Moss, American Express Company; Nancy Murphy, Student Loan Marketing Association (Sallie Mae); Martin Neilson, Seafirst Bank; Jim Newell, Student Loan Marketing Association (Sallie Mae); Michael O'Brien, MasterCard International; Kit O'Kelly, European American Bank; William Redman, European American Bank; Ruth Lambert Reeves, Georgetown University; Bruce Reid, AT&T Universal Card Services; Andrea Retsky, Congressman Joseph Kennedy's Office; Paul Richard, National Center for Financial Education; Ben Robinson, Congressman Joseph Kennedy's Office; Marcello Rojtman, Department of Education; Stephanie Schlant, Payment Systems; Dick Schliesmann, Wells Fargo Bank; Hans Schumann, AT&T Universal Card Services; Nick Sharkey, Ford Motor Credit Company; Lewis Siegel, Pirro, Collier, Cohen, Crystal & Bock; Jenny Smith, Oakbrook Bank; Art Spinella, CNW Marketing Research; Jennifer Spoerri, Nolo Press; Virginia Stafford, American Bankers Association; Amy Sudol, The Chase Manhattan Bank; Dr. Charlene Sullivan, Credit Research Center, Purdue University; Marcia Sullivan, Consumer Bankers Association; Terry Sullivan, General Motors Corporation; Ruth Susswein, Bankcard Holders of America; Greg Tarmin, American Express Company; David Tong, SRI International; Francine Van Nevel, Credit Union National Association; Dr. Elizabeth Warren, Harvard Law School; Gail Wasserman, American Express Company; Laura Weiss, Consumers Union; Dr. Jay Westbrook, University of Texas at Austin Law School; Lance Wilcox, J.D. Power & Associates; Jeff Wischerth, European American Bank; Labat Yancey, Equifax; Steve Zeisel, Consumer Bankers Association; Steve Zwillinger, Department of Education.

CHAPTER 4: BASIC BANKING

Kent Allison, Price Waterhouse; Caryl Austrian, Federal Deposit Insurance Corporation; Peter Bakstansky, Federal Reserve Bank of New York; David Barr, Federal Deposit Insurance Corporation; Richard Beebe, Bank of America; Brian Black, Bank Administration Institute; Alexander Bove, law offices of Alexander Bove, Jr.; Dan Brennan, Federal Reserve Bank of St. Louis; Diane Coffey, The Dreyfus Corporation; Jeff Comerford, The Equitable; Elda Di Re, Ernst & Young; Lorna Doubet, Wells Fargo Bank; Fritz Elmendorf, Consumer Bankers Association; Jennifer Harlan, Society Bank; Gunnar Hughes, Twentieth Century Services; Caroline Jervey, Bauer Communications; Jerry Karbon, Credit Union National Association; Cathy Keary, Merrill Lynch & Company; Ken Kehrer, Kenneth Kehrer & Associates; Tom Klipstine, General Motors Corporation; Dina Lee, Ernst &

Young; Ross Levin, Accredited Investors; Gail Liberman, Bank Rate Monitor; Jane Mahoney, The Equitable; Joyce Manchester, Congressional Budget Office; Brian Mattes, The Vanguard Group; Diana Mehl, BanxQuote; Michael Moebs, Moebs $ervices; Anne Moore, Synergists Research Corporation; Edward L. Neumann, Furash & Company; Steve Norwitz, T. Rowe Price Associates; Obrea Poindexter, Division of Consumer & Community Affairs; Barbara Raasch, Ernst & Young; Ellen Ringel, Price Waterhouse; Kevin Roach, Price Waterhouse; Richard Robida, Speer & Associates; Mimi Rossetti, Payment Systems; Dr. John Sabelhaus, The Urban Institute; Judith Saxe, Kronish, Lieb, Weiner & Hellman; Dr. Janice Shields, Center of Study for Responsive Law; Dr. Jonathan Skinner, University of Virginia; Barton Sotnick, Federal Reserve Bank of New York; Chrissy Snyder, Janus Capital Corporation; William Speciale, David L. Babson & Company; Virginia Stafford, American Bankers Association; Ellen Stuart, Chemical Bank; Michele Stuvin, Executive Enterprises; Jack Tatom, Federal Reserve Bank of St. Louis; Paul Thompson, Credit Union National Association; Joseph Votava, Nixon, Hargrave, Devans & Doyle; Sandra Weiksner, Cleary, Gottlieb, Steen & Hamilton.

CHAPTER 5: ALL YOU REALLY NEED TO KNOW ABOUT INVESTING

Lew Altfest, L. J. Altfest & Company; Jim Cain, Lehman Brothers; Lisa Cholnoky, Smith Barney; Peter Cinquegrani, Investment Company Institute; Mark Coler, Mercer; John Collins, Investment Company Institute; Bob Connor, Smith Barney; Peter Crane, IBC/Donoghue; Kim Crawley, Morgan Stanley & Company; Don Criniti, Fidelity Investments; Diane Cullen, Dalbar Financial Services; Jon M. Diat, Standard & Poor's; Richard Erickson, USAA; Dominic Falaschetti, Ibbotson Associates; Georgina Fiordalisi, Duff & Phelps Credit Rating Company; Lynne Goldman, Cerulli Associates; Rowena Itchon, T. Rowe Price Associates; Sheldon Jacobs, The No-Load Fund Investor; Charles Kassouf, Mercer; Teri Kilduff, Fidelity Investments; Patrice Kozlowski, The Dreyfus Corporation; Keith Lawson, Investment Company Institute; Marilyn Leiker, Lipper Analytical Services; Mark N. Lindblom, Morgan Stanley & Company; Stephanie Linkous, United Services Advisors; Jeanine Magill, Morningstar; John Markese, American Association of Individual Investors; Brian Mattes, The Vanguard Group; Patrick McVeigh, Franklin Research & Development; Norbert Mehl, BanxQuote; Bob Mescal, Institute for Econometric Research; Marilyn Morrison, Fidelity Investments; Chip Norton, IBC/Donoghue; Steve

Norwitz, T. Rowe Price Associates; Roger Nyhus, Frank Russell Company; Glen King Parker, Institute of Econometric Research; Chris Phillips, Frank Russell Company; Teri Redinger, IBC/Donoghue; Matthew Scott, Domini Social Equity Funds; Tom Taggart, Charles Schwab & Company; Thomas Tays, United Services Advisors; Jon Teall, Lipper Analytical Services; Maurice Turner, Working Assets Capital Management; Robyn Tice, Fidelity Investments; Julie Ann Urban, Ibbotson Associates; Michael Van Dam, Morningstar; Ken Volpert, The Vanguard Group; Bob Waid, Wilshire Associates; John Woerth, The Vanguard Group; Mark Wright, Morningstar.

CHAPTER 6: LIVING THE GOOD LIFE IN 2030

Kent Allison, Price Waterhouse; Harvey Berger, Grant Thornton; Andrea Bierstein, Western New England College School of Law; Joanetta Bolden, American Association of Retired Persons; Jack Bonné, Gateway Asset Management; Kent Brunette, American Association of Retired Persons; Anthony Burke, Internal Revenue Service; Steve Ciolino, Ernst & Young; Gloria Della, Department of Labor; Steven Enright, Enright Financial Advisors; Wilson Fadely, Internal Revenue Service; Karen Ferguson, Pension Rights Center; Martin Fleisher, pension consultant; Phil Gambino, Social Security Administration; Jerry Gattegno, Deloitte & Touche; Hal Glassman, Department of Labor; Mary Ann Green, MBL Life Assurance Corporation; Ed Hansen, Mercer; Tom Hakala, KPMG Peat Marwick; Cindy Hounsell, Pension Rights Center; Richard Koski, Buck Consultants; Ross Levin, Accredited Investors; Tom Margenau, Social Security Administration; John Markese, American Association of Individual Investors; Glenn Pape, Ayco Company; R. Michael Parry, American Planning Group; Carolyn Pemberton, Employee Benefit Research Institute; Mark Puccia, Standard & Poor's; Robert Runde, American Planning Group; Christine Seltz, Hewitt Associates; Greg Spencer, Bureau of the Census; James Velten, Coopers & Lybrand; Paul Westbrook, Westbrook Financial Advisors; Caryn Zappone, Hewitt Associates.

CHAPTER 7: OH, GIVE ME A HOME

Gopal Ahluwalia, National Association of Home Builders; Rick Beebe, Bank of America; Mark Berman, The Townsend Consulting Group; David Berson, Federal National Mortgage Association (Fannie Mae); Katherine Billings, Federal Home Loan Mortgage Corporation (Freddie Mac); Mary Burt, National Association of Mortgage Brokers; Michael Carliner, National Association of Home Builders; Andrew Carswell, National Association of Home Builders; Ed Chang, Interet; Brian Chappelle, Mortgage Bankers Association of America; Laura Clavier, Merrill Lynch & Company; Wayne Collett, Countrywide Funding Corporation; Nancy Condon, Federal Home Loan Mortgage Corporation (Freddie Mac); Willliam A. Connelly, Department of Housing & Urban Development; Josh Dare, Federal National Mortgage Association (Fannie Mae); Michelle Elliott, National Association of Home Builders; Robert Engelstad, Federal National Mortgage Association (Fannie Mae); Monica Gallagher, Hewitt Associates; Joe Gilvary, Bureau of the Census; Vince Gisonti, Deloitte & Touche; Keith Gumbinger, HSH Associates; Kevin Hawkins, Federal National Mortgage Association (Fannie Mae); Liz Johnson, National Association of Realtors; Ted Jones, Real Estate Research Center; Cathy Keary, Merrill Lynch & Company; Sam Khater, National Association of Realtors; Alfred King, Federal National Mortgage Association (Fannie Mae); Toni Langkau, New York State Housing Authority; William Lloyd, Norwest Mortgage; Dick Manuel, Department of Housing & Urban Development; Howard Marder, New York State Housing Authority; Laura Maxwell, Deloitte & Touche; Ken McKinnon, Department of Veterans Affairs; Naomi McLean, Department of Veterans Affairs; Ed Mierzwinski, U.S. Public Interest Research Group (PIRG); Paul Mondor, Mortgage Bankers Association of America; Larry Montague, Deloitte & Touche; Trish Morris, National Association of Realtors; Eileen Neely, Federal National Mortgage Association (Fannie Mae); Bonnie O'Dell, Federal National Mortgage Association (Fannie Mae); Forest Pafenberg, National Association of Realtors; Julie Reeves, National Council of State Housing Agencies; Cheryl Regan, Federal Home Loan Mortgage Corporation (Freddie Mac); Sharon Ridenour, Norwest Mortgage; Douglas Robinson, Federal Home Loan Mortgage Corporation (Freddie Mac); Margot Saunders, National Consumer Law Center; Michael Schlerf, Mortgage Bankers Association of America; Christine Seltz, Hewitt Associates; Jay Shackford, National Association of Home Builders; Dave Totaro, Dime Savings Bank; Rick Trilsch, Florida Public Interest Research Group (PIRG); John Tuccillo, National Association of Realtors; Robert Van Order, Federal Home Loan Mortgage Corporation (Freddie Mac); Andrea Waas, National Association of Mortgage Brokers; Margery Wasserman, National Association of Personal Financial Advisors; Sabrina White, Merrill Lynch & Company; William White, Department of Veterans Affairs; George Wilson, Department of Housing & Urban Development; Jean Wussow, National Association of Realtors; Catherine Zimring, Countrywide Funding Corporation.

CHAPTER 8: INSURANCE

Riad Assad, RBA Insurance Strategies; Rich Bailey, Provident Life & Accident Insurance Company; Bob Bland, Quotesmith; Phyllis Bonfield, American Society of Chartered Life Underwriters; Joseph Bosnack, Sr., Arthur Rothlein Agency; Ann H. Brockmeyer, Hartmann & Associates; Bruce Bruscia, Golden State Insurance Services; Karen Burger, American Institute for Chartered Property & Casualty Underwriters; Anthony Burke, Internal Revenue Service; John Calagna, New York State Department of Insurance; Brenda Cargile, Federal Crime Insurance Program; Dee Caruso, Illinois Department of Insurance; Diane Coffey, American Council on Life Insurance; Richard Coorsh, Health Insurance Association of America; Sam Cunningham, Anderson & Anderson Benefits Insurance Brokers; Glenn Daily, fee-only insurance consultant; Bill Dommasch, Geico; Henry Dowdle, Provident Life & Accident Insurance Company; Pam Drellow, Blue Cross & Blue Shield Association; Andrew Ede, MassMutual Life Insurance Company; Susan Farmer, American Society of Chartered Life Underwriters; Terrence Fergus, KPMG Peat Marwick; Anne Getz, Moody's Investors Services; Terrence Gordon, Avis Rent-a-Car System; Ed Graves, The American College; Gene Grebowski, American Council on Life Insurance; Paul Gribbons, Paul Revere Life Insurance Company; Don Haas, Haas Financial Services; Karen Hamilton, American Institute for Chartered Property & Casualty Underwriters; Ed Hansen, Mercer; Judith Hill, The American College; Rick Hill, 20th Century Insurance Company; Katherine Hoffman, National Association of Professional Insurance Agents; Charles Horne, Amica Mutual Insurance Company; James Hunt, Consumer Federation of America; Ted Huntington, Professional Insurance Agents of California & Nevada; Amy Ingram, Termquote; Kenneth Ingram, Termquote; Linda Jackson, Department of Labor; Donald Jayne, Executive Financial Systems; Jim Johnson, Paul Revere Life Insurance Company; Peter Katt, independent life insurance advisor; Susan Keller, Golden Eagle Insurance Company; Dr. Peter Kensicki, East Kentucky University; Amy Kraus, Mutual of Omaha Insurance Company; Arlene Lilly, American Council of Life Insurance; Eliot Lipson, independent insurance consultant; Jim Marks, Society of Chartered Property & Casualty Underwriters; Greg Marsh, Geico; Brandi Marth, Fireman's Fund Insurance Company; Judith Maurer, Wholesale Insurance Network; Keith Maurer, Wholesale Insurance Network; Mike Mayers, Beall, Garner, Screen & Geare Company; Larry Mayewski, A. M. Best Company; Wayne McHargue, American United Life Insurance Company; Annalise McKean-Marcus, Hertz Corporation; Robert Miller, New York Life Insurance Company; Al Minor, Health Insurance Association of America; Rhonda Moritz, A. M. Best Company; Todd Muller, Independent Insurance Agents of America; Tim Murphy, Northwestern Mutual Life Insurance Company; Nan Nases, Illinois Department of Insurance; Haig Neville, Haig Neville Associates; Eric Nordman, National Association of Insurance Commissioners; Mike Norton, UNUM Life Insurance Company of America; Mike Odom, Blue Shield of California; Bill O'Neill, Standard & Poor's; Kendal Leigh O'Neill, Time Warner; John Paganelli, First Transamerica Life Insurance Company; Jerry Parsons, State Farm Insurance Company; Carolyn Pemberton, Employee Benefit Research Institute; Nancy Peskin, Metropolitan Life Insurance Company; Chris Petrocelli, Petrocelli Group; Irving Pfeffer, insurance consultant; Tim Pfeifer, consulting actuary; Jerome Phillip, Mutual of Omaha Insurance Company; Diana Reace, Hewitt Associates; Donna Reichle, National Automobile Dealers Association; John Roman, American Association of Preferred Provider Organizations; Fred Rumack, Buck Consultants; Walter Runkle, Consumer Credit Insurance Association; Jeanne Salvatore, Insurance Information Institute; Bob Sasser, State Farm Insurance Company; Paul Schattenberg, USAA; Tracy Schauer, IDEA; Iris Shaffer, Blue Cross & Blue Shield of Illinois; Craig P. Shanley, Amica Mutual Insurance Company; Tracy Sherman, UNUM Life Insurance Company of America; Dr. Harold Skipper, Department of Risk Management & Insurance Research, Georgia State University; Camille Sorosiak, American Hospital Association; Judy Snelson, Allied Insurance Agencies of America; Steve Stark, Selectquote; Dale Stephenson, National Conference of Insurance Guarantee Funds; Morey Stettner, insurance consultant; Dottye Stewart, Wholesale Insurance Network; Jennie Storey, Provident Life & Accident Insurance Company; Ron Sunderman, Skogman Ralston Carlson; Doug Tillett, National Association of Life Underwriters; Julie Vokracka, American Express Company; Billy Watson, Anderson & Watson; Don White, The Group Health Association of America; Eric Wiening, American Institute for Chartered Property & Casualty Underwriters; Loretta Worters, Insurance Information Institute; Gay Yellen, Ameritas Life Insurance Company; John Zarubnicky, First Transamerica Life Insurance Company.

CHAPTER 9: HOW TO MAKE YOUR LIFE LESS TAXING

Nancy Anderson, H&R Block; Henri Bersoux, Ernst & Young; Anthony Burke, Internal Revenue Service; Joan Carroll, Coopers & Lybrand; John Collins, Investment Company Institute; Gary DuBoff, Ernst & Young; Ed Emerman, A. Foster Higgins & Company; Wilson Fadely, Internal Revenue

Service; David Fridling, Towers Perrin; Jerry Gattegno, Deloitte & Touche; Stephen Gold, Tax Foundation; Steven Gold, Center for the Study of the States; Jeffrey Gotlinger, Ernst & Young; Nadine Habousha, Arthur Andersen; Tom Hakala, KPMG Peat Marwick; Malin Jennings, Investment Company Institute; Judy Keisling, H&R Block; Sidney Kess, CPA; Stuart Kessler, Goldstein Golub Kessler & Company; John Koegel, Grant Thornton; Dina Lee, Ernst & Young; L. Harold Levinson, Vanderbilt University; Glenn Liebman, Ernst & Young; Norm Magnuson, Associated Credit Bureaus; Tom Margenau, Social Security Administration; Brian Mattes, The Vanguard Group; Marilyn Morrison, Fidelity Investments; Colette Murphy, Ernst & Young; Tom Ochsenschlager, Grant Thornton; Maggie O'Donovan, Coopers & Lybrand; Glenn Pape, Ayco Company; Jodi Patterson, Internal Revenue Service; Sylvia Pozarnsky, Ernst & Young; Ellen Ringel, Price Waterhouse; Diane Rivers, tax attorney; Don Roberts, Internal Revenue Service; Jeff Saccacio, Coopers & Lybrand; Sherri Sankner, BDO Seidman; Bertram Schaeffer, Ernst & Young; Martin Shenkman, tax attorney; Ronald Stone, Stone & Associates; Richard Stricof, BDO Seidman; Peter L. Tashman, CPA; Susan Van Alstyne, H&R Block; James E. Velten, Coopers & Lybrand; Mary Vogel, H&R Block; Sidney Weinman, Research Institute of America; Craig Wolman, Ernst & Young; Paul Yurachek, Gurtz & Associates; John Ziegelbauer, Grant Thornton.

INDEX

ABOUT THE AUTHOR

Beth Kobliner has been a writer for *Money* magazine since 1988. Before that, she researched and wrote more than one hundred columns for Sylvia Porter, the financial journalist, whose column appeared in 150 newspapers nationwide. Beth's television experience includes numerous appearances on CBS, NBC, CNN and CNBC. She has also appeared as a financial expert on *The Oprah Winfrey Show*, addressing the concerns of a group of people in their twenties. In 1994 and 1995 she was selected by *TJFR*, the leading trade publication for financial journalists, as one of the country's most promising financial journalists under the age of 30. Beth graduated from Brown University in 1986, and currently lives with her husband in New York City.

NFCC   1(800)557 7392
Questions for
Consolidation
application